Praise for *A World without Martha*

"*A World without Martha* is a painful, powerful, and ultimately hopeful story that will help the reader understand why we segregate some members of society, the terrible impact on them and their families, and what it means to be human."

> JOHN GUIDO, long-time member of L'Arche Daybreak and L'Arche Toronto, and Outreach Coordinator for L'Arche Canada

"Freeman's candid account illuminates the complex and far-reaching effects of institutionalization in the family and brings insight to essential human concerns including love, abandonment, and acceptance. It makes an important contribution to our understanding of families' experiences of separation and loss due to designations of 'difference.'"

> MADELINE BURGHARDT, author of *Broken: Institutions, Families, and the Construction of Intellectual Disability*

"Most memoirs written about people born with Down Syndrome have been authored by family members, often in a reassuring manner intended to destigmatize the condition for the general public. The tone of this book is strikingly different. It is full of regret, ambivalence, and conflict. There is no denying the honesty embedded in the author's raw, unvarnished reflections of her family's missed opportunities of acceptance and reconciliation."

> DAVID WRIGHT, author of *Downs: The History of a Disability*

"This is a raw, honest, and candid account of how institutional and ideological ableism – institutionalization and the separation of siblings as well as stigmatization, shame, and marginalization – impacts individuals, families, and their relationships in tragic, shattering, and unpredictable ways."

> PATRICIA DOUGLAS, assistant professor, Disability Studies, Faculty of Education, Brandon University

"Freeman's compelling memoir weaves together many stories about the lasting impacts of institutionalization. With power and honesty, she reveals how disabled people were, and continue to be, treated in Canada, and the deep, lasting effects this has on family relations."

> ELIZA CHANDLER, assistant professor, School of Disability Studies, Ryerson University

A World without Martha

A Memoir of Sisters, Disability, and Difference

Victoria Freeman

PURICH
BOOKS

28 27 26 25 24 23 22 21 20 19   5 4 3 2 1

Printed in Canada on FSC-certified ancient-forest-free paper (100% post-consumer recycled) that is processed chlorine- and acid-free.

Cataloguing data is available from Library and Archives Canada.

ISBN 978-0-7748-8040-4 (softcover)
ISBN 978-0-7748-8041-1 (PDF)
ISBN 978-0-7748-8042-8 (EPUB)
ISBN 978-0-7748-8043-5 (Kindle)

Canadä

UBC Press gratefully acknowledges the financial support for our publishing program of the Government of Canada (through the Canada Book Fund), the Canada Council for the Arts, and the British Columbia Arts Council.

Printed and bound in Canada by Friesens
Interior design: Irma Rodriguez
Set in Alright Sans, Baskerville 10, and Walbaum
by Artegraphica Design Co. Ltd.
Copy editor: Lesley Erickson
Proofreader: Judith Earnshaw

Overleaf: Martha's mother holding her sister Kate, with Victoria, shortly after Martha's institutionalization, 1960.

Purich Books, an imprint of UBC Press
2029 West Mall
Vancouver, BC, V6T 1Z2
www.purichbooks.ca

Dedicated to the memory of

Martha Ann Freeman
(1958–2002)

George Edwin Freeman
(1921–2017)

D. June Freeman
(1930–2017)

Monique (Monica) Szabadka
(1929–2015)

and to the loving vision of

Jean Vanier
(1928–2019)

Contents

Author's Note

A memoir is always a work of reconstruction and, inevitably, fiction's cousin.

The people who inhabit these pages reflect only certain dimensions of the real people who shaped my life; they would likely represent themselves quite differently, and others have experienced them differently. But this is who they were to me, in terms of the particular story I am telling. They – and others not mentioned here – have also been many other things to me.

The family dynamics that arose after my sister Martha's birth had a profound impact on my other siblings as well. Though this is my story, many aspects of it were shared by my sister Kate and brother, Eric, though some of their experiences were markedly different, and they have gone through their own struggles and learning.

In some cases, I have changed identifying details to protect people's privacy, particularly the staff associated with the Rideau Regional Centre, other than senior administrators, whose identities are well known. I have changed the names of many people who are not members of my immediate family, particularly those with whom I am no longer in contact.

Very rarely, I've combined or compressed incidents for clarity and a more streamlined narrative, but the essence of my experience was as it is described.

A word of caution about the language used in this memoir: the early chapters reflect the language used during my childhood, including the "r" word, which is the only way I can truly convey the power of those words to shape the social reality that my sister and I struggled within. For most readers – and especially people with intellectual disabilities – these words are profoundly hurtful. I hope the rest of the book marks a journey away from those words and that, in the end, I am able to make vivid the experience of oppression without reinscribing it. This is an ongoing challenge as I unlearn the ablist attitudes that so profoundly shaped me as a child.

There is no way to tell my own story without revealing personal details about my parents and siblings. I have thought long and hard about the risks of doing this. All I can say is that I love them dearly to this day, but I also believe that loyalty and honesty are not antithetical. I have had to balance the need to honour my sister's memory and speak of events in my own life on the one hand with shielding my family from hurtful scrutiny on the other. My siblings have had the opportunity to read and comment on this work; my parents, who were both afflicted with dementia for many years before they died, did not. I have tried to contextualize their actions and attitudes to the best of my ability.

I also want to acknowledge the ethical challenges in writing about my sister, who during her life had a limited ability to speak for herself and be heard by others, including me. I cannot represent her inner life except by asking a series of questions and drawing on the accounts of others who may have had similar experiences or at least lived in similar contexts, but how one interprets one's own experience is always unique.

I share my story not only to illuminate a difficult aspect of my own experience but also to encourage other siblings of people institutionalized for intellectual disability to break their often decades-long silence and share their own stories. We have been isolated and unknown to one another for far too long, our pain and loss often unrecognized in our families and in society at large. Our siblings endured more profound injustices, but we also have stories to tell ... and telling them is healing.

Ultimately, a memoir is not just a telling for others; it is also an accounting to and for oneself. We live by the stories we are told ... and by the stories we tell ourselves. I have had to dive deeply into this story – my past – and be open and accepting of the person who emerges on the other side.

A World without Martha

"We have hung a little chickadee like this in a window ... as an everyday memento of Martha."

1

Baby

Martha was my baby sister, and I had never known any other.

She couldn't talk, and I didn't expect her to. She did not sit up unassisted when other babies did, but I had no benchmarks to measure her by. She was simply a big, floppy baby, and I had come to love her with the proprietary love of the eldest child for a younger sibling who is no threat to her. She rarely cried. She didn't fuss. And she certainly was no threat since it was clear my mother loved me more. Indeed, my mother delighted in everything I did, lavishly praising each new accomplishment. I was smart enough for two, it seemed.

I enjoyed my sister even if she couldn't do much. I patiently played with her, dangled toys above her face, talked baby talk to her; I tickled her as my parents tickled me. She fascinated me, though she often also bored me. Like any baby, she slept a lot.

Luckily, Martha was a calm and happy baby – the easiest to care for, by my mother's own account. And Martha loved to watch me; from her, I learned that I was endlessly fascinating. I performed for her, making faces, jumping up and down on one foot, spinning around in circles, sticking out my tongue, goading her to react. It was easy enough to frighten her, but it took a long, long time before she learned to smile. I think, because it took so very long, her smile was all the more precious to me. I could see it in her eyes first, and then very slowly the corners of her mouth would lift. I played with her for hours, just trying to earn that smile. She would smile, and I would smile back; I smiled again, and she smiled some more. After a while I would make faces and play peekaboo, and I would be rewarded with her laughter. I remember a huge stuffed dog with yellow fur that was parked on the floor of her room. I would sit on it and boisterously sing snatches of imitation baby talk to try to make her laugh.

I'm not sure when Martha finally rolled over or sat up. My mother had kept a little diary in which she noted the date when I reached every one of these milestones, but she did not do the same for Martha. I was considered precocious: as I approached my fourth birthday, I was already sounding out words on the page and half-reading, half-memorizing the simplest children's books. I would show Martha the books my father read to me at night, *Tim and Charlotte Lost at Sea* or *The Cat in the Hat*, and pretend to read to her, pointing to all the pictures and saying the names of things, as my parents had done for me. Her eyes would move from the book to me, and back to the book, to my hand, and to me. Always to me. Her eyes followed me everywhere with a look of perpetual wonder.

My clearest early memories are of dancing. I was not yet four when I first started dancing to my parents' recording of Chopin's music for the ballet *La Source*. The story that I enacted through my dance was always the same, and it still comes back to me when I hear the music. I was a little seed that grew into something bigger and more beautiful, a plant or an animal or a baby human. I was the kernel of the thing itself. I grew towards the sun. I danced for joy. Like my baby sister, I had started from a seed, an egg, a small, inconsequential thing; the dance was always about growing, about being alive. I can still remember those wonderful dances, in the living room in the old house on Glengarry Road, my father setting up the record for me on the clunky old record player that also played 78s. I was inspired by the beautiful ballerina on the album cover, dressed all in diaphanous white except for the fleshy pink of ballet tights and ballet slippers. I'm sure Martha watched me from her baby seat or a blanket on the floor as I became that ballerina – or a princess.

A year later, I learned to dance the twist and loved to sing along to Chubby Checker's lyrics about a little "sis" who really danced up a storm.

> Yeah you should see my little Sis
> You should see my little Sis
> She really knows how to rock
> She knows how to twist
> Come on and twist yeah baby twist

But Martha was gone by then.

2
Conceptions

I was two years old when my sister was conceived and then imagined into being. She was never just herself; she was always also who my parents thought she would become.

As the tiny embryo became a fetus and made its presence known, my mother formed a relationship with it; she came to know it, though it was a felt knowledge rather than a knowledge based on sight. How strange that over nine long months a mother never lays eyes on the new being taking shape inside her, except through the thick and opaque skin of her abdomen, where an elbow or foot occasionally pushes outwards like a hidden actor disturbing the closed curtain on a stage. How easy it was for my mother to imagine that she and this new child would be united in a blissful, perfect love – as had been the case with me.

The Buddhists say we choose our parents before birth, when our souls have not yet entered a new reincarnation. I saw an image in a children's book once of a multitude of prospective parents calling out to the unembodied soul, "Choose me! Choose me!" and the unborn child selecting the mother and father who appeared most loving.

But I know now that every birth is a revelation and an extraordinary meeting, rather like the moment in some arranged marriages when the groom lifts the veil and husband and wife see each other for the first time and meet their future. I have also come to understand that birth is a separation. Each newborn sees the blurry outside of the world it has been inside. Its mother is no longer a rich, red glow of blood and tissue, a warm cushion of amniotic fluid, an ever-present heartbeat but a presence with skin and moving arms and legs, an expressive face, and milk-gushing breasts who holds her infant close but also inexplicably moves away from it. The whole world the infant has known is now only one element of a much larger universe, not the totality the child assumed its mother to be.

Now mother and child must navigate an imperfect and finite relationship, with all its stresses, strains, and strange twists of fate. It is a vulnerable time, for an infant is helpless and totally dependent, and in this new world it may or may not be loved, or even welcomed. Yet to be welcome on this earth is a profound human need.

My younger sister emerged into the light of a September day in 1958, in a delivery room in sleepy Ottawa, Canada. From the moment of her arrival it was evident that she had the telltale flat face, almond-shaped eyes, and other distinctive physical features then described as "mongoloid," a term not yet outlawed by the World Health Organization as an insult to the Mongolian People's Republic. Doctors would later classify my sister as an "imbecile," a being – she was hardly considered a person – who suffered moderate to severe mental retardation and who had an expected IQ of between 26 and 50, which ranked her between "moron" (IQ of 51 to 70) and "idiot" (IQ of 0 to 25). Others would simply call her a retard. Her birth was considered a calamity by all of those attending and all of those who might have loved her.

All my life I have had to contend with these words and their effect on my sister and on me, words that are now the shameful detritus of a less enlightened age but that still live on in various subterranean nooks and crannies, for all our belief in progress. Almost sixty years later, they still live on in me.

This is the story of how my sister and I were separated and what we each lost because of those words. It is also the story of how that was not the whole story between us.

I hold a photograph of my mother, pregnant and wearing a striped and polka-dotted blouse, sitting in a wooden Muskoka chair in our backyard on Glengarry Road, reading a book. It is date-stamped August 1958, a month before my mother went into labour and gave birth to the child who would become my sister.

That summer before my sister was born, I was a toddler with a toddler's volcanic passions but very limited understanding. How strange that I have no memory of my mother's swelling belly or of what I was told about it, that all of these absolutely foundational experiences are without conscious trace. I try to will myself back into that well of memory but only swim endlessly through clouds of grey mist, back, back, back ... to nothing.

My mother, pregnant with Martha, August 1958.

I believe, however, that my mother conveyed to me her sense of excitement. I believe she conjured in me a vision of this sister- or brother-to-be who would magically escape from the confines of my mother's body.

I believe I was there in the garden when this photograph was taken, just outside the frame, but perhaps it is only seeing the photograph that creates the illusion of remembering. Perhaps I have only imagined playing contentedly a few yards from her outstretched legs, picking dandelions and bringing them to her to make a flowery necklace.

My mother was twenty-seven, relaxed, expectant. She had married my father three years previously and had one healthy and much-loved child (me), and she believed she was gestating another. All seemed to be progressing as it should. She had a university degree, and her husband, although then making only ten thousand dollars a year, had prospects. In marrying a man with a master's degree, an economist employed at the Bank of Canada, she had successfully transcended her parents' social

My jubilant parents holding me, 1956.

class of small shopkeepers and hairdressers. She and my father socialized with other up-and-coming couples; the men were civil servants, the women educated and ambitious. They would have three or four children each, spaced rationally, not a herd of children all higgledy-piggledy.

The person I am now cannot remember the person I was then, before my sister was born. I am told I was a pink and golden baby, the apple of my mother's eye, and my father's too. I was definitely welcomed: I lived in a swirl of bliss. I was treasured, humoured, played with, coddled. My mother was instructed to feed me every four hours, but I don't think she stuck to this schedule. She read Dr. Spock and joined the Mothercraft Society, as modern, conscientious mothers did in the mid-1950s. But to her, motherhood was much more than a responsibility or social role; it was also, at least in its best moments, her glory. She would never do to me what her own mother had done to her, which was abandon her.

My father drove my mother to the Grace Hospital after her waters broke. I have imagined what came next many times, for I could not possibly have witnessed it, left as I was in the care of my grandmother.

It was a warm, beautiful, early autumn day. My mother and father passed through the city in the grey Studebaker, a large family car that had recently replaced the red MG convertible that my father had driven to the hospital with the top down when my mother was about to give birth to me. My mother was anxious but excited, not nearly as fearful as she had been the first time around. They passed through the doors into "Admitting," my mother leaning on my father's arm as the labour pains intensified, the antiseptic smell and slightly rundown look of the hospital familiar and oddly welcoming as she walked resolutely in.

A nurse handed my father my mother's clothes in a brown paper bag and told him to go home. My father would have stayed for the birth if they'd let him, but they didn't allow fathers in labour or delivery rooms in those days, so he told a joke to cover up his discomfort, kissed my mother goodbye, and went home with her underwear. They would soon telephone him with the good news, the nurse told him.

My mother was confident and as relaxed as one could be under the circumstances, but giving birth, like getting married, is one of those wild card moments in a woman's life. Once labour begins, you are not in control of either your body or your life; forces far greater than your puny will take over and deliver a child from your flesh, whether you like it or not. The pain rips through you and forces you to comply; the best you can do is accept it, breathe into it, go with it, accede to its rhythm. Then the pain can be yours, the incredible force of each muscular contraction can be yours, the power of birth can be yours in your own visceral moment of enlightenment as you align yourself with the forces of creation.

But my mother was now in the hands of a medical establishment that prevented such maternal epiphanies. Virtually all middle-class labouring women were sedated in those days. They went to sleep and woke up with a child – the stork brought it, for all they knew. That's what had happened two years earlier, when she had given birth to me. She had drifted into unconsciousness and the next thing she knew there I was, howling, the nurse wrapping me up tight, tight, tight in a towel. There had been no witnesses to my birth other than hospital staff, so there was no way to know what had actually transpired or even whose baby she had ended up with. My mother did not suffer the pain of my emergence; you could say I was born through her oblivion.

Later, my mother felt a vague sense of loss that she had not been conscious for my birth. It was as if it had been someone else's accomplishment, she later told me, the doctor's or the nurse's. But perhaps it was a mercy that she wasn't conscious that day when Martha was born, better for her not to have been alive to every moment of my sister's journey into life, to the incredible rush of encouragement and excitement when the child's head crowned, and one shoulder emerged, and then the other, and then the rest of the tiny body issued forth in a sudden viscous blurt, followed by an awful moment of silence when the nurse and doctor looked into the infant's face. It would be far worse to push, push, push, and pop out what everyone regarded as a freak of nature with your own effort – at least if you just woke up with it, maybe there was some mistake. Maybe it didn't come from *you*.

The first people to stare at my sister were the doctor and the nurse.

The nurse whisked away the child, and then a hushed and indistinct conference took place just beyond my mother's earshot. *The flattened face and nose. The upturned eyes that did not belong in the face of a Caucasian child. The telltale single crease in the palm of the hand. The big space between the big toe and the next one.* This was no ordinary child. Or perhaps I should say no "normal" child.

They did not tell her right away. She was too drugged, and they wanted to confirm what they suspected. They spoke to my father first, but it was not the phone call he expected.

"She's so big and healthy!" my mother exclaimed proudly when the doctor and my father first entered her room. Then she saw the doctor's face.

She would always remember what he said next: "I'm afraid I have some bad news ... She's not as healthy as she looks," and then, "an abnormality ... genetic ... no cure."

The words coursed through her labour-shocked body, their toxin travelling straight to her heart. From an ever-widening distance she heard Dr. McIntosh suggest that the baby could be taken away immediately and sent to one of those institutions that housed such children. There, it would be better off with others of its own kind, and she would be relieved of the lifelong job of caring for it. This was a child who would never grow up, he said. It would never leave home to support itself or raise its own family; it would always require extraordinary care and vigilance. My mother had her other children to think of, the one already born and the others yet to come, who would need her wholehearted motherly attention. She would undoubtedly go on to have more children, and she should not worry; they would all be normal. What had happened was a fluke, an accident, a freak of nature that thankfully was a rarity. If they took the child away now, my mother and father could quickly return to their normal lives and try again.

I imagine my mother lying in stunned and exhausted silence as she pondered the doctor's words. For nine months she alone had known this child as it grew inside her womb and drew nourishment from her blood, as it floated in the warmth of her own internal sea. How often she had spoken to it, rubbed its feet and buttocks as they pushed against her abdomen, heaved herself from one side to the other in the night, never complaining because she wanted this child, another child to love and a sibling for me.

My mother was a mother first and foremost. She asked to hold her child.

She took the blanketed bundle in her trembling arms and gazed into her daughter's face. The baby did not look too terribly different from other babies. Maybe the doctor had made a mistake. Maybe the child would be all right. Maybe the face had just been flattened in its passage through the birth canal and the eyes would soon resume their expected shape. Maybe she was confused and she would wake up from this nightmare and all would be as it should be, her daughter the beautiful second child she had imagined. But even as she struggled to reject the doctor's verdict, she knew somehow that it was true; the child seemed indefinably other, unalterably alien.

Birth anomalies had long been explained in European fairy tales through a similar motif: "Your precious babe is hence convey'd, and in the place a changeling laid."

My mother would never completely shake the feeling that she had been robbed ... or tricked ... that this was not her child.

Why is it so necessary for me to imaginatively revisit my mother's experience of my sister's birth? Because, in all our years together, my mother told me so little – except that this was one of the worst things that ever happened to her. Especially now that I am a mother, I need to understand both her feelings and her choices – and my father's – as best I can, since they had such a profound impact on my sister and me.

And so, in my mind's eye, I imagine her giving the baby to the nurse and turning her face to the wall, her heart now locked in a dead, dark place. No one dared to reach out to her or touch her. No one spoke. She could not, would not be its mother. It would be better if it were dead. Or if she were.

The doctor asked again: Did she want him to send it away? She could not answer, could not move. Did she want to discuss it with her husband? She did not answer.

Tears coursed down my father's cheeks, but my mother lay motionless, in a stupor, as the doctor patiently explained it. The problem was some sort of genetic aberration. There were new theories about the number of chromosomes in each gene, but nothing had been proven yet.

In fact, the exact cause of Down syndrome would not be definitely known until a year after my sister's birth, when Dr. Jérôme Lejeune in France and Patricia Jacobs in England proved almost simultaneously that Down syndrome was caused when the fetus received twenty-four instead of twenty-three chromosomes from a parent's egg or sperm, though a genetic cause had been suspected since 1932 and a trisomy (or triplication) of a chromosome since 1934. My sister was born with forty-seven chromosomes in every cell of her body, instead of forty-six, which resulted in various effects, both physical and mental ... though no two such children are ever the same.

I believe what my mother understood from Dr. McIntosh's explanation was that everything about her child was abnormal, that there was a "mistake" in every single cell of its body. And if there was truly something unalterably, genetically wrong with it, if it was not fully human, then she did not want it.

If my sister was not fully human ... what was she? The words "moron," "idiot," and "imbecile" would cling to my sister all her life like Pig-Pen's dirt. As with the word "retarded," these words had once aimed for neutral, even scientific, description but became insults in the pejorative creep to which all attempts to describe mental disability eventually succumb – today's "developmentally delayed" will likely go the same way. The roots of the words are telling. "Moron" comes from the Greek *moron,* the neuter form of *moros,* meaning foolish. The Greek word *idiotes* means not only an ignorant person but also a private person, a plebeian, or a layman, all derived from *idios,* "peculiar," "private." My sister was not technically an idiot, but from the moment of her birth she was relegated to a lower plane of existence that was both peculiar and private – the world of the subhuman. And the place where such creatures belonged was away.

No, in the eyes of the scientific experts of the time, my younger sister was not a moron or an idiot, but an imbecile. The term came from the Latin *imbecillus,* meaning weak or weak-minded. It referred not only to people with moderate to severe intellectual impairment but also to a type of criminal, a "moral imbecile."

The doctors did not refer to my sister as an imbecile in front of my parents; everyone called her a "mongoloid," a word first coined by John Langdon Haydon Down, the superintendent of the Earlswood Asylum for Idiots in Surrey, England, who in 1866 gave the first clinical description of the condition that would later bear his name. He chose this term because the epicanthic fold at the corner of the eyes of people with Down syndrome made them look vaguely Asian or Chinese. Reflecting the widespread scientific racism of the time, which held that the Caucasian was intellectually superior to the Mongoloid race, Down theorized that such children suffered from arrested ethnic development: "There can be no doubt that these ethnic features are the result of degeneration."

My mother was told shortly after my sister's arrival that she would have an IQ of no more than 45. I know now that the degree of disability in people with Down syndrome varies widely, and it is not possible to measure the extent of cognitive impairment at birth. But doctors were the experts: their pronouncements had the terrible dismissive finality, the utter infallibility, of the judgments of the Old Testament Jehovah, and my parents, in their terror and ignorance, believed them.

We soon experienced the tyranny of another powerful word that affected us just as profoundly but did not draw attention to itself the way those other words did. For years, my family used it without thinking, since it seemed to describe something so obvious, so permanently inscribed in human nature, so natural and unchanging, that we never questioned it. We had no idea that the word "normal" had only entered the English language a hundred years earlier, when Adolphe Quetelet, in 1842, conjured up the average man, something that disability scholar Rosemarie Garland-Thomson, in *Staring: How We Look*, would later call "a statistical phantom who stands in for us all." Before the concept of the normal or statistically average person was invented, the common view, expressed particularly in the Bible, was that all human beings were flawed at birth. One aspired to an ideal of human perfection, to be sure, but no living person could possibly attain it. Humankind reflected the infinite diversity of God's creation, even if the divine purpose in creating that variety remained inscrutable. God worked, it was said, in mysterious ways.

In the new, rational, and progressive world of the 1950s that my sister and I were born into, such mystery had been banished. On the one hand, North Americans imagined themselves as independent, unique, self-determining individuals; on the other, standardization proceeded apace, in universal education, mass production, mechanical reproduction of images, and advertising.

There were the normal people, as defined by science and statistics, who, it appeared, lived the only lives truly worth living –
and then there were the deviants and failures. In the Cold War
logic that prevailed through most of my childhood, these were
enemy others who had to be contained. As Ian Hacking, a philosopher of science, comments in *The Social Construction of
What?*, the word "normal" was "one of the most powerful ideological tools of the twentieth century."

I imagine my mother lying alone and awake in her hospital
bed in the depth of night, staring disbelievingly, uncomprehend-
ingly through the half-opened door at the lights in the corridor.
The hospital had given her a single room, out of consideration
for her feelings, or perhaps it was so as not to scare the other
mothers. Down the hall, she heard a mother-to-be moaning, and
somewhere else a baby cried. All around her, women were giving birth, infants were taking their first gasping breaths, and
husbands were greeting their offspring with excitement and joy.
She heard footsteps and hushed voices in the corridor. *Were they
talking about her? Was she the object of their pity or their scorn?*
In the dim light, she saw the outline of the flowers next to
her bed and the cards that had already started to arrive.
Her breasts were filling with milk, and she knew she should
nurse the baby.
Her eyes went to the call button. She could call and ask the
nurse to fetch the child from the nursery. Or she could call and
tell her to take it away. Her hand reached out, and then she sank
back into the bed and closed her eyes. She didn't want the responsibility of making that decision.
*But why had this happened to her? Why was she the loser
in some horrid lottery, when all her friends were winners? Why
should she alone be punished in this way? What had she done
wrong?*
She couldn't sleep. She pondered the dim outline of the empty
chair beside her bed. She wished her husband could be there to

comfort her and share her pain. She wondered if he had already spoken to me. How would they explain it if the promised baby sister or brother never arrived? Could they pretend that it had died? What if they told me the truth – that the baby was sent away because something was wrong with it – would I then fear that I, too, might be sent away if something was wrong with me or if I misbehaved? Surely at two years old I was too young to understand any of this. Maybe I would just forget about the bump in Mummy's tummy and all that it portended, forget all the talk of a new baby in the house and the guest room that was now a nursery. But what if I stubbornly demanded my sister? What if I could not let go of the idea?

I know I was a determined, persistent child.

Maybe it would be better to bring the baby home, at least for a time, then send her someplace where we could all go visit her sometimes. I would learn the truth, and they would not have to lie to me. Perhaps, my mother reasoned, that was more comprehensible and just. But what would it mean for me to have such a sister? My mother did not want me to have a sister who could never keep me company, who would always be a burden and an embarrassment.

They could send the baby away and start over. Other people would be paid to care for it. Some people, people who were more selfless than she was, might even enjoy caring for such children. She was not selfless at all, she knew; quite the opposite. She would not be a martyr – no, she wanted her own life back. If there was a way out of this, she would take it. This was not her life.

But what of her poor, sad, helpless baby? She wondered if she could really send away her own flesh and blood to be cared for by strangers. How could she be certain they would take good care of her? What if she were mistreated? What would it mean to grow up without love, without family?

Whatever this baby was, she told herself finally, it had come from her; it was her own intimate issue, her mess, her mistake. Maybe she would be lucky, and it would die. They often died young. She knew she was a terrible person to wish this.

Or maybe she would somehow grow to love this child. Maybe it was possible.

She knew that she should nurse it. She knew she should not deprive her own flesh and blood of this protection and nourishment. She was still its mother. She could not abandon it, much as she wanted to, even if she wanted to more than she had ever wanted anything. But, somehow, she couldn't, at least not yet.

Maybe she would nurse it for nine months to give it a good start in life, and then she would send it out into the world. She would find someone else to take care of it and let it go. Maybe she was an unnatural mother to even think of this. So be it. She would be the unnatural mother of an unnatural child.

She called the nurse, and the nurse brought the dreaded bundle to her. The baby lay limply in her arms. It did not cry. Mechanically, she put the baby to her nipple and tried to nurse it. But the baby was uncoordinated. She called the nurse again and asked her to take it away. Better not to get too close. Better the bottle than the breast.

Once upon a time, the fairies came and stole a mother's beautiful, healthy child and left an ugly changeling in its place. The fairies often did so to preserve and improve their race as human milk was necessary for fairy children to survive.

The parents could force the return of their own child by treating the changeling cruelly. The human mother was advised to brutalize the changeling by tossing it into the fire or throwing it into the lake so that the fairies would relent and return her child.

But the mother refused to harm an innocent child, despite knowing its nature.

Her own child now lived in the fairy mound. The little girl would grow up to be a beautiful woman; she would marry a fairy prince and live with the fairy folk forever.

3

One on Every Street

*S*cene: *A doctor's office, a doctor in a white coat, a woman sitting on a couch weeping, her husband consoling her.*

JOAN: There's been some mistake ... Tell me it's not true!

BOB: Please don't, Joan. Dr. *[inaudible]* is here to help us. Why don't you just listen to him?... Doctor, can't you give her something to calm her down?

DOCTOR: I'll give her a sedative ... But I think the best thing to give both of you right now is the truth. Nothing can be done until you both face up to the facts.

JOAN: It's true. You're asking me to face the fact that my little girl is ...

DOCTOR: Yes, Joan.

BOB: How could this possibly be, Doctor? There's never been anything like this [in my family].

DOCTOR: Mental retardation can happen in any family, Bob. It isn't inherited. It's an accident. A very common accident. The way statistics work it out, one in every thirty-three children is retarded, and you can bring it close to home if you realize that means there is a retarded child on every street ... You see

why I say it's a common accident ... One on every
street.

– *One on Every Street,* a film produced for the Ontario
government that aired on CBC Television, c. 1960

In a file of mementos my mother kept from my sister's birth,
there is a small card with a cascade of coloured baby toys alongside an ad for Carnation condensed milk. Next to these, there
is a printed form with handwritten notations.

The facts are so ordinary yet conceal so much; the little card
the first and lasting evidence that my sister existed, was born
exactly then, on a certain September evening, in a certain place,
before witnesses. Why was her length never measured? Was it
when they were measuring her weight that the nurse saw the
telltale signs and after that all else was forgotten? What was it
like for Dr. McIntosh, the same doctor who delivered me, to
be attending my mother on that day and to have to give her the
terrible news? What must the nurse have been feeling as she
filled in the standard card for "Baby Freeman"?

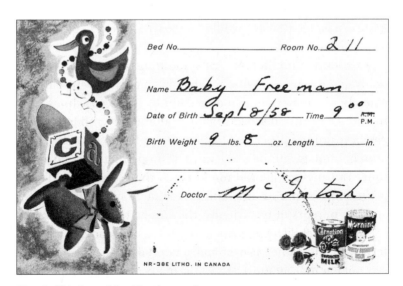

Hospital birth card for Martha, 1958.

Martha and my mother remained in the hospital for seven days while the doctors conducted tests to determine what other medical issues my sister might face. Did she have a heart condition, as so many Down syndrome children do? Yes, it seems she did. Hearing or vision problems? Gastrointestinal blockages? Guiltily, my mother took solace in the fact that half of such children did not live past their ninth birthday, though Dr. McIntosh told her that with modern medicine many were now making it into their twenties, a development that both she and the doctor regarded with considerable ambivalence.

Day in and day out, my mother lay listlessly in her hospital bed or sat bottle-feeding the baby in the chair beside it. Day in and day out, she pondered the meaning and consequences of what had happened. It was the same world, but not the same world. Things would never be the same. She would never be the same.

Although my mother did not want this baby, I believe that as the days passed the unhappy conviction settled over her that she deserved her. The more she pondered her fate, the more it seemed that Martha was the proof, the outer mark of her inner failure, a badge that she would now have to wear in public, her own scarlet letter.

Certainly, humiliation was something my mother was already deeply familiar with. She had been only eleven years old when her own mother abandoned her by fleeing the house and then the city after discovering my grandfather's infidelity. Perhaps my grandmother had had no choice but to leave her children behind, given the economics of single motherhood at the time. But my bewildered mother was then abandoned to the pursed lips, superior airs, and closed faces of the neighbours and the parents of her friends; they knew that no good could come from a child living in the motherless household of an adulterer and judged her as even more tainted when a woman who was not her mother moved in. Many of my mother's friends were not allowed to enter that household, and my grandparents only compounded my mother's shame when they divorced, the only parents to do so in the 1940s, a world of tenaciously married couples, a time when divorce was still unthinkable among "respectable" people. Eventually, her father remarried, and her mother moved back to Ottawa to run a boarding house and hair salon. But my grandmother then exacerbated her social sins by frequenting beer parlours with various men, to my mother's everlasting embarrassment.

From that early abandonment and its many social consequences, I suspect that my mother concluded what so many wounded children do: that she herself was flawed, unlovable, at fault. I believe she later saw my sister's birth as confirmation of her own unworthiness, her failure revealed and writ large in her "defective" baby. At the very moment when she most needed help, she couldn't bear for anyone else to see her shame.

That humiliation was renewed each day when she faced the mail. There were not as many cards and flowers as there had been at my birth, and most of those that did arrive must have taunted her. I imagine her glumly contemplating the image of a smiling baby swaddled in pastel-coloured blankets, happily floating down from the sky under a cloth parachute, while a teddy bear, duck, alphabet blocks, baby bottle, ball, christening gown, and flowers floated down alongside it. "Congratulations to All of You!" the card crowed in curly, gold-embossed script. Inside, she recognized the elderly, shaky hand that had written "Thinking of you often. Praying for you all. Love Aunt Jessica, Sept. 58." She did not want Aunt Jessica's pious sympathy.

On the table opposite her bed a nurse had placed red roses that had arrived in a brandy snifter along with a little card that read: "Dear June: Bob and I are looking at our own children and thinking very lovingly of you and George in your sorrow. We would like to see you at any time. Sincerely, Diane S." She knew Diane meant well, but it was hard to be reminded of other people's children.

Another card depicted exhausted parents, thin and angular, collapsing against each other, weighed down by a baby bottle, a rattle, a teddy bear, and a dripping diaper, with the words

"You've had it ... " just below. Inside the card, the parents celebrate with champagne as their baby sleeps peacefully in its crib, a long trail of *zzzzzzzz*'s rising like a telltale plume of smoke in a Hollywood western and "... ain't it wonderful? Congratulations!" the happy kicker. The senders obviously hadn't heard the news of Martha's condition.

They would all have to be answered. They would all have to be thanked. Some of her friends and relatives would insist on coming to see her, perhaps to gawk at her misfortune.

But there was one small card she tucked under her pillow and sometimes reread privately. It had a fuzzy, brown rabbit on the cover and inside only these words: "A gift for someone sweet and small, with warmest wishes to you all. Love Ron and Janice." It did not tear at her the way the others did, its offering as delicate as the baby's breath that accompanied the brash red roses, the gentlest reminder of Martha's innocence.

I know my mother did find comfort in a letter sent by Aunt May the day after Martha's birth, though she also could hardly bear to read it, for it spoke to her so directly.

Dear June and George,

We have all felt stunned and heartsick for you since the phone call came through a couple of hours ago. When I looked at my healthy, normal brood today, it seemed to me there was nothing I could say to you two that wouldn't be almost impertinence. It is so easy to bear other people's sorrows with fortitude, isn't it?

May recommended that my parents read Pearl Buck's *The Child Who Never Grew*, a book that had greatly helped several families she knew who had had a baby like Martha. Buck emphasized that such children

were real human beings, in as much need of love and affection as normal children. She was certain that their capacity for affection was not damaged, and their need for the secure knowledge of being loved was the same as for a normal child. She was angry when she saw how many defective children were just abandoned to an institution, and how wistful they were when the others had visitors.

May concluded that she and her husband were thinking of my parents a great deal: "I know that the baby's older sister will be a wonderful comfort to you these days."

If a famous writer had had such a child and had written about it and found something worthwhile to say about the experience that other people wanted to hear, perhaps my mother could also survive this tragedy. But she was wary, too, for she suspected that Pearl Buck was a much better person, more noble and self-sacrificing, than she could ever be, and she feared that May expected her to rise to this laudable standard. She could not bear to think that caring for this defective child was now her moral duty. But May's words may have influenced her or my father, for they did not send Martha away immediately at birth, as so many parents did.

Every day my mother would make resolutions that she would overcome her antipathy, get over her discomfort with the child, and be a good mother to it. She would stroke the baby's soft red hair as she fed her and breathe in her warm baby smell, relaxing for a moment, almost loving her. But then she would take the baby's hand and stare intently at the single crease in the palm or search the irises of her not-yet-brown eyes for the telltale Brushfeld spots that marked her difference, and she could not stop her tears. She told me later that she cried for six months.

It was always there, that difference; it could not be erased. She could not forget the child my sister might have been, the daughter she had dreamed of, for to do so would be to acquiesce and accept this cruel fate.

A few days after Martha's birth, one of the nurses on the ward, who I will call Mrs. Johnson, came to visit my mother. She sat down in the chair by my mother's bed and asked her how she was.

"As well as can be," my mother answered guardedly.

Mrs. Johnson made a few perfunctory comments then brought out a photograph of her own child, who also had the telltale eyes, the "mongoloid" look.

"It's not so bad," she told my mother. My mother looked at her dubiously. "You'll get used to it."

"I never will," my mother said.

"But you do," the nurse persisted. "You'll see. You meet other parents, and it's not so bad."

"I don't want to meet other parents. I don't want to see more of those children."

"There's a retarded children's association that we formed two years ago, so the children have somewhere to play where nobody will make fun of them."

"Great," my mother said, with a notable lack of enthusiasm.

"I know," the nurse said softly, and my mother's lower lip began to tremble. "I cried for months."

"I won't cry," my mother said, but the tears were already welling in her eyes.

The nurse silently took my mother's hand. My mother shrank back but did not pull it away.

"It's OK," the nurse said. "It's hell and you got a bum deal. It's not your fault. It's bloody unfair ... I know."

The tears suddenly coursed down my mother's cheeks, and she turned her face resolutely away so Mrs. Johnson wouldn't see them.

But my mother never forgot that nurse's compassion.

My mother came from a long line of Presbyterian Scots with closeted hearts and constricted feelings, and that was just normality. "I trust there will be no unseemly display of emotion," her stern and formidable grandfather had warned his children and grandchildren on the day of his wife's funeral. No one had dared disobey and face the dreadful consequences of his wrath, the only emotion, apparently, that he considered seemly.

But alcohol could loosen the tongues and swell the hearts of my mother's family. The men of the older generation would likely have agreed that there was nothing more desirable than to be anaesthetized from the full force of one's emotions, though one could sentimentally linger over the remaining traces of them with other men in a similar boozy condition. And the women? It was not seemly for a woman to be drunk (though one could be pleasantly tipsy in the right company); perhaps the feelings of the women went into their sharp tongues, which lashed their children or husbands and gossiped about their neighbours, or perhaps they were long-suffering and cried alone. My mother did not want to speak harshly, so she held her tongue and turned her feelings inward. It was her silent resentments, her wordless depressions, that would suffuse my childhood like the dank and heavy air of an August heat wave.

The first day after Martha's birth, my parents mourned together, but over the next several days, while my mother remained in hospital, they largely mourned apart. For a while my mother withdrew into herself, perhaps fearing she had failed my father by giving birth to an abnormal child. The woman she had imagined herself to be, the beautiful and capable woman she had seen in his admiring eyes, she was no longer. When my father visited her in hospital, she asked how I was doing at home or talked about the practicalities of Martha's care, rarely about what she felt. She did not want to lose her dignity in front of him, because he was all she had. Or perhaps her dignity was all she had. Perhaps deep down she also felt that he had failed her. He was older and stronger and a man, and she had always looked to him for protection, but this time he had not protected her. He must have felt helpless before the defeat he saw in my mother's haggard face, and knowing him, I can imagine he blamed himself for it.

My mother told me several years ago that while she was still recuperating in hospital, and while her mother looked after me (my grandmother being somewhat rehabilitated in my mother's eyes after she had re-entered my mother's life and offered her services as a babysitter), my father went on a three-day bender. He was a professed atheist, she told me, but the day after Martha's birth he asked God what he had done to deserve this – not in my mother's presence but at a bar in the company of Victor Sterling, his friend and my godfather. Victor later told my mother that in the depth of his despair my father had cried out: "What have I ever done that such an awful thing was visited on my daughter?"

It would be the pattern throughout their long marriage that my parents would rarely talk directly about their deepest feelings with each other, though they might intuit them. There was a circumspection in their relationship, a horror of being intrusive, of prying, which I think was characteristic of many marriages of the time. According to this code of behaviour, your partner's feelings were none of your business, and you did not burden your partner with your own. It was up to each of them to master their emotions privately or to turn to friends if all else failed. I know my mother did share her feelings about my sister with at least some family and friends, and I'm glad that she had that outlet and their support. But my parents' manner was to be considerate of each other in allowing silence and emotional space; they sympathetically imagined what the other might be feeling or discerned it through close observation (as I am doing here) but never insisted on disclosure. It was a way of showing respect that acknowledged their respective roles, their separate spheres as man and woman, husband and wife. They later took the same approach with me, rarely discussing emotions openly, theirs or mine.

There were other ways to communicate, of course, and of them laughter was my father's secret weapon, for he could disarm my mother and many other people with his warm and inoffensive humour and masterful storytelling. In a lot of ways, laughter was the glue that held them together, for he could always delight my mother with his wit and silliness – but he was not clowning now. Instead, as he later told me, his mind dwelt on the poor creature in the nursery, the child who would never be witty or beautiful or charming, who would need so much help just to live, who would never be sought after, who would never marry, who would be ridiculed and scorned. He knew others would point fingers and stare or mock. He wanted to protect his daughter, to care for her, as he wanted to care for his wife – in that, he was unfailingly generous.

As a child, however, he had observed that to be smart was the single most valued attribute in a person. His parents had claimed it was better to be generous or charitable, but he quickly learned that only those who were highly intelligent were truly deserving of respect. Only top marks were acceptable in school; his mother and father simply expected him to be brilliant and the best. War was wrong, and you shouldn't beat people up, but if you trounced or bullied them with your mind, if you demolished them with the logic of your argument, a natural hierarchy prevailed. Luckily, my father excelled at his studies and learned to win arguments by fair means or foul. In high school, he had taken extra subjects – Latin, Greek, and Hebrew – and won the B'nai Brith prize, a goy beating out all the Jews in Hebrew, reportedly to his parents' immense satisfaction. His intelligence was his ticket in life, his parents' pride and joy, and his defence. When he entered university at the age of sixteen, he was two years younger and a foot shorter than all his classmates, including the girls, who at first openly scorned him. It was only his quick and lively wit that saved him.

Although the doctors had reassured my parents that Martha's disability was an accident, there was still a popular train of thought that related mental retardation to parental intelligence and a lingering suspicion that the parents of Down syndrome children were somehow defective themselves, and this made my parents vulnerable. Only three years before my sister was born, these issues were still being debated in the scientific community. For example, on October 14, 1955, at a meeting of the Ontario Neuropathic Association at the Ontario Hospital School, Smiths Falls, one D. Gibson had given a paper titled "The Correlation of Parental and Mongol Intelligence and Its

Relation to the Etiology of Mongolian Imbecility." I wish I could locate the paper to know what it argued.

My parents had grown up in the 1920s and '30s, in a society shaped by a popular belief in eugenics, as Angus McLaren describes in *Our Own Master Race: Eugenics in Canada, 1885–1945*. The British statistician Francis Galton, the "father of eugenics" and a cousin of Charles Darwin, was the first to assert that "intelligence" was a scientifically valid concept, that it was inheritable, and that breeding techniques could and should be applied to human reproduction to improve the race. In his view, genetically superior beings should be encouraged to reproduce and the unfit stopped from doing so, by sterilization, if necessary. Intelligence testing was subsequently developed to quantify intelligence through a single number – one's intelligence quotient or IQ – allowing people to be ranked by supposedly intrinsic ability.

At first, eugenics enjoyed widespread scientific respectability. In 1912, the first international eugenics conference in London was presided over by Leonard Darwin, son of Charles Darwin, and the vice presidents of the association that sponsored it included Winston Churchill, Charles Eliot (the former president of Harvard), Alexander Graham Bell, and Sir William Osler, the renowned physician. Over seven hundred delegates from around the world attended, including professors from McGill University and the University of Toronto, the universities my parents later attended. They heard that "feeble-mindedness" (which according to North American definitions included both "morons" and "imbeciles") would rapidly disappear from human populations through segregation and the prevention of breeding.

In the ensuing decades, and especially during the Great Depression, which so shaped my parents' childhoods, social reformers warned about the scourge of deviancy and the moral, social, and financial burden of the feeble-minded on society. Many people believed it was necessary to stop the reproduction of the feeble-minded through incarceration or sterilization. The widely circulated story of the infamous Jukes family of New York State lent support to this view: five "mentally deficient" sisters had reportedly produced 1,258 descendants, costing the state an estimated $1.3 million over a seventy-five-year period. Even Tommy Douglas, the now revered founder of the Co-operative Commonwealth Federation (later the federal New Democratic Party), initially shared these concerns. He wrote his 1933 master's thesis on "The Problems of the Subnormal Family," though he later distanced himself from eugenicist views. While some moral reformers, particularly social gospellers such as my father's parents, attributed social "degeneracy" primarily to environmental rather than genetic causes, often focusing instead on the ills of urbanization and industrial capitalism, eugenicists popularized a vocabulary of deviance and degeneracy that even their opponents ended up using.

Canadian eugenicists were influenced both by American eugenicists, who decried the rapid breeding of supposedly inferior races and considered miscegenation a prime cause of degeneration, and by British eugenicists, who generally attributed feeble-mindedness to the supposed genetic inferiority of the lower classes. Nonwhites, immigrants, and poor people were thus variously blamed for transmitting mental deficiency, crime, sexual immorality, prostitution, syphilis, illegitimacy, and vagrancy from generation to generation, overburdening hospitals, schools, jails, and charitable organizations. In all cases, the feeble-minded were seen as impediments to progress, and reformers emphasized the role of scientific experts and the necessity for state control and interventionist approaches to solve the social problems the feeble-minded reputedly created.

It was certainly the general view through most of the twentieth century that "mental defectives" like my sister had nothing to offer either their families or society at large. They were economically unproductive, without value. As Thelma Wheatley notes in *"And Neither Have I Wings to Fly": Labelled and Locked Up in Canada's Oldest Institution*, even Dr. Beaton, the doctor who headed the Ontario Hospital for Idiots at Orillia, the first institution of its kind in Ontario, referred to such people as "the loathsome ones," while Helen MacMurchy, a renowned early twentieth-century Ontario public health pioneer, worked tirelessly to disseminate eugenicist ideas. In fact, the most vocal defenders of eugenics were medical doctors.

Many people, not just hard-core eugenicists, felt it would be better for all if such children died so that "survival of the fittest" prevailed. The severely disabled were described as monstrous, as throwbacks to a distant evolutionary past, half human and half ape. In various contexts, so-called merciful infanticide was practised, sometimes by not tying the umbilical cord. Hitler took this attitude to its extreme: in addition to killing Jews, homosexuals, and others, he killed from 70,000 to 95,000 mentally and physically disabled adults and 5,000 children between October 1939 and August 1941. Such ruthlessness gave eugenics a bad name, and it was increasingly discredited after the defeat of the Nazis, at least officially and scientifically, but such beliefs were not eradicated in the general population in Canada or elsewhere in the Western world. All of these associations were still in the air when my sister was born and classified as an imbecile.

My sister was considered a mental but not a moral imbecile, thankfully, and in any case, she never had children (she was later given the pill to make sure she wouldn't). But in spite of these precautions, she did reproduce – not in the usual sexual sense but more subtly.

It may sound strange, but she reproduced herself in me.

4

Substitutions

The mother who came back from the hospital was not the same mother who had gone in. Pale and lethargic, with deep circles under her eyes and a general air of sadness, she tried to make the effort to mother me, but even a two-year-old could sense that something terrible had happened. There was still the warmth of my mother's body when I snuggled in her arms, but something was dreadfully wrong with her spirit.

It bothers me that I have only the faintest impressions of those early weeks of Martha's life. I do not even know if I was taken to visit her in hospital. My early blurry recollections of my mother nursing an infant in a rocking chair in the baby's room, or my mother's back bending over a fidgeting, smelly wriggle of arms and legs at the changing station, all viewed from a low perspective, may well be confused with similar scenes after my sister Kate's birth two years later, when Martha had already been taken away and I was four years old.

I do know, from later conversations with my mother, that there was no celebration upon her return home, though my father's father jumped on a plane immediately upon hearing the news, and other relatives and friends did eventually come by to see Martha and offer their support. My mother had mixed feelings about those obligatory visits, though in truth she needed her friends and family. Some of those who came to see the baby

My mother holding Martha, with me beside her on
the couch, 1958.

said that Martha was still a pretty baby regardless. One friend
mentioned a friend's sister who also had a "mongoloid"; the
child eventually learned to make her own bed, brush her teeth,
and help with the household chores. My mother could only
shudder at such good news. Some people insisted on telling her
every irritating detail about Down syndrome they had gleaned
from the numerous books and newspaper articles they had consulted. She knew they meant well, but she could not bear to hear
about it. Because no one really knew what to say to my mother,
many of her visitors said little or avoided the subject of my sister
altogether, which also hurt and angered her. She soon developed
a sixth sense, discerning in each friend or relative what she felt
they were trying to hide – their secret disgust, their terror, their
sense of superiority, their condescending pity – though she also
was nourished by the genuine love and concern of some. But
no matter what they said, a painful and invisible wall separated
my mother from everyone else, for she felt she had to keep up
appearances and pretend she loved her baby.

My mother did most of the things one normally does with babies: that much I do remember. She fed Martha, changed her diaper, put her down for her morning and afternoon nap. She washed her diapers and hung them out on the line, she fed her strained carrots from the little Heinz baby food jars she had picked up at the supermarket, or she prepared soft food herself. But as the months passed there were some things she didn't do much at all, such as read baby books to my sister. What was the point? She didn't talk much to her either. There wasn't the delighted chatter that fills up much of the time of caring for a small child who can't talk herself yet. Instead, my mother often lapsed into silence. She did not spend long minutes lovingly looking at my sister, engaged in that intense reciprocal gazing, "each held in the sustaining view of the other," that Rosemarie Garland-Thomson sees as foundational to a child's sense of self-worth and its attachment to others. Did Martha feel seen? By anyone? I know my mother tried. But sometimes she would stare off into the middle distance, as if Martha and I were not there at all.

Where did she go when her mind went elsewhere? Perhaps, in a state of disbelief, she replayed certain scenes from her life before Martha – dances at the tennis club, lazy summer days at the cottage at Lake Clear, the night my father proposed to her, the proud moment of her wedding, her happiness at my birth. She could not believe she was the same person who had done those things – how could she connect that life to this? Perhaps she felt she was no longer in her own life, that a part of her had become detached, had gone missing, or perhaps had died.

For me it was different. I loved my parents, but Martha was the first being in my family who I saw as separate from me since I could not yet fully discern the boundaries between my parents and myself. She was someone who came after me, who was not originally part of my world or the initial grounding of my life. She was mine in a way my parents weren't – I belonged to my parents, but she belonged to me.

Me feeding Martha, c. 1959.

I would not know for years that my parents had decided within a few days of Martha's birth that they would not keep her. They knew her stay with us was temporary. It must have been hard to endure the waiting; they could not help comparing Martha to me and other "normal" children, and they wanted to try for another baby as soon as possible. They tried to be charitable and patient, but sometimes my mother couldn't really manage it.

It was disturbing to me as a very young child to observe how my parents treated Martha. My mother never neglected her, but there was a stiffness, a frozenness, as if she never relaxed. She was not the warm, motherly self she was with me. My father was more generous in his affection and more accepting, but he always deferred to my mother when it came to Martha, and he was never judgmental of my mother's treatment of her. I had no words to describe any of this, but something made me uncomfortable in the way they behaved with her.

I grew used to Martha watching me, always watching me, following me with her eyes, but sometimes she seemed anxious, and that annoyed me. Maybe she was envying me, resenting me, wanting what I had, that coveted place in my parents' hearts. Perhaps I only imagined that, but very early on I was aware of the difference in their treatment of us and of my privilege in enjoying my parents' love.

And yet I was happy in that house on Glengarry Road. It was my world, along with our friendly neighbours and the park down the street, though there was also the big elm in the backyard that eventually died of Dutch elm disease, the first pestilence that I knew of. How strange that even big, beautiful trees could be attacked by something small and invisible and would have to be cut down.

I know my mother tried to do her duty, but she was young and did not want to be chained to this child for years to come, and there was almost nothing in the way of support for her. Pearl Buck had written: "Now my eyes can find in any crowd the child like mine. I see him first of all and then I see the mother, trying to smile, trying to speak to the child gaily, her gaiety a screen to hide him from others. Those mothers' cries were always the same: 'The schools won't take our children. The neighbors don't want them around. The other children are mean to them ... What shall we do? It's not a crime to have a child like ours.'" But as my mother had foreseen, she was no Pearl Buck. She knew she did not have it in her to care for Martha for decades as Pearl Buck had done with her child. She simply could not accept Martha for who she was. She knew her own daughter was still in the fairy hill.

It has taken me a long time to recognize that there was something else that contributed to my mother's decision to send Martha away. I do believe it was largely my mother's decision, which my father then supported. My mother rejected the assumption that women should put their own desires aside and devote themselves to caring for others, that it was their lifelong obligation and duty. In Western societies, women family members had long been expected to care for children, aging parents, or sick relatives, and often they had no choice. Caregiving was considered a "natural" female activity, and nurturing was thought to be part of women's essential nature, a central component of what a woman was and should be. Self-denial and sacrifice were supposedly a mother's noblest attributes. Yet my mother at least partially rejected that role. She was the first woman in her family to earn a university degree and one of a minority of educated women of her generation who studied commerce rather than a traditional women's field of study such as nursing or education. Her own mother, despite her faults, had been an independent and successful businesswoman at a time when that was rare. It is undeniable that my mother would have had to carry the burden of caregiving. No one expected my father to quit his job and devote himself to the care of my sister for the rest of his life. And in this case, they believed that the caregiving would never end, that the child would never grow up. Although my mother had been forced to leave her job when she got married and fully expected to be a stay-at-home mother for some years as she and my father raised their family, she was a "modern," middle-class woman in that she also wanted to direct her own life as she saw fit.

My parents did not expect to keep Martha at home forever, but they could not easily send her away either. Nine months came and went, and Martha was eating solid food and starting to roll over. My mother certainly wanted Martha to be gone, but the awful thing was she had started to care for her child. Not in the same way as with me – it would never be the same – but still, there was an inescapable tie she couldn't deny. It was the thinnest, darkest thread of connection, but it was there.

But my mother was already pregnant again, had in fact become pregnant two weeks before Martha's first birthday. I doubt it was an accident, and it may even have been my parents' act of defiance, their attempt to reclaim a normal life. It was during this time that I believe my mother made some kind of psychic bargain, though I don't know with whom: if only she could send Martha away in exchange for this new child, a normal child, all would be right with the world. It seemed like a good plan but for one thing: all was not right with my mother.

Once the fact of her pregnancy was established, my father made inquiries to the Rideau Regional Hospital School in Smiths Falls, a small town within a two-hour drive of Ottawa. The initial response was not encouraging.

Smiths Falls,

Nov. 17, 1959

Re: Freeman: Martha Ann

Dear Mr Freeman,

This is to acknowledge your request and documentation in connection with the admission to this hospital school of the above mentioned child.

I regret that we have no vacancies at the present time and our waiting list is very lengthy, and is increasing rapidly due to the fact that our turnover of patients is, as you will realize, very small.

We are overcrowded now and unfortunately it will be several months before admission can be arranged. The child's name, however, has been placed on our waiting list, and as soon as a vacancy is available for the patient we shall communicate with you.

Yours very truly,

H.F. Frank, MD
Superintendent

As with my mother's previous pregnancy, I have no clear memories of my mother's changing shape or my own expectations, though this later pregnancy must have occurred in an atmosphere of tremendous tension and fear, a chronic anxiety that my sister Kate surely absorbed in the womb. Would my mother give birth to a second child with Down syndrome, rare as that occurrence was, but as the nurse, Mrs. Johnson, had done? Our family and friends were cheerful and encouraging but sometimes in a forced way that betrayed their own worries. My mother's terror ate away at her confidence, an insidious worm destroying the flower from within, to borrow a famous image of the Elizabethan poets. She knew only too well that nothing was assured.

My mother was not a religious person. She did not believe in God or go to church, but I suspect in her heart of hearts she prayed every day for a normal child, a replacement child, a better child, one who would develop properly. Perhaps she feared to love her unborn child until she could see that it was normal. She would not be fooled again.

And what would she do about Martha? It must have been so painful for my mother to think about the change that was hovering just beyond, waiting for her, a choice that she couldn't escape. At least she knew that my father would help her do whatever she needed to do when she was ready.

The months passed, and my mother was more and more convinced she would not be able to manage a new baby and Martha at the same time. Not physically. Not emotionally. Martha had only begun sitting up by herself when she was eleven months old, and it seemed she might not walk for years. My father was gone from 8:15 a.m. until after 6 p.m. each weekday, and he sometimes worked at home in the evening or on weekends. Who would help her manage? Still, they waited, and there was no word from the hospital school.

I've wondered since how Martha's admission came about since there were long waiting lists and, at that time, admissions to all institutions were almost invariably arranged through members of the provincial legislature. Decisions were not necessarily based on greatest need, and the superintendent of the institution was often told whom to admit. I've since read some of the letters sent by doctors on behalf of families to the Honourable J.W.

Spooner, minister of municipal affairs, who handled these admissions from 1962 to 1967, and it's clear that many families were desperate for some kind of help. For example, "John, aged 5 ... wears diapers and has to be fed. He eats only pablum and milk ... He gets very angry and bites his tongue until it bleeds; also bites other children. He does not walk and will not put any weight on his legs. He sleeps from 7:00 pm until 3 a.m., then wakes up and shakes his crib. He also frequently bangs his head." Other letters described the difficulties of a parent "looking after a child as badly retarded as this one in a family of seven other children, all of a comparatively young age"; the problems of a widow with a disobedient eighteen-year-old son, "a big husky fellow," whom she feared "might attack some young children"; or a mother on the verge of a breakdown, whose daughter was very difficult: "She is also physically sick and the father is also sick and unemployed."

According to my parents, it was at a meeting of the Ottawa and District Association for Mentally Retarded Children, a recently formed support organization for parents whose children were either in institutions or at home, that they were finally able to secure a place for Martha. It was there that they met and talked with Dr. Harold Frank, the medical superintendent of the Ontario Hospital School at Smiths Falls, later known as the Rideau Regional Centre. According to my mother, he took one look at her swelling belly and said Martha should be admitted right away. My father then received a letter stating that "arrangements for the admission of the above mentioned can now be made." My father was required to submit two medical practitioner's certificates for admission of a mentally defective patient, which certified that "(s)he is mentally defective and is a proper person to be confined in an Ontario Hospital or Hospital School." Dr. McIntosh also filled out the "Mentally Defective Patient's History" form:

Father, *38 years,* school grade reached: *masters of arts, economist*
Mother, *29 years, bachelor of commerce,* former occupation: *research worker in government*

Brothers and sisters: *Victoria Freeman, 3 years, not at school*
Age of parents at marriage: *34, 25*
Not blood relations,
Have any relatives been mentally ill, feeble-minded, epileptic,
   neurotic, eccentric? Give particulars. *No: One uncle can be
   called depressive on his father's side*

The form asked for the particulars of Martha's personal and development history, educational history, economic history, social history, and "moral history":

(a) Is there a history of petty thieving or stealing? *No*
(b) Does patient do injury to himself? *No*
(c) Is patient cruel to people or animals? *No*
(d) Is patient a fire-setter? *No*
(e) Describe patient's sex interests and experiences,
   if any: *No*

Habits: Is patient quarrelsome, quick or violent tempered,
   suggestible, stubborn, seclusive, suspicious, obedient,
   etc.? *No – age 13 months* [sic] *– she is very easy to attend and
   a very lovable child.*

My father soon received a reply from Dr. Frank: "All documentation has been received and is in order and we are now prepared to receive the patient on Wednesday May 11, 1960. The child should be brought to Hospital by responsible relatives who should be prepared to give a complete history for our records."

As children were generally admitted at birth or a number of years later, my sister's admittance at twenty months seems to have been somewhat unusual. According to a government film, made circa 1960, "Doctors agree that retarded children should be kept home until the age of six, but sometimes exceptional conditions make this impossible." I do not know why Martha's case would have been considered exceptional. My parents had more money and fewer children than many other parents, so their need was certainly no greater than anyone else's. Perhaps it was their class privilege that pushed them to the front of the line.

Was it at this point, when her departure was assured, that my parents finally told me of Martha's condition, or was it at this point that I finally understood? Again, I have no recollection of this pivotal moment. But somehow I came to understand that Martha was different from other little sisters. She had a mistake in her genes (blue jeans I imagined they were talking about) or in her chromosomes (which was surely one of the first big words I learned). Something was not normal, not right. She was slow. She was slow to sit and crawl. In fact, although a year and a half old, Martha was nowhere near walking yet. There was something wrong with her, something I couldn't see or understand, but she would never be like me; she would never do what I could do. She would never be as smart as I was. A mistake.

From that time, I developed an air of superiority and condescension towards her. *Poor Martha, poor little sister.* I felt exceedingly virtuous in taking care of her. She was damaged goods, inferior, not quite human. I would look at her, observe her carefully, assess her limitations. She became alien to me, not one of us. She didn't just have Down syndrome; she *was* Down syndrome. Increasingly, she was *only* Down syndrome. All I saw was her inability and lack.

I, too, began looking for signs of her difference. It was the subtlest thing, but it was also a physical thing, and it became ugliness in my eyes. I saw her short, thick neck, her big tongue lolling out of her mouth, her squat body and stubby fingers. She was the opposite of the princess I wanted to be. The only beautiful thing about her was her red hair, but it was wasted on her, for she would never find a prince.

My friends Susan and Eleanor, who were two and four years older than me, respectively, were obsessed with princesses, princes, and weddings, like most girls born in the Dominion of Canada in the 1950s. Even my mother grew misty-eyed when she remembered the royal coronation, the first thing ever broadcast on television in Ottawa, when the young Princess Elizabeth had been crowned Queen four years before I was born. Elizabeth had travelled in the royal coach to Westminster Abbey with dashing Prince Philip – a real live fairy tale.

Susan's older sister had paper dolls of the two royal princesses, Elizabeth and Margaret, swathed in a dry-cleaner's plastic bag and stored in a drawer, frozen in time. Susan's sister would take them out from time to time and allow us to change their beautiful cut-out clothes, which had little white tabs that folded neatly over their shoulders to secure their elegant gowns, a precarious arrangement that sometimes resulted in their severe embarrassment (much to our delight) at the royal balls we concocted for them. Our lives were filled with Snow White, Cinderella, and the two princesses, and the point of it all was weddings. I remember spending a whole afternoon practising how to walk correctly up the wedding aisle. We took to wearing our mothers' slips and crinolines, and we filled out our bosoms with socks or tissues. We took turns wearing the glittering tiara that had been part of Susan's Hallowe'en princess costume as we walked in slow, measured steps up the make-believe wedding aisle in all our royal dignity.

"Why does Martha look so funny?" Eleanor asked one day in the midst of our royal preparations. "She looks like a monkey."

I kicked the carpet morosely with my shoe.

"There's something wrong with her," Susan chimed in. "She's retarded."

"I know," I said hotly, flushing a deep crimson, not sure whether to defend Martha or abandon her. "She's a slow learner."

"A retard!" Susan added, with a sick kind of glee, singing out the word several times for effect. "Retard! Retard!"

"She's a mongoloid," I offered, trying to mollify them.

"I don't know how your mother touches her," Eleanor confided with a patently false sympathy. "Isn't she afraid of cooties?"

Cooties? What were cooties? I looked anxiously from Eleanor to Susan.

We were called to lunch, and that was the end of it. But from that day I knew the shaky ground I stood on, even with my friends.

In April 1960 I turned four. We played pin the tail on the donkey at my birthday party and gobbled crustless party sandwiches, made with bread, peanut butter, and banana that had been wrapped in a roll and then sliced to make pinwheels. There were favours in the cake, nickels and dimes wrapped in wax paper that you had to be careful not to bite into. My favourite present – a baby doll that wet her pants through a hole in her plastic bottom – was given to me by my parents so I could practise changing diapers and learn how to be a mother. She had blue eyes and curly golden hair and a beautiful expression. I called her Gwendolyn, and she was a princess. She and I were immediately inseparable.

One day in early May, a few weeks after my birthday, I was playing with Gwendolyn in Martha's room while Martha crawled on the floor and attempted to pull herself up. Curious about how Gwendolyn was put together, I pulled and twisted her arm until it popped out of its socket. Try as I might, I could not reattach the arm. Martha grabbed it and put the end with the little plastic hand in her mouth. I tried to get it away from her, but she wouldn't give it back to me.

"Mum," I cried. "Martha's got my doll's arm, and she won't give it back! She's wrecking it!"

My mother came into the room and swiftly pulled the arm from Martha's mouth. Martha began to howl.

"Stop that," my mother shouted, and even I was startled by her vehemence. Martha gaped at her open-mouthed for a moment and then howled louder. My mother picked up Martha and plopped her roughly in her crib. "You stay there until you learn to behave."

"She's so stupid," I shouted.

"Did she pull off your dolly's arm?"

Miserably, I nodded. I didn't want to admit that I had done it. "She's a retard," I said sullenly. My mother stared at me, and all the anger went out of her.

She sighed deeply. "You mustn't say that, Tut. She can't help it."

"She's a moron," I shouted petulantly. I marched out of the room and slammed the door.

My mother tried to reattach Gwendolyn's arm, but she couldn't. I threw my broken doll into the back of my closet and never played with her again.

A few days later, Martha was gone.

It is shocking to me that I remember nothing of Martha's actual departure. I don't remember what I was told or when I was told or even if I was told that she was leaving. One day, she simply wasn't there. Did I go with my parents to Smiths Falls on the day she was taken there? Was that the first day I saw the huge sprawling complex of the hospital school?

No. My parents made that sad journey, a two-and-a-half-hour drive through the scrub and deadwood of eastern Ontario, without me. It was May and likely beautiful weather, though when I imagine this trip in my mind it is always grey and raining. They drove up to the school and left her there, a twenty-month-old baby, in the care of strangers, in the home for children with damaged brains and orphans and others who were not wanted. That was the end of her brief stay in the world of the normal.

The hospital records document that Martha was admitted on May 11, 1960. Her file reads, "Admitted carried in father's arms."

Mental condition: Quiet, happy.
Assigned to female infant ward.
28 pounds, 32 inches tall.
Clean, well-nourished,
6 upper and 4 lower teeth.
Attitude of patient on admission: co-operative, quiet during admission routine.
Articles brought with patient: rocking horse.

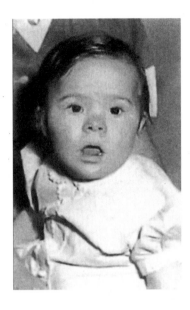

Institutional photo of Martha, shortly after her arrival at Rideau, 1960.

It would be more than fifty years before my mother spoke to us of this day. She told my sister that when they first took Martha to her ward, my sister happily crawled towards the other children. But as my parents turned to leave, Martha suddenly realized what was happening and began to crawl after them, crying piteously. Somehow, they kept walking, down the long hallway, out the door, away.

May 26, 1960

Dear Dr. Frank,

It is now about two weeks since our child was admitted, and we would very much appreciate hearing anything there is to tell us about how she seems to have settled in, if someone could find the time to drop us a line – especially since we won't be able to visit her ourselves for a few weeks yet because of the imminent arrival of a new baby.

Yours very truly,

George E. Freeman

May 27, 1960

Dear Mr. Freeman,

In reply to your letter of the 26th of May 1960, we are pleased to report that Martha Ann has made a satisfactory adjustment to the hospital environment and is happy and contented. Her physical health is satisfactory.

Please rest assured that she is receiving the best possible care and attention.

Yours very truly,

H.F. Frank, M.D.
Superintendant

JOAN: But can't Betty be cured? Can't she grow up to lead a normal life?

DOCTOR: No, Joan, she can't be cured. Helped, yes, but not cured. *(He walks over to the couch and sits down beside Joan in a solicitous manner.)*
With proper care and training, Betty may reach the mental age of eight, but that will likely be the limit, and this is a hard fact to have to face and learn to live with ... But remember this, there are 500,000 mentally retarded people in Canada. That means a million mothers and fathers have gone through this thing before you. You're not alone.

BOB: Well, doctor, we now know beyond a doubt that our little girl is mentally retarded, and we know, too, that we'll have to live with it somehow. Now what can we do for Betty?

DOCTOR: Just what comes naturally. Love her, look after her. Someday, we may have to see about putting her under the care of one of the Ontario hospital schools.

JOAN: *(Reacting in horror.)* You mean in an institution?

DOCTOR: Well, you can call it that if you like. I prefer to
          think of these places as communities where a child
          can be happy ... sometimes very useful ...

          Joan, we find modern living a little overwhelm-
          ing at times, don't we? Just think about how dev-
          astating it must be for the retarded to cope with
          the world. Your little girl may even be happier,
          better off, in a community which she can under-
          stand, a community where she is understood.
          Try to remember that.

                    – *One on Every Street*, c. 1960

5

The Fairy Hill

My sister had disappeared. I did not know where she was. I did not know why she had gone. I could not comprehend her absence or why my parents seemed to be so accepting of it. I felt a kind of horror, a dead nothingness. I could not name what wasn't there.

Where was my sister? I became obsessed with this question. I asked my mother, and she patiently tried to explain, but the words didn't make sense to me. Where was my sister? Where was Martha? Who had taken her? Where had she gone? My mother grew short-tempered with me and told me to "buck up."

Where was my sister? Day in and day out this question tormented me. *Martha, where have you gone?* She had disappeared into nothingness. It seemed it was up to me to keep her memory alive because my parents never spoke of her. It was up to me to speak to her, to encourage her to keep living, wherever she was. *Martha? Are you there?*

Martha was gone, and there was nothing I could do and nothing I could say that would change that. No one wanted to hear what I thought or felt about it. My parents said it was for the best and that they did it for me. I knew I should be grateful, and I did feel so privileged that they did this for me. Eventually, I stopped fighting it. I became complicit. I agreed with it. I accepted it.

Two weeks later, my mother gave birth to Kate. I can't imagine my mother's mental state at this point. She had given up one child and was due to have another at any moment. She could not have been sleeping well. What a horrible mixture of grief, guilt, and fear my sister Kate was born into.

If I had been my mother, I would have wanted to be totally unconscious for the birth. I cannot imagine her fear as she went into labour for the third time. But my mother was brave. She gave birth to my sister without general anaesthesia, and for the first time my father was at her side, for the newly formed Ottawa Natural Childbirth Association had successfully agitated for fathers being present in the delivery room. Even so, those first few moments must have been stressful as my new sister emerged to claim her place among the living, when she was visible but not yet known. Once it was confirmed that she was a fine, healthy infant, my mother was triumphant, my father ecstatic. The doctors and nurses celebrated along with my parents. Now, at last, my mother and father were back on track, living the life they had dreamt of and felt they were entitled to. There was cake when they came home, a celebration with friends, replete with champagne, cigars, flowers, the works. I was buoyed along by the good spirits, the chatter, the oohs and aahs over the new arrival.

I remember the curious and then annoying sound of my new sister crying in the night. Kate had a very different cry from Martha's: sharper, more grating, like sandpaper; it made you get up and pay attention to her. I remember my father holding her in his arms and walking her back and forth in the hallway, trying to get her back to sleep. I remember my mother explaining to me the miracle of a baby's mustard yellow poop, which didn't smell as bad as normal poop, and I remember how Kate's tiny baby's bum would get chapped and bright red and have to be smeared with white diaper cream thick as clown makeup. I remember the smelly diaper pail, the reek of ammonia, and the man from the diaper service who picked up the used diapers in a huge bag and in return left a stack of clean white diapers. I helped my mother fold them in threes and then once over the long way before we arranged them in the bottom of the changing station. I was so happy helping her with this new baby because she was finally happy again. The baby slept in a wicker bassinet in my parents' room for the first few months, and I liked to slip into their room to watch the gentle rise and fall of my sister's breathing as she slept.

The house was brighter now, but after the initial celebrations my own mood darkened. I was bewildered and there was no place for my grief.

I can see that darkness in a photograph taken a few months after Kate's birth. Once again, my mother sits in the lawn chair in the garden in the late summer or early fall. There are a few fallen leaves on the grass. She wears earrings and a pretty dress, and her long, shapely legs are crossed at the ankles, her slender feet encased in stylish pumps. Her face is soft and relaxed, her body lush and contented. All her attention is focused on the new baby in her arms. She looks down at my sister, and a gentle smile plays across her face. My sister's eyes are half closed, and she is reaching out with one arm across the arm of the Muskoka chair, looking off into some indistinct space.

I stand beside her in a short dress with puffy, short sleeves, white socks, and patent leather shoes. My hair is short, and my bangs are ragged because I had attempted to cut them myself. I am leaning my right arm against the arm of the Muskoka chair, beside my mother and Kate, but in no way am I connected to them. There is a look on my face that haunts me. My defiant eyes meet the camera, but everything is contained, my jaw clenched, the lips slightly pursed to hold it all in. Something is choked down, my body refusing to discharge its energy. My pudgy arms are those of a four-year-old, but my expression is of a much older child, all intensity and disillusionment and anger. I am looking out at the world, and I don't like what I see. I am trying to smile, but I can't. I am determined not to show what I feel.

**My mother holding Kate, with me by her side, shortly
after Martha's institutionalization, 1960.**

My parents didn't seem to recognize that I lived in a state of
silent, impotent rage. No one seemed to understand that my
world had been taken away from me or that I felt I couldn't
trust anything. It felt wrong that Kate was being nursed in the
same rocking chair that Martha had been held in and was being
changed at the same table. My mother seemed to like this baby
better than Martha, but I could not forgive this interloper for
taking the place of my sister. And my father became completely
wrapped up in Kate, which was somehow much more of a betrayal than just the regular birth of a sibling would be. Perhaps
my father poured all of his pain about Martha into his love for
this new child. Perhaps he turned away from me because he
couldn't face my bewilderment and pain.

Even now, more than fifty years later, I can't begin to express the rage I felt, the bitter sense of loss. I was never able to speak it then. I swallowed it down, was a good girl, denied my pain to lessen the pain of others. I did this out of love for my parents but also out of fear, for if my parents did not love Martha perhaps they only pretended to love me. Perhaps one day I would also be sent away. I had not just lost Martha, then; I had lost the security of my parents' love.

I was afraid they would send me away if I misbehaved, but I was overwhelmed by my feelings and couldn't control myself. My mother was busy with the new baby, and I began to act out to get my mother's attention. One day, for some unremembered reason, I was so overcome with rage that I began to throw things at her. I must have been completely out of control because my mother locked herself in the bathroom to get away from me. This only enraged me further, and I erupted in a torrent of screeching, pounding, and hitting. Despite my small size, I picked up a wicker-and-wood clothes hamper and hurled it against the bathroom door, screaming "I hate you! I hate you!" Horrified by my own words and the power surging through my body, I collapsed in a sobbing heap outside the door.

My rage didn't change anything, and over time it dissipated. Eventually, my feelings about my sister were locked away, hidden in a place so private that even I did not acknowledge its existence, a tiny windowless room with a locked door that rarely opened and was guarded, a place where no one looked in and from which no sound escaped. What went on there no one knew. Whatever lurked in there could die, could starve, and I wouldn't care. No one would. It was a place without air, a place of radical emptiness, where nothing could or should exist. And yet something did.

At some point, many weeks or perhaps it was even months later, my parents took me to the hospital school to see Martha. It may have been quite a while later because my parents first had to get over the exhaustion of having a new baby, and then

Martha got trench mouth in August and was in isolation for two weeks. We didn't see her on her second birthday in September either, so it may have been after that. I can only wonder what my parents felt on that anniversary.

Dear Mr. Frank,

Re: Birthday Party for Martha Ann Freeman

I understand that it is possible to arrange a party for patients on their birthday. My daughter will be 2 years old on Thursday, Sept. 8, and I would very much appreciate it if a party could be held in the ward to mark the occasion. I enclose $5.00 to cover expenses.

Could someone let me know whether Martha needs anything in the way of new clothes, etc.?

Yours very truly,

George Freeman

Sept. 13, 1960

Dear Mr. Freeman,

In reply to your recent letter, I am pleased to inform you that the birthday party was held for Martha last Friday. The children all had a very enjoyable time.

Sincerely,

H.F. Frank, M.D.
Medical Superintendent

Finally, the day came when we headed out to the hospital school. We drove for about an hour and a half through the scrubby forests and struggling farms along Highway 7 and then turned south on Highway 15 to Smiths Falls. We followed the signs out of town and then turned off the highway and headed up a long drive through a phalanx of trees. We emerged at the top of a hill before a sprawling complex of over fifty interconnected two-storey brick buildings. For the first time, I saw where all the mistakes of nature and the mistakes of society were collected and isolated, kept away from all those upstanding citizens who feared and hated them.

On that first visit, as we passed through the double doors of the imposing main entrance, I was assailed by the industrial stink of disinfectant that was undoubtedly used to scrub down the tiled hallways and possibly the children themselves. We walked down corridors so long and unfriendly I imagined one could get lost and never find one's way out. We passed long lines of strange-looking beings – *What were they? Children? Adults?* – shuffling and grunting as they were shepherded to unknown destinations. I couldn't help staring after them with a mixture of revulsion, curiosity, astonishment, and dread.

Why did I stare? In *Staring: How We Look*, Rosemarie Garland-Thomson discusses how we stare at what seems illegible, inexplicable, unruly, and strange, how the extraordinary excites but alarms us, because it is unpredictable. To stare is to ask, "Why are you different from me? What happened to you?"

We walked down one and then another hallway past various shut doors until we came to the glass door of the female infant ward. We pushed it open and entered a small waiting room. A woman in a hospital uniform greeted us. We identified ourselves and asked for Martha. She invited us to sit down, and then the nurse or aide disappeared into the inner sanctum; after several minutes, she came out with my sister, having retrieved her from its mysterious confines like a storekeeper obtaining an item from the stockroom.

The nurse led Martha to my mother. In the time between Martha's arrival at Smiths Falls and our visit, she had begun to take a few faltering steps, though she was still wobbly. My mother exclaimed over this, gave her a perfunctory kiss, and then set her down on the floor of the waiting area. She brought out some toys from her bag, a small teddy bear and a cloth ball, which

Main entrance to the "hospital school."

The endless main hallway at Rideau.

she set in front of Martha. My parents sat on the two vinyl-covered chairs and talked at her.

Martha sat there. She blinked but was otherwise without expression. She just sat there and looked off into the distance. She did not try to crawl or play with the things in front of her. None of us knew what to do. I sat cross-legged on the floor beside her and began to make faces at her, an old game. Only gradually was I able to tease a smile out of her. I redoubled my efforts and started making loud farting noises until my mother shushed me. Only then did Martha laugh, but it did not last long. She sat there listlessly, her legs splayed out before her, and stared at me.

We spent a miserable hour there under the watchful eye of the nurse. Eventually, I rolled the ball, and she crawled after it several times in a row. My mother kept trying to interest her in the teddy bear, but Martha ignored it. Only my father took her hands and proudly guided her wobbly steps up and down the hall. Then it was time to go. My mother stood up awkwardly, took Martha's two hands, pulled her to a standing position, and led Martha to the nurse. A worried look crossed Martha's face, and she began to twist and whine.

My mother remonstrated with her, "It's time to go now, Martha. We'll come back and see you another time. No, don't cry. There's a good girl. Here's the nurse."

Martha clung to my mother and would not let go.

"Let go, Martha. It's time to let go. Come on, now. Don't make a fuss." But Martha made a fuss. She made an awful moaning sound that was both despairing and defiant, and I started to cry too.

"Martha, stop it now. It's time to say goodbye. We'll come back soon," my mother said. And with that, she pried Martha's hands from her own and handed her over to the nurse, who picked her up and carried her away. "Now don't you start," she said to me. But I was sobbing loudly.

My father scooped me up in his arms as we headed back out the glass door and down the long corridor. It seemed to take forever to get out of that miserable building, but finally we stepped outside and gulped fresh air. We walked silently over to the parking lot.

My father and Martha at Rideau, c. 1960.

Martha with my father and I at Rideau, c. 1960.

My mother slid into the passenger seat, slamming the door behind her. My father helped me into the back seat then went around to the driver's side to take his place at the wheel. The engine turned over and hummed into life, and we were off, leaving that hideous place and poor, miserable Martha behind.

My mother turned on the radio, and we escaped to the sound of Elvis Presley singing "Are You Lonesome Tonight?" Once we turned onto the highway and made it through Smiths Falls, my mother abruptly switched off the music, and we travelled the rest of the way home in silence.

But stop. There is something wrong with this account. Where was Kate? Did she come with us? If not, where was she? Perhaps she was left behind with my grandmother, but it's also possible she was with us that first time we visited Martha, and I've simply obliterated her from my memory. Now, I imagine the moment when Martha saw the baby, if not on that visit then a subsequent one. She saw the new baby and saw everything; she didn't need words to understand betrayal. She simply stared open-mouthed at the baby. She knew. I swear, she knew.

The next time we went, we turned down the wrong hallway and ended up in the wrong ward. This one was for hydrocephalic babies, babies whose heads were grotesquely swollen from too much fluid on the brain. We saw one being visited by disconsolate parents before my parents realized their mistake and hurried me out of there. I did not know what I had seen, but I knew I had seen something terrible. Their spinal cords were not closed properly, my father told me, and most of them would die. Those that didn't would have irreversible brain damage. My father was so compulsively honest. I had smelled the sadness of that ward, and I did not want to go there again to see the bereaved parents hovering over the infants.

So that was how I learned about children who were not wanted or who were abandoned or who caused their parents unbearable heartache.

And that was how I learned about dispossession, that the things that have been taken from you are the things you love the most, as any exile knows.

I do not remember consciously deciding I would remain connected to Martha forever. Even to think of Martha was to be disloyal to my mother and all she was trying to accomplish, the normal life she was trying to give me. But my deepest, darkest secret – and also my most terrifying fear – was that it was now entirely up to me to keep Martha alive. For I had come to the terrible realization that my mother actually wanted Martha dead.

Somehow it seemed that only I could sustain her existence by never forgetting her, by never severing our connection. So when safely alone, I would talk to her, and she would talk to me. I didn't even have to say things out loud because Martha knew what I was thinking. She was always there, in a secret part of me. No one could take her away from me. And she wasn't retarded. She was normal like you and me. She was my beautiful sister, and she was mine. And she knew everything about everybody and about what was going on, because she was smart.

And so I, too, became a strange child, a child caught in another reality, a child split in two, the two parts never co-existing in the same time and place – and my parents didn't even realize it. And neither, really, did I.

Changeling:

1. a child surreptitiously or unintentionally substituted for another.
2. (folklore) an ugly, stupid, or strange child left by fairies in place of a pretty, charming child.
3. (archaic) a half-witted person, idiot, imbecile.

6

Jesus Loves Me

Four months after Martha's expulsion from the family, I started
junior kindergarten. On my first morning, my mother left Kate
with Madame Latour and walked hand in hand with me up Beck-
with Street, along Main Street for a very long way, and then right
onto an unfamiliar street, Evelyn Avenue, a journey that would
be repeated so often over the next seven years it still forms an
indelible pathway in my brain. I remember how long it took to
walk that route and the seemingly aimless collection of houses
we passed – the somewhat unkempt one on the first corner that
had rangy bushes and bare patches in the lawn; another just before Main Street that looked like a small cottage but had brightly
coloured, slatted metal awnings over some of the windows, hooded
eyelids over sightless eyes; a third covered in ugly brown stucco
that looked sad, especially in the rain; a fourth so completely
covered in ivy I imagined the house underneath being choked
and obliterated. Such unprepossessing houses, built after the
war for returning soldiers, and they got shabbier as we reached
the far end of Main Street.

The most important landmark was on the other side of the
street and about halfway to the school: McTier's, a variety store.
Just the sight of McTier's heavy sign hanging over the dusty
sidewalk would awaken in me an intense craving for sweets, for
it was stocked with licorice, Bazooka gum, toffee, jujubes, and

other delights. On that first day, however, we walked right on by, past all the familiar landmarks, into unknown territory.

Finally, we turned onto Evelyn Avenue, and I became aware of a cacophony of shouts, calls, squeals, and screeches that filled the air with a strange and relentless energy. The noise came from two playgrounds full of raucous children, one on either side of an imposing red brick building, three storeys high, with banks of tall windows and pale yellow trim. This was Lady Evelyn Public School, our destination. We walked right past the first playground, a swirling panorama of girls, some skipping double dutch to a chanting singsong, others playing with yo-yos or balls and jacks, still others shrieking and chasing one another in games of tag, and others quietly talking in pairs. We continued past the impressive front entrance of the school, which was never used by children, then turned into the teeming, seething, unbelievable chaos of male energy that was the boys' playground. I held my mother's hand tightly as we dodged the yelling, hurtling boys, continued past the boy's double-doored entrance, and came to a newer addition at the back of the building, where there was a flight of stairs leading to a big wide cement verandah. My mother led me up the stairs, pulled open a big heavy door, and we walked in.

Before me was a big, bright room with tall windows shaded by yellowing venetian blinds. It smelled of some kind of cleaner. There were large posters on the walls of enormous coloured letters of the alphabet and others of friendly baby animals with large, cloying eyes. Everywhere I looked there were children, some standing at a big sandbox, scooping up sand with plastic shovels and packing it into pails, others rooting through a rack of clothes and transforming themselves with red firefighter's hats or grown-up dresses covered in sequins, others seated at a big table drawing pictures with big, thick crayons. I was amazed to see, a little to my right, a child-size painted wooden stove with an oven door that opened. Beside it stood a play sink that had a real tub of sudsy water in it, in which a little girl scrubbed plastic dishes, and beyond that a wooden refrigerator, painted white, with doors that opened. Children sat at a kitchen table set with plastic plates, and they were even pretending to cut up imitation fried eggs and toast with plastic knives and forks! It was the most marvellous play kitchen I had ever seen, and I was itching to go explore it.

But something about this room also made me uncertain, and I hesitated in the doorway, unsure about whether or not I wanted to enter. A slender, dark-haired woman waved us in and came over to meet us. She had a kindly face and told us her name was Miss Sloan. She took my hand and began to lead me farther into the cavernous room. Suddenly, my mother gave me a kiss on the top of my head.

"I'll be back to pick you up at lunch time," she said in an excessively cheerful voice, and she began moving away from me, heading towards the door.

A strange and awful sound came out of me, and my mother turned back, a look of panic on her face.

"She'll be fine," Miss Sloan said to my mother and waved her out.

I stared in horror as the door closed behind her.

For a moment, I went still. Then I began to whimper and then wail. Miss Sloan held me in her arms and repeated that my mother would be back at lunch, but I could not be consoled. I wept with every ounce of my being, every last breath of oxygen, on and on. I could not believe what had happened, that my mother had abandoned me. I did not know how she could do that. I knew full well that, whatever she said, she might not be coming back or that she might never let me come home. I did not want to be given over to strangers as my sister had been.

It felt like the shudders and heaves would never stop coming out of me. It was like the violent act of retching, when you expel every last vestige of food or drink in your body and then it feels like your insides will come out too until you are turned completely inside out. The room was spinning. I was completely beside myself, unconscious of who saw or what they thought of me. Eventually, finally, the shudders diminished, and everything was spent. I lay curled in a fetal position on the cold floor with my eyes scrunched shut, willing myself somewhere else, anywhere else but there in that room, without my mother. Finally, I opened my eyes and stared disconsolately at the door, but I no longer had the energy even to will my mother back into the room. All I wanted to do was sleep, to escape into unconsciousness. I shut my eyes again, and all went mercifully dark.

When I woke up, Miss Sloan was beside me. She helped me to my feet and led me into a circle of children. "Children, this is Victoria," she said, and I felt all those children's eyes on me. I didn't know any of them. She said it was hard for everybody on their first day and that some of the other children had been coming for several days now, that I would get used to it, just as they had, and that I would make some new friends. Maybe it was true, but I didn't know if I could believe her or if she even knew that my mother might not come back. Miss Sloan told me I could sit in the rocking chair for as long as I wanted but that she was going to lead an activity now, and I was welcome to join in.

She laid out a big clump of green playdough on a low table covered with a plastic cloth with a yellow-and-white gingham pattern. She set out cookie cutters and two rolling pins and invited several children to join her in making shapes from the dough. She invited me as well, but I sat morosely on the chair while the other children played. Then I listened to them sing. Every once in a while I would start to cry again, and great shuddering heaves would take over my body. I did want to play with the play kitchen and the playdough, but my body had become incredibly heavy, and I couldn't move from the chair.

Suddenly, there was a scrape, and the outside door opened again. My heart raced in a single moment of expectancy, but it was not my mother returning. It was another new child arriving with her mother. This girl, Amy, was also nervous and shy but not nearly as distraught as I had been. She cried for about three minutes and then joined the other children for story time. I was beginning to feel embarrassed over how much I had cried. I was a big crybaby, and now Miss Sloan and all the other children knew that about me. Now, I was too embarrassed to play with the other children, so I sat and sulked all morning, waiting, waiting, waiting for deliverance.

Finally, just before noon, a bell rang, and we put on our sweaters and jackets and lined up by the door. Then we marched out, two by two, onto the veranda. I could hardly bear to look for fear she wouldn't be there, but there, waiting below, was my mother amid a crowd of other mothers. We children broke rank and flew to them in a single movement like a flock of birds. My mother smiled broadly and gave me a big hug. I felt the tears rush to my eyes, but then I was so angry I did not hug her back, and then I couldn't stop crying. She took my hand, and to my immense relief we turned and walked out of the schoolyard, heading for home. Along the way, we stopped at McTier's, and my mother bought me a bag of jujubes. The sun shone brightly on the way home, and I began to feel better and less confused. But I knew I had narrowly missed being abandoned, and I resolved to be a very good girl to make sure I would not be.

The next morning, my mother walked me to school again, and I had the same fearful reaction when she left, though perhaps I cried a little less. All morning I waited anxiously to see if she would be there again when school was let out, and thankfully she reappeared, this time with Kate in the perambulator, and once again we walked home together. After lunch, she let me lie beside her on the couch while she watched the afternoon movie and Kate napped; I had never felt more appreciative of her bodily presence, her physical warmth.

On the third day, although I still cried when she left me, I began to relax a bit and joined the class activities more wholeheartedly. For the next two weeks, the moment of separation was still difficult for me, but one day I simply hugged my mother goodbye and then ran off to join my new friends – and that was that. School became a new and welcome adventure, an alternative society that had nothing to do with the hidden misery at the core of my family or the rampant abnormality at the only other institution I had ever been exposed to, since I had never gone to church. To be sure there were many strange rules in this new kindergarten society, such as the no-talking rule at certain times, but I adored Miss Sloan, my teacher, and I quickly became her pet.

I remember the rows of cubicles or "cubbies" on one side of the room, where we kept our jackets and a blanket that we would stretch out on the floor and lie on for naps, each of us confined to our own separate rectangular territory. It was hard to get to sleep during nap time, and I would often toss and turn as I endured the half hour of silence and inactivity. It was only then that I would sometimes feel lonely and miss my mother. But after nap there was a snack, cookies and apple juice in tiny white paper cups, and I felt happy again.

Every day we sang, and there were actions to go with some of the songs, such as the hokey pokey. We had bells and triangles, tambourines, and a drum, and we made a terrible racket as we accompanied our singing. I remember holding hands in a circle and singing "Old MacDonald Had a Farm," and in each verse we would sing "And on that farm he had a ...," and then Miss Sloan would point to one of us to shout out the name of the animal – "Cow! Horse! Duck!" – and then that person would go into the centre of the circle and act it out. There were some children who were too shy to do this, but every day I was less and less shy, and I soon became a show-off.

Lady Evelyn Public School was mysterious and wonderful to me, full of arcane rules and practices, from the bells that ran at the beginning and end of our school day, to the mysterious staff room and the principal's office down the hall, to the school assemblies in the gym, where we sat cross-legged in long ragged lines. I remember how the telephone in our classroom would sometimes ring, and Miss Sloan would engage in a one-sided conversation as we listened. If she was summoned from the classroom, an uneasy excitement would prevail once we were alone and momentarily free to act as we pleased, subject to the uncertainty of when, exactly, she would return. After the first few minutes, our silence would give way to the first conspiratorial whispers, and then more and more talking, a rising hubbub. Eventually, some of the braver, rowdier boys would get up to some kind of mischief, like going up to the front of the room and mimicking the teacher's motions or tickling or poking someone else or taking something from another student. I remember the sense of conspiracy in those stolen moments and then the sudden desperate hush when we heard Miss Sloan's heels clicking down the hallway (if we did) or our dismay if she caught us in the act of disobeying. Yet I never minded Miss Sloan's authority, which she carried so easily, so gently, not like Mrs. Potser, in senior kindergarten. You could hear old Pots and Pans yelling from the room across the hall, even with both doors closed.

Most of all, I remember Miss Sloan's soprano soaring above us as she led us in "Jesus Loves Me," which quickly became my favourite song.

> Jesus loves me, this I know
> For the Bible tells me so
> Little ones to him belong
> They are weak and he is strong.
> Yes, Jesus loves me! Yes, Jesus loves me.
> Yes, Jesus loves me!
> The Bible tells me so.

At home we didn't talk at all about Jesus; he was not part of our vocabulary. My father considered religion to be superstitious claptrap, especially because his father had been a United Church minister and his parents had expected him to follow in his father's footsteps. We never went to church or read the Bible and were secretly disdainful of people who did. But here in school I puzzled over the powerful father God whom we were required to pray to each morning in the arcane language of the Lord's Prayer, and I was secretly in love with the bearded young Jesus in flowing robes who appeared in book illustrations and whom we sang about in "Jesus Loves Me." I sang it emphatically, shouting out the crucial line, "Yes, Jesus loves me!," as if daring the world to disagree, as if by sheer volume I could convince myself and the world that I was entirely deserving of such unconditional

love. And yet Jesus was also confusing to me. It was good of
him to love the little ones, the babies and small children such
as myself, but did he love the weak because they were weak? If
so, why? Did he love Martha and all those other children like her
shut up in that place at Smiths Falls? Did he love them because
he could feel superior, because he was stronger? On the one
hand, that was good, because they certainly needed someone to
love them; on the other hand, it seemed that if he loved retards,
Jesus was not very discriminating.

Was I weak? I certainly didn't think so. I certainly did not
want to be.

It was a new experience, being in a group of children, with
its own social dynamics. When Miss Sloan's attention was elsewhere, all kinds of things happened between the children. I
discovered I could be bossy, and I enjoyed being a leader, convinced of my superiority and willing to ostracize others to make
sure I would not be the one ostracized. "She's so stooopid!" we
would say of others we didn't like. I was Miss Busy Body, Miss
Goody Two Shoes, Miss Teacher's Pet, Miss Know-It-All. Sometimes, other children would call me things like that, but they
somehow sensed that it was dangerous to call me certain names:
nobody ever dared call me a retard to my face.

Miss Sloan saw none of this, for she wrote in my first report
card: "Victoria is a delightful child in all respects. The children
love her and she treats them all with respect. She joins in all our
activities with enthusiasm and is capable of very good work. She
has a good singing voice for her age." I was immensely proud of
her assessment of me and did try to live up to it, though I didn't
always succeed in suppressing a strong competitive spirit that
could be ruthless. Following the dictum of my father's family, I
had to be the smartest; I had to be the best.

My mother walked me to and from school every day, pushing
the baby carriage. By this time, I was happy to have my new sister, who I knew was a better sister than Martha could ever be.
I knew that nobody was going to send her away, though sometimes in my darker moments I might wish it. We didn't talk
about Martha or where she was. I don't recall ever thinking of

her as also being in school, learning things. I never thought of that similarity.

In fact, once I had established my place in the new social world of Lady Evelyn, I rarely thought of her at all, to tell the truth – or perhaps it would be more accurate to say I now avoided thinking about her, since I couldn't articulate or comprehend the enormity of what had happened or find my way through the labyrinth of dark emotions that thoughts of her evoked. Our secret conversations had been replaced by new friendships with "normal" girls and boys. Increasingly my secret self, that innocent child who loved Martha and still held on to her, was split off from consciousness – unacknowledged, unsafe, yet persisting and continuing its subterranean life. Mostly, to my everyday self, it seemed that my sister was lost, left behind somewhere, in an alternative reality, outside of regular time. It was as if the lethargic child we sometimes visited was no longer my sister. I hated going to Smiths Falls; my whole family did. Martha was among her own kind, her own people, my parents reminded me. I thought of them as different from us, defective. They would never progress as we did. I did not belong there. She did.

Maybe they understood one another, and recognized one another, and understood one another's grunts and grimaces, but we could not understand them and did not want to. Perhaps she really was better off with them. Perhaps it truly was best to leave them alone, to keep them hidden away.

They all looked alike to me, at least the "mongoloids" did, and how I felt about them affected how I saw Chinese people as well, since they had similar eyes. They, too, I thought, were not as good as us, the white people, the normal people, the nice, educated middle-class people who lived in well-kept houses and were polite and did well at school and loved our parents. There was one Chinese boy in kindergarten who liked me, but I avoided him. He made me think both of "Siamese twins" and mongoloids, and I was afraid that he had cooties or that other children would think he did. There were risks I could not take.

There was also Brenda Vachon in her ugly worn-out clothes, saggy tights, scuffed shoes, and ragged haircut. She smelled funny, and I suspected she didn't take baths often. I didn't want her for a friend, even when she tried to follow me everywhere – maybe she knew I had a sister who was also a reject. And yet I couldn't just drive her away as the other kids did. I would edge away from her when she approached me, but I would never quite leave. I tolerated her, at least for brief periods, before I ran off to join my more socially acceptable friends. I never wanted to listen to her complaints about the other children in the class, although she sometimes said things that interested me. I felt very virtuous spending time with her. After all, I knew I was good. I knew I was normal, and I wasn't poor like she was. I don't know how she stood my insufferable pity, but I was the only girl who would deign to spend time with her at all.

By then, my family was settling into a routine, going to visit Martha every four to six months. My parents hoped that in time we would get used to these pilgrimages, but we never did. It was always an ordeal. Although the hospital school became ordinary to us in some ways, it remained monstrous in others, a nightmare world of strange and piteous creatures. I tried to be brave when we went to see Martha, armouring myself with my supposed normality, and I pretended I was unaffected, but sometimes huge versions of Martha crowded round us, blocking our way, lunging towards me to hug me or stroke me or otherwise touch me, and I would cling to my mother in abject terror. I did not know that they were overly friendly because they were starved for love and attention. The sooner we got out of there, the better.

Martha eventually learned to walk more steadily. We could then escape the hospital school and take her out for an afternoon in Smiths Falls. To me, the town was itself suffused with Martha's inferiority, with its sad little Main Street, its grubby little restaurants, and its dejected little clapboard houses or brick ones with no porches, just a door leading out abruptly onto the street. I felt sorry for everyone who lived there, especially the hundreds of people who worked at the hospital school and had to deal with people like my sister all day.

The part of town I liked best was the park by the Rideau River, with the waterfalls, and the canal beside it. There was also a lift bridge for the railroad, which we sometimes saw swing up to allow a large boat through the canal or swing shut to let a train pass. A Second World War plane on a pedestal in the park provided a dramatic backdrop to our picnics.

I remember playing on the swings on the grounds of the hospital school in the summer time, the only thing I enjoyed there. I loved the sense of freedom when I pumped with my legs and got going so high the chains holding the wooden swing would give a little hiccup as I reached the top of its arc. We only used the swings when the children from the hospital school were inside; we never mixed with them. Sometimes, as we drove up the long laneway to the school, the first thing I saw was children playing on the swings and the attendants pushing them. If the car windows were open, I could hear the sound of children laughing and calling out in the playground, and from a distance I couldn't tell that they were different from the children at my school. But when we pulled up and parked, when I opened up the car door and stepped onto the pavement of the parking lot and then followed the paved sidewalk past the playing children to the entrance of the building, I saw and heard and remembered why I could leave and they couldn't.

Gradually, over time, the Martha we visited at the school was less and less like the sister I had loved. The Martha we visited was slow, clumsy, and boring because she couldn't even talk. It seemed to me that she got more funny-looking, more retarded-looking, and just plain uglier each time we saw her. It was embarrassing to be around her. She just grunted and waved her hands about or cried and whined. In theory she was my sister, but in reality she was like Brenda Vachon. Everything about her said "loser."

But in that inner place I no longer had conscious access to, I held a different Martha so close to me that we had become one, like conjoined twins. I carried her with me always, just by

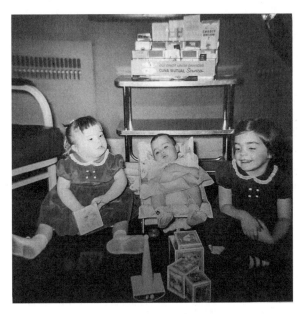

Martha, Kate, and I at Rideau, c. 1960.

my heart. I could no longer tell where she ended and I began, what in me was Martha and what was me. I held her so tightly because if I let go of her, I was afraid that she would die, that she would be swallowed up into that netherworld of the hospital school forever, never to be seen again, that she would never come back out to the world of humans. I held her so tightly because, if I let her go, I feared that I would die too.

Yet, if you asked me then or even now, I would have to say my childhood was mostly happy. I was loved. I was cared for. I never wanted for anything. I had friends, a nice house, a new baby sister, loving parents, lots of attention, lots of toys, adventures, great holidays. I was the little girl who had everything, and it was a great life. I knew my parents thought the world of me. . I was mostly a thoughtful, considerate child, if perhaps overly protective of my parents. For them, and particularly for my mother, I was the strong one, the dependable one, the repository and symbol of my mother's normality. If Martha was the ugly toad, I was the princess, pure and good. I realize now, in ways I sensed then but never articulated, that my mother needed me to be those things. She needed me to be that sterling child. She needed me to shine to counteract her own internal darkness.

Why was I always protecting my parents rather than myself? Because I did not want to face that darkness – my mother's shame, her guilt, her rage. Most of the time I related to my parents as if my sister didn't exist and they hadn't done what they had done. We all pretended she didn't exist and that the monstrous hadn't happened.

I remember one incident, however, that speaks to the contradictions I tried to paper over. I remember a get-together with family friends when I loudly asked my mother why Mr. Bobb was so fat. My mother shushed me and pulled me aside and said sternly that I must not criticize people or talk about them in front of others. I was embarrassed by my faux pas and from then on it seemed wrong to criticize people even in my mind. I always tried to think the best of people and suppress any negative thoughts. It never occurred to me to question why I couldn't criticize my parents' friend for being fat when my parents could send their child away for being slow.

My childhood memories after Martha's departure exist in pleasant abundance. I remember the snow mazes that my father made in the backyard and how I loved to play in them with my father and the neighbourhood children. He was my playmate on the weekend in a way my mother never was. She was always too busy with Kate, or maybe it just wasn't her nature. Her games were wan, half-hearted things, no fun really, whereas my dad made me shriek with delight. He always pushed the game to its limit, throwing me up in the air and letting me fly. He invented the game of the three robber girls, in which Susan, Eleanor, and I robbed banks from our flying bathtub, an old trunk in the basement. It was a silly game, but it was great to have a place to be bad, to act out our malevolence and evil. We could imagine anything, do anything. Even violence was allowed, at least in fantasy. In one robber girl book we created, the three robber girls hit their bratty neighbour Johnny with a baseball bat, stuffed him in a garbage can, and kicked it to the moon.

I loved make-believe. Sometimes I was a fairy. I looked normal, but I was not. I came from another world, and I liked to play tricks on humans, bewitch them, render them speechless or paralyzed. I could transform frogs into princes, princes into retards, or retards into normal people. I could tie up my victims in spider webs and take them to my fairy mound or make a hundred years pass in a blink of an eye. Sometimes I was a queen, not a mere princess – I wanted power, like the red queen in *Alice through the Looking Glass*. I could boss everyone around, throw them into the dungeon, or chop off their heads.

My days may have been filled with imaginative games and fantasies of power, but at night I started having recurring nightmares. In one, my father made a well of snow in the backyard but then fell into it and disappeared. The hole kept going down, down, down, and then he was gone. And then my playmates tried to find him. When they looked down into the hole, they too fell into it and disappeared. And then my mother went to investigate, followed by my sister Kate and my grandmother. Finally, everyone I knew, my whole family and all my neighbours, had disappeared into the abyss, and I was alone and crying by myself.

In another dream, I had to drive the family car, even though I was only six years old. I tried desperately to avoid crashing it or running into people. It was terrifying because I didn't know what I was doing or how to stop it or where I was going.

We lived near a park by the Rideau River, and one night I dreamt I went down to the park, where there were little flying alligators everywhere. They tried to land on me and take bites out of me like giant mosquitoes. In another dream, the alligators were bigger, walking on their hind legs like people in a strange alligator world. When they came after me with their hideous glinting eyes and menacing teeth, I woke up, trying to scream but unable to.

As Christmas approached, my kindergarten class began working on our pageant, which we'd perform before the whole school at the assembly. I was cast as Mary and was proud to have been chosen for the lead role. I liked the boy who played Joseph, and it seemed romantic to be playing husband and wife. Other children played the three wise men, the shepherds, and angels, and some of the more troublesome boys were assigned roles as sheep or donkeys, which allowed them to act up for laughs. This was the most exciting thing I had ever done – so I was devastated when I got bronchitis and missed the performance. I had to stay home for two weeks, and when Dr. McIntosh came over to put a burning mustard plaster on my chest, I cried from the pain of it.

While I was at home coughing and wheezing, a Christmas card arrived in the mail from the hospital school. On the front were the words "Seasons Greetings" in ornate red lettering above a photograph of the children in Martha's ward. Two nurses beamed as they held children on either side of a Christmas tree, and Santa was holding a child – was it Martha? – on his lap in front of the tree. Eight small children in dress clothes sat in front of Santa, all two or three years old.

I examined this card with intense interest. Martha would not be coming home for Christmas, my mother had said. It was too hard and, besides, she would have her own Christmas at the hospital school. We would go to see her after Christmas. But in that other world where Martha resided, it seemed Santa had already been and gone, which puzzled me – or maybe he lived there, though that also seemed unlikely. Maybe, like Jesus, he

Christmas at Ontario Hospital School, Smiths Falls

Christmas card, Rideau Regional Centre, no date.

especially loved the weak, which made me a little anxious,
perhaps even jealous. Maybe I wasn't weak enough, or meek
enough. I wondered what it was like to be held by those very
proper nurses or by Santa Claus himself and what it was like to
sit in a neat and ordered row with the other retarded children.
There were so many of them there, a whole other tribe. Maybe
they would grow up to be Santa's elves or Snow White's dwarves.

I was too young to read the message inside the card:

> The Christmas Season brings to all of us a renewed and
> deeper appreciation of the age old story of the Birth of Christ;
> and with this the implicit recognition of the dignity of all
> human beings and the rights of all children to opportunities
> for happy living and full development. We hopefully feel that
> we have been providing the type of programming and the
> adequate environment in which this philosophy can be main-
> tained and developed. We have received many comments of

your appreciation and all of us at the Hospital School are constantly heartened by your approval and support.

We regret that our hospital population continues to increase; and the problems of overcrowding are adding to the burdens of an already hard-pressed staff. To those who have been, and are waiting, many months for the admission of their child, may I say that we are very appreciative of their patience and unselfish waiting.

The past year has been a milestone in the field of mental retardation. The London Scientific Conference pointed to the tremendous surge of interest in the problem in a score of countries: research activities are being stimulated in many lands including our own; better facilities and more progressive methods of training are being developed. At our own Hospital School the approach to the children is benefitting from all these activities.

We are ever mindful of the needs of our children and particularly so at Christmas time. An effort is made to bring joy to each child; and we strive to provide an atmosphere in which all the children can derive, in as full a measure as possible, the same enjoyment they would derive if they were in a home. Children love gifts. We know you will be generous. Suitable gifts are toys, games, books, records, etc.

It would be appreciated if you would arrange to have your parcel reach here not later than December 12th PROPERLY ADDRESSED. THE PARCEL SHOULD BE ADDRESSED TO THE PATIENT (OR IF NO NAME IS KNOWN, TO "THE FRIENDLESS" IN CARE OF THE ONTARIO HOSPITAL SCHOOL, SMITHS FALLS).

I sincerely thank you for your co-operation in making the Christmas Season a bright and happy one in the lives of the children here, and may I wish you, on behalf of all members of the Staff, a VERY MERRY CHRISTMAS AND A HAPPY NEW YEAR.

Yours sincerely,
H.F. Frank, M.A., M.D.
Superintendent

The school was far over capacity and did not have the resources to adequately care for its charges. There were now "hospital schools" like this all over North America, and they were bursting at the seams warehousing the unwanted. In fact, they had become dumping grounds for every kind of "problem" child: some residents were not intellectually impaired at all but emotionally troubled, autistic, or simply friendless.

I did not know that the institution had staged a Christmas concert just as my school had or that relatives had been invited to attend. My parents never considered going, as far as I know. I imagine the gymnasium full of excited children and adults and even some parents. I know the institution's choir sang on those occasions and that that was where Martha learned her favourite Christmas carols, such as "Rudolph the Red-Nosed Reindeer" and "Frosty the Snowman." I can imagine the pride of those on the stage who had been chosen to play Mary or Joseph or the three wise men, some of them so overwhelmed by performing in front of an audience that they forgot their roles and simply stared out at the vast sea of faces or waved at friends or hammed it up, just as children did at my school. They, too, celebrated the birth of the heavenly child, a child more perfect than any of us.

On Christmas Day, I woke up early and discovered a huge pile of presents under the tree. My mother put on carols, and we drank eggnog as we opened presents. Later, we went over to my grandfather's house for a turkey dinner, and I got to drink Coca Cola, which my mother never had at home. It was wonderful. We were a normal family, and we were happy.

I returned to school for the spring term and had my theatrical debut in the class production of the *Three Billy Goats Gruff* as the littlest billy goat. At the end of the year, I received an "honours promotion" to senior kindergarten. Miss Sloan wrote: "I could not be more pleased with Victoria's progress." I was well

Christmas 1960 at my grandfather's house. Dad is holding Kate, and I'm peeking over the tabletop.

on my way to learning to read, which I knew was the ultimate achievement.

I can still feel Miss Sloan's gentle presence, her love for me, her encouragement. I don't know if she ever sensed the pain in me, but it didn't matter. She sensed something in me that was worth loving and that needed her, and she gave me a pure and steady love that helped me all my life, including the next year, when my teacher was the terrifying Mrs. Potser.

April 3, 1961

Dear Dr. Frank,

My wife and I had planned to visit Martha Saturday April 1 but were told that the Female Nursery was isolated because of dysentery. Could someone tell us whether Martha is ill or not, as we are rather worried? If at all possible, we would like to visit her next Saturday or Sunday (April 8 or 9) around 2 pm, whichever is most convenient, even if only for a few minutes ...

Sincerely,

George Freeman

April 6, 1961

Dear Mr. Freeman,

Thank you for your letter of April 3, regarding your daughter.

She is not ill, but has to be isolated because of dysentery cases on the female ward. Unfortunately, we still have positive cases there and I do not think it advisable for you to visit her on April 8th or 9th, unless you wish to see her through the window.

In fact, my sister tested positive for dysentery on April 12 and again on April 18. On May 31, a full two months after the outbreak began, the quarantine was finally lifted. Two months later, my mother wrote to Dr. Frank to arrange for my sister's first trip home. She was with us for five days.

By then, Martha had become a stranger, a foreigner in our midst. She had lived for more than a year in a highly regimented environment and had never been alone in all that time. She could not talk and communicated only through gestures and cries. She was not yet toilet trained. She could perhaps sense but certainly could not fathom the complicated guilt-laced emotions that her presence evoked in my parents and in me. I viewed her with distaste, for I saw her only in terms of deformity.

In this, I was shaped by many things, including the huge painted signs advertising the freak show that I had gawked at as we travelled through the midway at the Ottawa Exhibition every summer. The Ex fascinated me with its grime and noise and tawdry splendours: the rides, the games, the candy floss, the candy apples and caramel corn, and the insistent, wheedling voices of the barkers trying to reel us in, tempting us to forget our manners, pay our money, and stare at the strange and bizarre, the morbidly obese, the deformed, the overly hairy, the monstrous, the grotesque, the exotic. Where else could one contemplate with equal parts wonder and horror the two-headed baby or the monkey girl? I never actually went inside the freak show, but it was always there (in fact, freak shows persisted into the 1970s in Canada), and it definitely influenced the way I looked at my sister.

Rosemarie Garland-Thomson writes in *Extraordinary Bodies: Figuring Physical Disability in American Culture and Literature* that "when the body becomes pure text, a freak has been produced from a physically disabled human being." This "spectacle of Otherness" undoubtedly confirmed the rest of us in our supposed normality. But if my sister was one of those others – a freak, a monstrosity like those exhibited and scorned in this seedy, dirty way in the marginal, alternative reality of the Ex – I knew that by virtue of our familial proximity I was also tainted.

Those five days Martha spent with us in 1961 must have been a disaster. According to the hospital records (which may not be accurate), there wasn't another visit home for the next four years, and after that my sister never again stayed longer than two nights with us for the whole time she was at Rideau. We all agreed that she belonged with her own kind – not with us.

Sept. 21, 1961

Dear Mr and Mrs Freeman,

I wish to let you know that a Birthday Party was held for your little daughter Martha Ann, as you requested in your letter of Sept. 5th. The hospital staff enjoyed very much having a little party for her, and we appreciated your generosity in providing the necessary funds in order to have a special treat for the kiddies. A little Birthday Cake with candles to light and ice cream was served. Balloons and party hats were also a part of the celebration, and indeed all had a very happy time. Thank you very much for your thoughtfulness.

Sincerely, S. Lippard, O.T. Reg.

7

Fair Exchange

My parents were now happy with their little family and understandably cautious about having more children. Having received what they wanted – a healthy replacement for Martha – they didn't want to press their luck. My father didn't want to put my mother through such terrible anxiety again, although he also regretted that he didn't have a son.

A phone call one evening in 1962, a few months after Kate's second birthday and a few days after Martha's fourth birthday, changed all that. It was a cousin of my mother's, who was also a doctor. Their conversation became part of our family lore.

"June, there's a bit of a crisis here, and I wondered if you and George could maybe help us out for a few days."

"Oh, why, sure ... What can we do?"

"I need someone to take care of a little baby for a few days, just until we find a new foster family." He explained that the baby's mother was a patient of his and only sixteen. An older woman who had fostered other children was taking care of the baby for the Children's Aid, but she had decided she was too old to care for a newborn and wanted to give him back. The baby was only ten days old.

"Oh, geez, Tom, I'd like to help, but my hands are kind of full at the moment."

Tom persisted. "The kid's had a rough start in life, you know. Born six weeks premature. Just needs a stable family situation for a few days to help him settle down ... I couldn't think of anyone better than you and George."

"Uh ... well ... let me talk to him and get back to you."

So my mother hung up and went to talk to my dad. They shut the door to the kitchen and conferred. When she opened the door again, she headed to the phone and called Tom back.

"I guess we can take him ... if it's only for a few days. We're not exactly set up for another baby."

"I'm not asking you to take him permanently. He just needs a good place to be for a few days so he can settle down and gain some weight. He's got a few allergies ... nothing serious ... just a bit of eczema, a bit of colic ... Poor kid just needs some stability and not being shuttled from place to place."

"Well, uh ... I guess we could be ready by the weekend."

"The thing is, the old lady wants him off her hands, so I was hoping you could take him tonight."

"Oh ... well ... I guess we could manage ... What time, then?"

Kate was ever after convinced that it was men who brought babies into the world, because after dinner my father headed off in the car. My mother hurriedly got out the big wicker bassinet that she had used for all her newborns, and I helped her unpack the tiny baby sleepers that she had been about to pass on to another family. My father returned with a wee baby boy, pretty much the size of a small loaf of bread. He had indeed been born too soon, and he wasn't happy about it.

He cried constantly. He woke up every hour in the night with a hunger that never seemed to be assuaged, although he often wouldn't suck on the bottle. He woke up screaming every morning because his eyes were gummed completely shut with goopy yellow mucous, which we had to soak off with a warm washcloth. His rough, reddened cheeks were as irritated and sore as his flaming red bottom. He farted and pooped and spit up volumes of formula. It seemed that none of his systems were working properly, and nothing seemed to soothe him except holding him constantly.

By the end of the week, my mother was a nervous wreck, but I thought the baby was adorable – if one thing was clear, it was that he was not another sister. One day, my father went to change him, and a great arc of pee shot out of the baby's tiny penis, hitting my dad full in the face and wetting his glasses, to my great horror and amusement. Evidently, there was a very different standard of normality for boys.

Tom called a week later and asked my parents if they could keep the baby for a few more days because he was still having difficulty finding a new foster parent. My parents had an argument about this, the first that I can remember – my father obliging, my mother reluctant. The thought of sending this helpless and extremely sensitive child out into the unknown world of the Children's Aid was too much for my father; they should keep him, he argued, since they were reasonably well off and could care for him. My mother was worried, rightly as it turned out, that Kate would get short shrift if there was a needy new baby usurping her place. But, this way, my father could have a son without my mother having to go through another nerve-wracking pregnancy, and besides, they already knew the baby was normal.

My mother, who in three tries hadn't produced a boy, let herself be talked into keeping the child, in spite of her misgivings and exhaustion. There was a kind of reciprocity in this arrangement that made sense and could perhaps assuage her guilt about Martha: they could take care of this little boy in exchange for someone else taking care of Martha. And so my parents made yet another substitution, a final psychic bargain. They signed the adoption papers, and their family was complete.

Eric joined our family and became my brother. His adoption was highly irregular, for my parents were never screened or given time to prepare. They knew next to nothing about Eric's background other than that his mother was young, unmarried, and had tried to disguise the pregnancy by binding her stomach, and little about the psychological stresses of adoption, for parents and the adopted child. Why the presiding doctor rather than some functionary for the Children's Aid was playing the role of finding a foster family remains a mystery.

What I do know is that my father was smitten with this baby boy, my mother less so, mainly because Eric needed a lot of attention, and she already had a two-year-old and a six-year-old (and somewhere in the back of beyond a four-year-old). My mother assumed she would come to love my brother, but she was also conscious that his presence in her life was not fully her choice. At least there was some relief in the thought that Eric would definitely be the last child in her family.

He was a cute little guy with golden hair and thick, sturdy ankles and big square feet that everyone said would make him an excellent hockey player. My father tried to be practical and realistic, but he would never be interested in going to hockey practices or throwing softballs; in his view of the future, he and Eric would play chess together and discuss economics and European politics. His role would be to mentor his son as he succeeded brilliantly at university, established his career, and found an accomplished and beautiful wife of his own.

But Eric, like Martha, was his own being and already had his own history. He had been born more than a month before his due date, before his bodily systems were fully developed. He had been separated from his mother at birth. He had not had those crucial moments of bonding or the boost to his immune system that breast-feeding supplies. His first ten days of life had been chaotic as he had been moved from the hospital to the foster home and then to our home. His first and defining experience was abandonment.

My parents assumed that Eric would quickly settle down and become one of us. And in some ways he did. He eventually outgrew the colic and eczema. I had a new sibling to play with, and this one was not the one who had displaced Martha. Perhaps I was even a little bit happy to see the child who had displaced

Martha being displaced; certainly, I stopped paying attention to Kate and devoted myself to playing house with the baby. But Kate was bewildered at being suddenly pushed aside by this interloper. There was a new and demanding being in the family, one who had stolen her place without warning. Now she was the one who felt neglected and abandoned, as she was crowded out by a bossy and overachieving big sister, the invisible Martha and all that she represented, and Eric's screams.

My mother saw Kate's distress and was tormented by a new source of guilt. She had not managed to trade it away after all. She now saw how deeply Kate was affected by Eric's arrival, but it was too late. My mother blamed my father for pressuring her into keeping Eric, and her deep resentment about this would flare up suddenly in the middle of minor disagreements. She was not the kind of person to forgive and forget; it was something she held over him. When she turned on him accusingly, he in turn was riven with guilt for all the pain he had caused her, and he acquiesced to her wishes.

From the time I was six, I watched this guilty dynamic between them with puzzlement. Why didn't my father stand up for himself? Why did they fight over the decision to keep Eric when it was clear that giving Eric back was now unthinkable and they just had to get on with it? Couldn't they just open their hearts and love him as I did? My mother tried to love him, but she was always conscious that he wasn't her child. His arrival in the family had been accidental. He had never been a tiny pinprick of hope and possibility that she had nurtured into being day by day, month after month. She had never willingly suffered the pain of birth so that he might live. There had been no rich river of blood between them, no umbilical cord, no bridge.

But it was more than that. Many adoptive parents do come to love their children deeply and truly, but something happened to my mother after Eric's arrival. It was more than the family version of the Peter principle, whereby parents end up with one more child than they can sanely cope with. The birth of Kate and the institutionalization of Martha had seemingly offered my mother a new beginning, reassuring her of her ability to be a normal mother of a normal child and offering her a way to grow, a path forward that at the same time did not deny the tie to Martha. But when Eric arrived, that healing progress was arrested; something stalled, got stuck, became frozen.

Perhaps, in time, she could have come to love him more deeply if she had not developed, early on, the conviction that he had rejected her as his mother. Looking back, I'm not sure he actually did so, but I can see how his behaviour could have been interpreted that way. Once Eric's colic passed and he became a toddler and then a young child, he did not like to be hugged and caressed; he usually squirmed to be released from her lap. Although my mother was his primary caregiver (my father now increasingly busy with demanding senior positions at the Bank of Canada), Eric did not seek her out when he was upset or afraid, and he often ignored her when she called him to her. He seemed wary or even suspicious of her motherly attentions, as if he intuitively sensed their fragility. He would not listen, would not admit connection or accept her proffered love. It's now widely known that such behaviour is an early sign of attention deficit disorder, that such children dislike being held and experience it as restraint rather than comfort or love, but my parents did not know that. My mother was quietly, privately, devastated.

It is disconcerting to be rejected by a small child, even one you meet casually on the street or in a bus or store; you smile, only to have that child burst into tears or shriek in terror. We sense that a child is a pure being in some way; it does not know you, but its clear eyes observe you, sense you, seem to grasp and assess your very essence. We know that children go through this phase of "making strange," but if we are vulnerable, we may still take this behaviour personally, feeling judged or exposed as untrustworthy. So it was for my mother.

"I don't know what's the matter with this child," she would mutter, when, as a toddler, Eric would humiliate her in public by running away from her, hitting other children, even defiantly laughing in her face as he disobeyed her. His apparent rejection of her ate away at her self-confidence, revealing to any passerby her failure as a parent and compounding a deeper sense of failure that had everything to do with my sister. Yet she also felt keenly that it wasn't fair, that she didn't deserve any of this – not Martha, not Eric – so his behaviour also enraged her.

No one told my mother that bonding could be far more difficult with an adopted child. She didn't understand that Eric's behaviour was not due to a permanent lack of love for her or any inadequacy on her part but instead might have been a reaction to his early experiences of abandonment, isolation, and powerlessness, to a lack of nurturance in those critical first days. He had already learned that the world was a dangerous and frightening place and that he couldn't depend on anyone. He hadn't learned to bond with her – or anyone. He didn't know that she could be a source of love and comfort, so he rejected her efforts to calm, soothe, and connect with him. Nor were my parents aware of the phenomenon of post-adoption depression, which often sets in when parents' expectations about the adoption experience aren't met.

Our family dynamics became even more complicated when Martha and Eric started interacting with each other, often negatively. I remember when Martha was brought home for a visit when she was nearly six years old, almost two years after Eric's arrival. She was still not talking much. In fact, other than learning to walk and say a few basic words, she hardly seemed to have progressed in the four years she had been at the hospital school. Oddly enough, it was because of her irritation with my brother that she suddenly shouted her first connected sentence, or at least the first we recognized. She shouted it at the closed door behind which my brother was supposed to be napping but was instead crying relentlessly to be released from his crib. Martha knocked on the door and suddenly shouted, "Shub up, kib!"

The indistinct blur of her speech would remain her peculiar idiom throughout her life, one we would always struggle to comprehend, but those first words were unmistakable. We knew how slowly she learned, how many repetitions it would take for her to remember such a phrase and reproduce it so accurately. Her "Shub up, kib!" connected us with a thud to the reality of her life at the institution where my parents had been assured she would always be "cared for."

It was bad enough when my mother was trying to cope with my demanding little brother, Kate's emotional withdrawal and fearfulness, and busy, attention-seeking me, all while cooking meals and cleaning house in a sleep-deprived haze. But when Martha began coming home again for infrequent weekend visits, she simply lost it. I'm not sure why my parents started bringing her home rather than simply visiting her in Smiths Falls. Perhaps it was because of the effort of getting all of us suited up and keeping us all amused during the long car rides there and back, or perhaps my parents had realized that it wasn't good to expose us to that terrifying place. But there was soon an awful predictability to these home visits.

On the first day, my mother would be nervous but upbeat. My father would fetch Martha from the institution, and she would arrive in a state of excitement at seeing us again because, miraculously, she still recognized us as her true family. In those first moments, as she joyously cried out our names – "Mameee!" "Daee!" "Towee!" – her happiness would be met with hugs and laughter, and we all briefly felt the possibility of being one big happy family together.

My mother would hustle Martha into the kitchen and offer her grilled cheese sandwiches, because Martha was always most content when she was eating her favourite foods. After lunch, my mother would give her a little gift that she had bought for her at the five-and-dime store, sparkly costume jewellery or a colouring book and crayons. They would occupy Martha for a while, but eventually the moment would come when she would tire of these diversions. Then she would look expectantly at my mother, and my mother had the rest of the visit to face up to.

My parents privately thanked God for television. Martha would sit a foot in front of its flickering images, entranced, for hours. Sometimes my brother would join her, and that would keep both of them quiet for a while. But even so, there were the yawning hours ahead, hours that my mother knew she should spend with Martha, talking with her, playing games with her, singing with her, but she simply couldn't make herself do those things and hated herself for being so ungenerous. We children would play with Martha for half an hour, but then we'd get bored, and my parents would have to figure out what to do with her. My dad was the hero of the family. He would take her out for a doughnut or amuse her with the sort of games one plays with a toddler, such as peekaboo or making faces or building towers with blocks so that she could knock them down.

Soon, my mother would begin to retreat into herself. She would start muttering about how she really wasn't a nice person; it seemed she was desperately trying to hold on till Martha's departure. She would also get more and more irritated with Eric. Finally, she would head for the aspirin bottle in the bathroom – she had a huge bottle containing one thousand tablets – or my father would pour her a stiff drink.

The next day, my parents would face the next challenge, which was taking Martha and the rest of us out into the wider world. My parents always did this somewhat defiantly, getting us all zippered into our snowsuits and then going to the shopping centre or the park, and we would go through this elaborate charade of pretending that Martha's presence with us was perfectly normal. No one was fooled. We were on display, pretending that we were not the freak show yet hyperconscious of Martha's difference and our ambivalence about her. Everyone we passed would stare at her and then at us and then look away in embarrassment. When Martha was with us, our interactions with others were almost always strained because even friends and acquaintances did not know what to do with their feelings of pity, fear, fascination, or repulsion since none of that was expressible according to social protocol; they did not know how to act towards her or what they could ask or say.

I myself acted the part of the nicest, kindest, most benevolent sister who did good works for the handicapped. Truly, I was embarrassed to be seen with her, but it seemed she was our cross to bear, and we did bear it, holding up our chins, stiffening our upper lips, acting as if nothing at all were amiss. But why were we afflicted with a disabled child when none of our friends were? Why had we alone been visited by what we all thought of as a family tragedy?

Well, we did know of a couple of other unfortunate families. There were the friends of friends who had a thalidomide baby, an otherwise beautiful child born with flippers instead of arms. There was also the boy down the street who had cerebral palsy and was confined to a wheelchair. In those days, all we saw was the wheelchair, certainly not the person. Really, we did not want to associate with any other families with handicapped children; we did not want to be classified in this way or be part of such a group.

We'd get home from our excruciating excursions in the outside world, and my mother would either go straight to her bedroom and shut the door for a lie-down or my father would pour her a drink and shoo us out of the kitchen. By then they would be watching the clock for when it would be time for my father to take Martha back to the hospital school.

I could not understand what my mother was feeling. I could not touch my mother's pain. It seemed so vast and unfathomable, a dark ocean, as heavy as molasses. I could not help her. I could not cross that ocean to be with her on the other side. It was a grief, a rage, that was expressed nowhere and so came out everywhere. All of us were affected by it, and it never seemed to end. I wanted her to get over it, but she couldn't.

My mother could not wait for Martha to leave, but Martha herself felt differently. She always protested, looking from one to the other of us for signs that we would relent, but we never did. Often, she would cry, and even in the peculiar way she cried – a pitiful whimpering or a bleating cry – we saw her difference.

8

"Progress and Happiness"

What sort of people cared for Martha all those years and knew her so intimately? Who bathed her, wiped her bottom until she could do it herself, dressed her, and taught her to make her bed, brush her teeth, and tie her shoelaces? Who cared for her when she was sick? Who trained her, disciplined her, and comforted her? Somebody did all those things, I now realize, though I never gave it a thought as a child. In fact, many people must have done those things since the staff at the institution worked in shifts. I never knew her caregivers or spoke with them. I never thought of them as anything other than the faceless employees of the hospital school. What did her caregivers think when they went home at night to their own families? How did they cope with the overcrowding and overwork? How did they deal with the stigma of working there? I have searched in recent years for staff members who may have looked after my sister, but so far I have not located them. I may never know who most of these people were, and many are likely now dead. Yet these were the people who taught my sister to sing and to dance, introduced her to Santa Claus (or "Kagua," as she called him), and wiped away her tears, though it seems from her "Shub up, kib!" that they also yelled at her.

They did so in a situation of terrible overcrowding. In 1963, the population of the Ontario Hospital School, Smiths Falls, as the Rideau Regional Centre was then known, peaked at twenty-six hundred, which was eight hundred more than originally intended. The institution that housed my sister was the largest facility of its kind in the Commonwealth and in some ways a wonder. Imagine five miles of corridors linking fifty buildings and over a mile of underground tunnels. The 523-acre property included a working farm that had 80 acres under cultivation and a 2,500 square foot greenhouse. In 1971, according to the *Rideau Regional Centre Memory Book, 1951–2001,* the farm produced 433.5 tons of vegetables, including 9,000 bags of potatoes, 10,000 early cabbages, 2,000 midsummer cabbages, 2,500 lettuces, and 3,500 tomato plants. In 1972, staff and residents washed 4.5 million pounds of laundry (43 tonnes each week), which consisted of 20,000 pounds of clothing, 27,000 sheets, 3,750 pillowcases, 26,400 bath towels, 50,000 diapers, 7,000 tea towels, and 1,500 thermal blankets and required 200,000 gallons of soft water, 700 pounds of soap, 200 pounds of soda, and 14 gallons of bleach. Much of this was accomplished through the unpaid, involuntary work of residents. My sister, like almost all long-term residents who could be trained, was destined to become a slave labourer.

The hospital school, as we called it, had originated as a Conservative Party campaign promise during the Great Depression, although construction did not begin until 1947, and it didn't open until 1951. For decades it provided steady employment in the otherwise struggling town of Smiths Falls, which lost its tractor factory in 1955, a casings plant in 1964, and many railway jobs as diesel engines replaced steam in the 1950s. In 1971, the Rideau Regional Centre, employed 2,200 people, 709 in full-time jobs.

When it opened, it was seen as an improvement over much of what had previously passed for care of those with intellectual disabilities. As investigator Walter Williston would later recount in a groundbreaking 1971 report on Ontario's institutions for people with intellectual disabilities, the first asylum had opened in January 1841 at the Old York Jail in Toronto, though it made no distinction between people who were developmentally disabled and those who were mentally ill. Subsequently, people with intellectual disabilities were locked up in the unoccupied east wing of the Parliament Buildings in Toronto, and then they were moved, in 1850, to the new Provincial Lunatic Asylum at 999 Queen Street (now the Centre for Addiction and Mental Health). A branch of the asylum was established in a modified hotel in Orillia in 1859. The branch was transferred to London in 1873 and operated there until 1876, when the Orillia Institution reopened as the Hospital for Idiots and Imbeciles, Canada's first hospital training school for so-called feeble-minded children. The hospital moved to new premises in 1885. Until 1950, Orillia (also known as Huronia) remained the main site where people like my sister were warehoused. That year, faced with severe overcrowding and long waiting lists, a new institution in Aurora was opened "for the most difficult and unwanted men." It was followed by the institution in Smiths Falls in 1951 and Cedar Springs in southwestern Ontario a decade later. By the 1960s, there were sixteen institutions across the province, though Rideau and Huronia remained the largest. Despite good intentions on the part of some of those involved and the rhetoric of progressive treatment, these huge and isolated institutions can be seen as the ultimate expressions of "the hopelessness, revulsion, ignorance, and fear" that spurred neglect and cruelty towards people with intellectual disabilities in most Western societies over centuries, if not millennia (though there have also been countervailing tendencies at times).

The history of attitudes towards intellectual disability was entirely unknown to me as a child. According to disability scholars David Lawrence Braddock and Susan L. Parrish, ancient societies, such as the Greeks and Romans, attributed illness or disability to angry gods and often killed infants with congenital deformities, though some slaves with intellectual disabilities are known to have been kept by wealthy men as fools for entertainment purposes. In later Roman times, people with intellectual disabilities must have reached adulthood because they were forbidden from marrying. The Old Testament portrayed disability as punishment by Jehovah but also called for charitable treatment. Because Jesus miraculously healed some impairments, Christians sometimes interpreted disability as a sign of the power of God. Despite these more positive interpretations, in medieval Europe, intellectual disability was widely believed to be caused by supernatural or demonic forces, hence its association with both the wondrous and the monstrous – and the folk explanation of supposed theft of infants by fairies in the trope of the changeling.

Yet, as Braddock and Parrish recount, there was a remarkable hospice in fourth-century Turkey that offered an early example of progressive care. And while "idiots" in medieval Europe were often left to wander the countryside as beggars, lacking any sort of protection, they were not as stigmatized as they would later become, partly because some Christians adopted voluntary poverty and partly because beggars provided the wealthy with opportunities to demonstrate their virtue by providing alms. By England's Poor Law of 1601, families caring for intellectually disabled relatives at home could apply for relief payments, although the mentally ill were increasingly incarcerated.

Perhaps the biggest changes to attitudes towards disability – and the origins of many of the modern assumptions and practices that so affected my sister – came about through the scientific spirit of the European Enlightenment. As Rosemarie Garland-Thomson notes in *Extraordinary Bodies*, by the eighteenth century, "the monster's power to inspire terror, awe, wonder, and divination had been eroded by science, which sought to classify and master ... the extraordinary body." A new curiosity led scientists to conduct both individual case studies and postmortem studies of anatomy to investigate mental faculties, mind-body interactions, and the differences between humans and other animals in the expectation that, through experience and reason, the individual human being and human society could be improved.

Scientific efforts to educate children like my sister dated from this period. One famous experiment was the attempted education of the "wild boy of Aveyron," a feral child of roughly twelve years of age who had reputedly survived for years alone in the French woods before being captured in the 1820s. He was reportedly unable to talk, walked on all fours, drank while lying on the ground, and attacked those who came too close. His teacher, physician J.M.G. Itard, like many early to mid-nineteenth-century experts, initially believed that intellectual disabilities could be cured through education, though after much experimentation it became clear that this belief was overly optimistic and that this boy and many others would need lifelong care and supervision. Yet Itard's work inspired educational reformers Edouard Séguin and Maria Montessori to develop new educational approaches for children like my sister. Meanwhile, in Germany, classes for the so-called feeble-minded were integrated into public schools beginning in the mid-nineteenth century.

In the United States, some early institutions enjoyed moderate success in returning intellectually disabled children back to communities as "productive workers," but by the 1870s educational failure as well as economic hard times had reduced employment opportunities, fostering the widespread view that people with intellectual disabilities were hopeless cases who needed charitable care and protection rather than schooling. They were gathered together in large institutions, often farm colonies in isolated settings, and put to work so as to be self-supporting. They were kept there for the rest of their lives.

It was the late nineteenth-century eugenic concern to halt the reproduction and social burden of the genetically unfit or deviant that led to much harsher regimes of incarceration for people with intellectual disabilities. Increasingly, they were separated from the rest of society and warehoused in under-financed and overcrowded institutions or colonies, where they were stripped of all comforts, segregated by sex, and generally regimented and dehumanized. This was certainly the experience of generations of people who were confined at Huronia, the Ontario Hospital at Orillia, the central institution of the system in Ontario that later engulfed my sister.

In Ontario, as Thelma Wheatley notes in *"And Neither Have I Wings to Fly,"* the brutal fact was that money spent on institutions for people with intellectual disabilities did not garner votes. In the nineteenth century, Huronia administrator Dr. Alexander H. Beaton sought better accommodation and further development of the educational component of the school, but beginning in the 1890s political attacks on the high cost and the supposed futility of education for "idiots" resulted in reductions in the number of teachers and even temporary closures of the institution. Later superintendents focused on reducing costs and ensuring that the institution largely paid for itself through the unpaid labour of its inmates.

Only in the 1950s, the decade of my sister's birth, did new patterns of care develop in the wake of public reaction to the horrors of the Second World War and the racial and eugenic ideologies that had fuelled Nazism. The 1948 UN Universal Declaration of Human Rights proclaimed that all members of the human family had equal rights to human dignity and freedom, and in 1959, the year after my sister's birth, the United Nations proclaimed the Declaration of the Rights of the Child, which affirmed, among other things, that "the child who is physically, mentally or socially handicapped shall be given the special treatment, education and care required by his particular condition." Similarly, in 1954, the World Health Organization proclaimed that each child had the right to develop his or her potential to the maximum. This was new thinking, but on-the-ground care was slow to change.

By the time Martha arrived at Smiths Falls in 1960, all of these various influences had resulted in a large, overcrowded, and understaffed institution with immense power over its charges. In 1957, sociologist Erving Goffman coined the phrase "total institution" to describe institutions such as penitentiaries and insane asylums where every aspect of the lives of residents was regimented, controlled, and monitored by others, and Rideau fit the bill. Residents had few opportunities to make choices for themselves. At all the "hospital schools" in Ontario, residents lived in locked wards and had no means to communicate with the outside world or complain about their treatment, especially since many could not speak and had been abandoned by their families. Reflecting on conditions in 1960, Walter Williston wrote that the hospital school was truly a closed institution: "The attitude of the staff from central office right through to ward staff was, 'We can take care of the retarded better than their families – that's why they were sent to us ... families should release their children to us and not interfere with our management.'"

Five months before my sister was admitted, Pierre Berton, the well-known journalist, toured the Ontario Hospital School in Orillia, the sister institution of the Smiths Falls institution, and wrote a scathing article in the *Toronto Star* titled "What's Wrong at Orillia – Out of Sight, Out of Mind." He described deplorable conditions, including overcrowded and badly deteriorating buildings, physical and emotional abuse, and neglect. The article ended with a reference to Nazi death camps: "Many Germans excused themselves because they said they did not know what went on behind those walls. No one had told them. Well ... you have been told about Orillia."

The article caused such a stir that the matter was debated in the Ontario legislature. My parents must surely have been aware of this. For a time before and after my sister was institutionalized, they had attended meetings of the Ottawa and District Association for the Mentally Retarded – in fact, my father had briefly served on the executive – so they must have heard of Berton's article through the parents in that network, though I never heard them discuss it. Did they believe that conditions were as bad as Berton claimed, or did they dismiss his shocking story as journalistic muckraking and sensationalism? Did they just not want to know, or did they have reason to believe that things were better at the newer facilities at Smiths Falls?

Certainly, they were in contact with other parents who were familiar with the situation at Rideau. In 1958, the same year that Martha was born, nine women who were members of the

Ottawa association and who had children at Smiths Falls had formed the Rideau Regional Hospital School Auxiliary (renamed the Smiths Falls Hospital School Welfare League in 1964 and the Rideau Regional Centre Association in 1971), which initially operated as a subcommittee of the Ottawa association. Despite confidentiality restrictions that made contacting other parents difficult, the committee recruited 634 mothers to fundraise, purchase toys and other extras, and in many other ways support and improve the school. "It was always the women's prime purpose to support the administrator and staff in every way possible. They have never wavered in this objective," the *Memory Book* recorded. Encouraged by Dr. Frank, in December 1964 they undertook a letter-writing campaign to federal and provincial government members, calling on them to improve living conditions and staffing at Rideau.

More critical parental activism, in the form of outright opposition to the large isolated institutions, had also begun long before my sister was born. In 1949, Victoria Glover wrote a letter to the editor of the *Toronto Daily Star* and asked, "Why not a day school?" Three years later, a group of mothers set up a nursery school in Toronto, which was later moved to a local school. In 1956, the Canadian Association of Retarded Children (now the Canadian Association for Community Living) was founded, and their first conference was held during Retarded Children's Week, November 16 to 20, 1958, two months after my sister's birth. That was when the association began a campaign to close institutions and adopted the slogan "Placement is not the only solution."

Perhaps my parents had been reassured by the film commissioned by the Ministry of Health called *One on Every Street*. It aired on CBC Television in April 1961, almost a year after Martha went to Smiths Falls. The narration, by one of my parents' favourite CBC Radio hosts, Allan McFee, offered a story of determined progress:

> A community where the retarded are understood: our Ontario government maintains a number of these communities. Some

are old, like this one [an image of Orillia], which first came into being almost a hundred years ago, when the clouds of ignorance and misunderstanding hung low. What was once called an asylum for idiots has now become, with added buildings, modern knowledge and equipment, plus a highly trained staff, a crowded but well-run community called the Ontario Hospital School, Orillia. Progress, often slow but inevitable, is symbolized in the up-to-date buildings of the Ontario Hospital School at Smiths Falls [an image of the main building, followed by another image of children skating on an outdoor rink at the school], where another expert staff cares for and teaches another community of children ... children, who through no fault of their parents, are victims of retardation.

"Progress" and "happiness," McFee continued, were the key words describing the aims of these institutions, where progress was adapted to a "slowed-down intellect." Each new patient was "a complex individual puzzle" who was thoroughly examined and tested through IQ tests and the latest scientific equipment, such as the electroencephalograph, to determine the patient's degree of intelligence so that a training program could be tailored for him or her. Meanwhile, at another hospital school in London, Ontario, McFee said that "a great step forward" had been taken in research into the causes and control of mental retardation. This would have given hope to many parents, as the genetic cause of Down syndrome had been identified in a breakthrough only two years earlier, and many were optimistic that this would lead to a revolution in treatment. The Ontario minister of health, Dr. Matthew B. Dymond, appeared in the film to solicit more public support to help the schools and "the thousands who probably should be hospitalized."

The film also showed the residents of the schools learning baking and woodworking, sewing and shoemaking and spoke of the "need to feel useful." Children learned in classrooms, and some even reached Grade 4 or 5 and could read for their own pleasure; they also received speech therapy as "clear speech is one of the greatest difficulties for the retarded." Accomplishments were important to retarded children, the narrator continued, and "women are taught to take an interest in their appearance." At the same time, the film did not gloss over the problems: "Even in the newer buildings there is often the problem of overcrowding," and McFee noted the shortage of specialized staff, the fact that some residents were also mentally ill and required restraints, and that some never gained control of their limbs or bodily functions.

One on Every Street asserted that the children at these institutions would never grow up: "The infants grow and become adults but mentally they will always remain children and they must be treated and cared for as children for the rest of their lives." Yet the film suggested a less than optimistic future for many adults, particularly men, who had "the minds of infants shrouded in the imperfect bodies of adults." Over sinister music, the film showed a procession of adult men, some with huge goiters: "There are these hopeless ones, the ones for whom there has never been any hope. They live in their own world, separated from the children, separated from those who may eventually leave the school. One day they will have their own hospital, but meanwhile they are happy in this community within a community." But they did not look happy, and the ominous tone of the soundtrack suggested they were dangerous, particularly to children.

"Many parents and friends come to see their children," the film's narrator said, "and after a visit home with the family, they are often very happy to get home to the hospital school." And this did seem to be the case with Martha. She was always sad to leave us but did not display any fear or aversion to the school when she returned. It was very likely the only home she could remember.

The school may have been one of the main employers in Smiths Falls, but it was not high-status work. Because the institution was distant from major cities, it was hard to attract qualified staff. The people who worked there had minimal training, and many likely held the same negative attitudes as the general population. If they, too, regarded their charges as subhuman, and if the residents had no recourse in the case of abuse, the situation was ripe for callous treatment, insensitivity, and abuse of power, just as it was in other institutions, such as "Indian" residential schools and orphanages, where beatings and other forms of abuse, including sexual abuse, were common, though this wasn't well known at the time. I had no inkling of this possibility while my sister lived at Rideau, and I don't think my parents seriously considered it either.

In fact, I knew next to nothing about my sister's life there, and my parents couldn't have known much more as communication doesn't seem to have been frequent. Even the institutional record of Martha's thirteen years at Rideau reveals little. Her file begins promisingly with daily entries, recorded in the first week after her arrival, that chronicle her height, weight, medical condition, and overall adjustment to life in the institution. After that first week, however, the number of entries drops off precipitously, save for entries detailing ongoing medical issues. Whole years go by with only a few paltry sentences recording anything else. The very paucity of comment speaks to the lack of attention to individual needs at Rideau.

What I can gather from her file is that she was often sick and struggled emotionally:

January 16, 1963 feeds herself with a spoon, toilet habits improving, using a few more simple words, understands simple commands. Enjoys television and will sit for long periods watching a programme. Enjoys music and tries to "twist" (dance) – keeps time to music well. Plays with other children well but rough and aggressive, likes dolls and dishes.

Feb. 16, 1963 Infectious hepatitis, transferred to isolation.

Jan 7, 1964 Martha often has a cold that becomes croupy or becomes pneumonia. Her eating habits have improved. Enjoys helping with small errands on the ward – still very aggressive with other children and enjoys ward school and activity room.

March 23, 1964 infection on left leg/inside.

Aug 5 64 infected area on buttocks.

January 11, 1965 Martha's chest condition has not improved this past year – frequent colds and pneumonia – also prone to skin infections. She is a determined child who likes her own way and tends to throw a temper tantrum if she is crossed. She is abusive to others – scratching and pushing often for no apparent reason. Martha's speech has improved – speaking in phrases.

August 27/65 progress note
Martha is a fairly quiet child, but becomes very annoyed and abusive with other children if she cannot get her own way. On the whole she plays fairly well in a group. She is able to walk well; speaks in rough undetermined phrases; can sing simple songs with other children. She enjoys music and some TV shows. Table manners are very good; toilet habits are improving; brushes her own teeth and washes her hands and face. Enjoys doing simple ward tasks; does as she is told.

Sept 20, 1965 boil on wrist.

Oct. 4, 1965 dysentery, transferred to isolation unit, age 7, released Nov. 4.

Nov. 8, 1965 infection on left heel.

Dec 1 1965 progress note
A seven year old mongoloid, who is toilet trained and can feed herself. Goes to ward school, is quick to learn. Enjoys ward activities. Talks, can form sentences. She is very good to help when asked.

March 23/66 She enjoys ward school – able to thread beads, build blocks, use peg board and colouring books. She plays well alone – but plays with others. She is able to dress and undress herself with some assistance – tries to help dress the other children ... Toilet habits good. Sleeps in a bed. Responds well to correction and follows instructions and simple commands fairly well.

Sept. 7 /66 Progress Note PW
Age 8 years ... Likes to be by herself; does not enjoying playing with other children.

Dec. /66 Martha was in the Christmas Concert this year as a "go-go girl." She follows instructions well and enjoys helping the staff with small errands and helps with serving of plates at supper time; takes children's boots off and helps dress and undress other children.

July 27/67 Progress Note EK
Can undress and folds her clothes, but when dressing she puts her dresses on backwards. Can lace her shoes but ties the laces in numerous knots. Helps with ward duties; assists other children. Converses readily in pleasant conversation and fully understands her peers. Although speech is guttural can be easily understood. Attends all ward activities.

A few of the entries in her file suggest she had good relationships with some of the staff:

July 17/66
Go out with M Couch (a staff member) for the evening.

Aug 23/66
May go out with Miss Couch (staff) today for the evening

But she also seems to have become increasingly withdrawn and quiet. On her tenth birthday, four community college students

who spent some time on her ward as part of their training recorded what they had observed about Martha.

Sept. 8, 1968 Barbara S

Personality: Martha is a quiet, affectionate little girl. She
doesn't have the trust in adults that most youngsters seem
to have. Martha is well behaved and is always ready to
please.

Sept. 8/68 Sandra C

Martha is a quiet girl but not unsociable; she likes to play
with the other girls.

Martha has to me seemed a happier child. When I first
came into the ward there was no sign of any kind on her
face. She never smiled. Now she smiles and is happy to
see me. I think Martha may be able to learn some small
trade, a very simple one.

Sept. 8/68 Mary R

Martha is a pretty, ten year old mongoloid. She is quiet
when around adults but tends to be bossy when with her
own peer group.

We both got along well but Martha does not ask or
like extra attention.

Martha enjoys the groups but is quiet unless spoken to.

Sept. 8 1968 Bea D

She is a very affectionate quiet little girl. Martha gets
along very well with the other girls in the group. She
likes to help you a lot ... Martha likes to be neat and tidy.
She dresses herself very well and her personal hygiene is
excellent. Her manners are very good and never
forgotten. She helps the other girls get dressed and
washed for school. Martha is one of the smartest ones
in the group.

It's clear from my parents' surviving letters to the institution
that her frequent illnesses concerned them and made it that

much more difficult for them to see her on a regular basis. Also, it's clear that they worried about how she was adjusting and what was best for her, even at one point offering to take her home for a while to help with her emotional adjustment.

Feb. 27, 1963

Dear Dr. Frank,

We understand that our daughter Martha Ann, who is in the female nursery, has jaundice and is now in the isolation ward. We have not been able to visit her for some time and we would appreciate any news of her condition – particularly when she is released from isolation and we can visit her again.

Yours very truly,

George Freeman

PS We are very much interested in your staff's assessment of Martha's capabilities and their views on whether taking her home for a while might help her emotional development. Who should we talk to?

I wish I knew what it was that prompted my parents' concern about Martha's emotional development at this juncture. Was it something a staff member told them about her rough and aggressive behaviour towards other children on the ward? Was it some way that she behaved on visits with us, perhaps towards my infant brother? Was it the "Shub up, kib!" incident? All I know is that they must have been quite worried about Martha's state of mind to offer to take her home for a while, and they must have had some serious concern about the quality of care she was getting to think that bringing her home might help her.

The reply they received was blandly reassuring but did not really address their concerns or even acknowledge the behaviour mentioned in her file:

Smiths Falls Ontario, March 12, 1963

...

Re: FREEMAN: Martha Ann

Dear Mr. Freeman,

I am writing to you further to your inquiry concerning Martha's progress.

Martha shows a typical picture of children suffering from Mongolism. She functions intellectually at about forty to forty-five per cent of the normal for her age and this is quite typical of such children.

She has learned to say a few simple words and understands a great deal of what is said to her. She looks after some of her own needs. She is able to feed and toilet herself to a degree. She is always happy and cheerful and enjoys the company of other children.

Yours very truly,

H.F. Frank, M.D.
Superintendent

What could my parents do? They were not inclined to rock the boat. They resigned themselves to the fact that her situation was not ideal but that there did not seem to be any realistic alternative. There was no way my mother would ever take Martha back permanently, especially now that she was struggling to cope with Eric as well as her two other children who lived at home. In fact, what seems to have happened is that my parents started to keep her infrequent visits home as short as possible. And yet in my sister's file, there is still undeniable evidence of my parents' concern for her.

November 23, 1965

Dear Dr. Frank,

I would like to know how my daughter Martha Ann Freeman is – whether she has recovered from dysentery; if there is anything she needs or that might be useful, and when I might be able to visit her.

Yours truly,

June Freeman

———————

November 30, 1965

Dear Mrs. Freeman,

We regret that you were not notified that Martha has completely recovered from dysentery and has been released from the isolation unit and returned to her ward. You may visit her any time at your convenience.

Sincerely,

H.F. Frank, M.D.
Superintendent

———————

Sept 28, 1967

Dear Mrs. Freeman,

We are enclosing a picture which was taken at Martha's Birthday party. Two of her little friends were also celebrating birthdays and so they shared the honours as well as the expenses. The children had a very happy time. They just love to have parties and had great fun blowing out their candles and singing the "Happy Birthday" song. We wish to assure you of our appreciation for your thoughtfulness in having requested the party.

Mrs. S. Lippard OT Reg.

My parents still did not celebrate that day with her. That my mother could not do. Nor, it seems, did she keep the photograph.

As the decade of the 1960s progressed, there were more and more calls for reform of these institutions and some improvements in both Canada and the United States. In 1961, President John F. Kennedy appointed a panel of experts to study the issues, and an American program for national action was announced in 1962. In Canada, a groundbreaking Federal-Provincial Conference on Mental Retardation was held in October 1964, and a blueprint for action was presented to the Ontario legislature in 1965. Subsequent legislation provided financial assistance for community residences and support for the further development of training programs and sheltered workshops, which were segregated spaces where adults with intellectual disabilities could be employed and receive a minimal wage. Stung by reports in the newspaper that hospital schools were not providing adequate educational opportunities for their charges, the Ministry of Education took over education at Rideau and the other institutions in 1965.

By the mid-1960s, there was also much more public discussion of the deplorable conditions in these institutions. In the United States, Robert Kennedy, the brother of President Kennedy, vehemently denounced the shameful neglect and abuses of children he had personally witnessed in several large, overcrowded, and unsanitary American institutions and talked publicly about his own sister Rose, who was intellectually disabled – a courageous move since most people's disabled relatives were still hidden away and never mentioned for fear of the stigma. In 1966, the book *Christmas in Purgatory* revealed shocking photographs of abuse and neglect surreptitiously taken by two US journalists who had visited several US institutions. That same year, the President's Committee on Mental Retardation called the poor status of residential care a national disgrace. There was similar upheaval closer to home. Most notably, in the 1965–66 Toronto Study, researcher John Fotheringham compared the effects of home versus institutional care and concluded that home care was better, as did Douglas Jackson's heartbreaking 1969 National Film Board film, *Danny and Nicky*, which offered shocking footage of life at Huronia.

I was not aware of these particular developments, but even I noticed that attitudes were changing. People like my sister were no longer called mongoloids or retarded; they were handicapped, and they had Down or Down's syndrome. We began to notice the occasional child with Down syndrome in Ottawa, on the street or on the bus with his or her family, and we could tell sometimes that the child actually lived with the family and was not just visiting, or at least they didn't seem to have that self-conscious awkwardness that we did. If anything, they seemed unselfconsciously normal, but maybe they were just better actors than we were. Even so, we never knew where to look; I'm sure we gawked like everybody else. We certainly didn't go up to them and introduce ourselves. Sometimes my mother would say things under her breath like "You couldn't pay me to do that," "What about the other children?," or "That's all very well if you are the martyr-type."

Increasingly, such comments embarrassed me. They seemed mean-spirited and bitter, not loving and generous, the way I wanted my mother to be. I had always thought of her as the best mother in the world, the most progressive and open-minded, and also as the main victim of our family catastrophe, but such lapses threatened to undermine that narrative.

In this new environment of increasing attention to the needs and rights of people with disabilities, I decided I needed to do something to make things better for my sister. In 1966, when I was ten, I heard that the hospital school was trying to raise funds to build a swimming pool. It had become popular to raise funds for charitable causes through walkathons, so I decided to organize one to raise money for the pool. I persuaded my family and some of our neighbours to pay me five cents each time I walked around a long block of houses near my home one Saturday, and in that way I raised $24.35, which my father dutifully sent off to the hospital school. Looking back on it, I realize that marked the birth of my own social activism.

9

Revolutions

Outwardly, when Martha was not there, we were to all intents and purposes a normal family. None of us had unusual physical or mental characteristics, and we all went to school and wore nice clothes. We socialized with the families of my parents' friends, who were also white, upper-middle-class, polite, well educated, well fed, and well groomed. Over the next few years, we rented cottages and ski chalets with some of these families; we went on wonderful family holidays to Florida and the Maritimes. It was in many ways an idyllic life. But, eventually, mysteriously, each of the remaining children in my family began to falter. The reasons are undoubtedly complex, but I can't help feeling that the silences and unhealthy dynamics that developed after Martha's institutionalization contributed to this diminishment.

What strikes me now is how isolated we were as Martha's siblings. My parents were initially active in the Ottawa and District Association for Retarded Children – my father became vice-president – and they helped develop its first sheltered workshop, which was considered a progressive move by many at the time though not today. But some time after Martha went to Smiths Falls, my parents dropped all contact with the association and distanced themselves from the other families. I don't know why they did so.

It may have been that once Martha had been institutionalized for some time they felt no need of it, but I suspect that my parents may have withdrawn from the association because of political disagreements over institutionalization. Within a couple of years of Martha's arrival at Rideau, such associations were riven with dissent between two opposing groups: the more radical community parents, who were fighting to close the institutions altogether and increase services so they could care for their children at home, and the more conservative institutional parents, who still wanted institutional care but in smaller institutions with improved services and staffing, arguing that "Bricks have a soul – Staff & Volunteers." My parents sympathized more with the latter group, because they definitely did not want Martha at home, but they also were no longer inclined to volunteer.

The unfortunate result was that we never compared notes with other families; we never went to any events for families affected by intellectual disability. Although some of my childhood friends knew about Martha, few of them met her. Only Belinda White really understood what it meant to have such a sibling. She was my best friend in Grade 5 and, like me, wanted to be an Egyptologist and go on excavations and learn to read hieroglyphics. Every day we walked home from school together, discussing books and archaeological digs and boys and our families. Eventually, we revealed to each other that we each had a sibling with Down syndrome – except her brother was younger and still at home. The more we talked, the closer Belinda and I became, even as her little brother was sent off to the Rideau Regional Hospital School, just as Martha had been.

Unfortunately, after only a few months of our friendship, Belinda's father was transferred out West, and the family moved to join him, though I don't know if the institutionalized brother did. She was the only person I ever knew as a child who also had a sibling like mine, other than the family two houses over who had sent their daughter away at birth and never spoke of her or saw her again. I used to play with the other children in that family, but I didn't know of their sibling's existence until my mother told me decades later. (In our case, there was more than one on our street.)

Other than those few months with Belinda, I knew no one else in a similar situation. No one seemed to realize that, as the sibling of a child who had been institutionalized, I might have needed companionship or support to process what had happened. It is only in the past few years that I have met siblings of other people sent to these institutions, and I have been struck by our collective woundedness and ongoing grieving and the nonrecognition of our pain when we were children, made all the more difficult because our siblings disappeared from our day-to-day reality, rendering our trauma invisible. It was out of sight, out of mind, just like Pierre Berton had said.

In fact, most of the time I forgot that I had another sister, and given my experiences at the hospital school, there was little that I wanted to remember.

Martha, Kate, Eric, and I were all in school by 1969, but Eric was having difficulties. Three years earlier, within the first couple of weeks of starting kindergarten, Eric's teacher had remarked to my mother that he could not sit still and didn't listen, that he talked loudly to the other students and disrupted the class. My mother began to get an uneasy feeling; he'd been like that in nursery school as well, but then she had attributed it to his immaturity and boys being slower to develop socially. Now it was clear the problem wasn't going away; if anything, it was getting worse because Eric was now expected to sit still for much of the day. He simply couldn't.

Perhaps he was hyperactive, my mother thought. This was a new term that some experts were using, and there were articles in the newspaper about it. She consulted various doctors and educational specialists, but to her dismay everyone assured her he was perfectly normal. She wasn't convinced. She felt in her bones that he had some kind of problem paying attention, but she couldn't find any professional who would take her concerns seriously. There were no relatively objective or visible markers of his disability, as there were with Down syndrome. The experts she consulted treated her like she was the problem, one more neurotic mother, one more silly, anxious woman making things up or making things worse. After all, neo-Freudian mother blame routinely attributed all children's problems to bad mothering (rarely bad fathering). In fact, professionals were now diagnosing increasing numbers of children with more ambiguous and controversial social, emotional, and behavioural disorders, and they often held rejecting mothers, overprotective mothers, dominating mothers, or overly affectionate mothers responsible. Yet the experts my mother consulted do not seem to have made any kind of diagnosis at all; instead, they simply dismissed her concerns.

Something was definitely amiss, however. In spring 1969, Eric failed Grade 1. Unfortunately, with that failure, my little brother became convinced that he was stupid, a loser, though he covered up this lack of self-confidence with bravado. That's when the real hell began, because Eric began to torment Martha when she came to visit. Now that he was seven and more capable than she was, he would mimic her and taunt her, even play tricks on her and then call her a retard. She would get a very troubled look on her face, begin to remonstrate, and start to cry. Then my parents would get upset, and they'd yell at Eric or spank him. That was another reason I didn't like it when Martha came home and why her visits home were limited. Kate and Eric were always fighting too. I regularly took Eric's side against Kate, but I didn't like it when he made fun of Martha.

What did Martha understand from my brother's teasing, from the stares or comments of others, from my own condescension? What did she see when she looked in the mirror? Did she know that she looked different or that she had an intellectual disability and that everyone judged her for it? Did she know that she was "different" from "normal" people? From us? Did she understand that it was the stigma of disability that had deprived her of sanctuary in "the safe shadows of ordinariness," to borrow Garland-Thomson's memorable phrase, propelling her into "the bull's eye of judgment"?

Yet it was not only Martha who suffered such judgment. Eric also did. He was always the odd one out in our family when Martha wasn't there. He didn't like to read (in fact, he had difficulty reading), which was what the rest of us wanted to do whenever we had a free moment. He wanted to play sports, which didn't interest us much, except as spectators. He went his own way, often defying my parents' rules. My parents did not know how to handle him much less help him.

In 1969, when Martha was eleven years old, the institution issued a report card like the ones the rest of us received. It noted that her physical development – in posture, walking, running, jumping, using toys, and so on – was satisfactory; that she was independent, neat, and tidy in her cloakroom routines; and that she was independent in all washroom routines ("She is very clean"). "She can do simple puzzles, bounce and catch a ball. She enjoys music and has a good sense of rhythm." She had some articulation problems in speaking but could describe simple pictures in short sentences, recognize her name, count to ten, and write the numbers from one to six. In a section on housekeeping, Martha was "satisfactory" in drying dishes and sweeping, "improving" in food preparation, and received no mark in laundry, table setting and clearing, and folding and ironing clothes, which she presumably hadn't been trained to do yet. Her progress was "satisfactory" in all areas of social development. The teacher described her as self-reliant, courteous, dependable, accepting of criticism, respectful of the rights of others, considerate, willing to share with others, able to practise self-control, cooperative, and obedient. Her work habits were apparently also "satisfactory": she was neat and orderly, listened and followed directions, and was showing improvement when it came to accepting responsibility, completing work and working independently, and using her time, energy, and materials well. Her teacher concluded, "Martha is quiet and well behaved and does not talk out of turn. She seems to enjoy school and tries to do her best at all times [and] has made some improvement in class."

By the time of that report card, Martha had been at the hospital school for nine years, but she was still basically in kindergarten. That same year, I began high school and was admitted into the accelerated class, where I would do five years in four, as I had also done in junior school, putting me two years ahead of my peers by the time I was ready to go to university. I was the accomplished one – excelling at school, playing the viola in the youth orchestra, going to Italy on a school trip, winning prizes and scholarships – and my sister Kate was soon following in my footsteps. Gradually, a hierarchy emerged in our family: there were the good children and the flawed children, the children my parents were proud of and the other ones.

But even that distinction became blurred over time. Eric left school before completing Grade 10, never having received the help he needed for what was probably some form of attention deficit disorder or learning disability. Kate was a gifted student in the accelerated class but became increasingly unhappy as she progressed through high school, eventually rebelling against the expectation that she should be like me – one of the top students, one of the "good" kids. She started skipping school, letting her grades fall, and hanging out with the "wrong" crowd, asserting her need to find her own path. And while outwardly I seemed to be a high-achieving, well-liked high school student, I was not nearly as outgoing and confident – or as "normal" – as I appeared to be.

Just as I entered that most vulnerable time of puberty, my sense of what was normal was shattered. My hero, Martin Luther King,

My Grade 9 school photo, 1969.

was assassinated on April 4, 1968, a week before my twelfth birthday, and on TV I watched six days of race riots erupt in over thirty cities across the United States. In Washington alone, over twelve hundred buildings were burned down, thirteen people were killed, thousands were injured, and more than six thousand were arrested. That same week, in Canada, Pierre Elliot Trudeau was elected leader of the Liberal Party in a wave of Trudeaumania. He was hip, and he talked about a just society; even my aunt laughingly admitted that she had dreamed of being kissed by him.

Then there was Robert Kennedy's assassination, the shooting of demonstrating students at Kent State University, massacres by US soldiers in Vietnam, oil spills, bombings, and huge antiwar demonstrations. Even though most of these events took place across the border, they did not seem far away. What to make of hippies, yippies, free love, psychedelia, rock concerts, drug overdoses, and people tuning in and dropping out? Everyone seemed to be questioning authority or rebelling against something. No adult could tell me what rules made sense anymore, because they were as bewildered as I was.

Then in 1970 the October Crisis brought revolution to our doorstep. A British trade commissioner and then a Quebec Liberal cabinet minister were abducted in Montreal, and the latter was murdered by the Front de libération de Québec, or FLQ. Our hip prime minister declared martial law through the repressive War Measures Act, the army moved into Ottawa, and just up the street from my house the Cuban Embassy was under twenty-four-hour guard amid several bomb scares. No one knew what would happen or where the FLQ would strike next, but Ottawa seemed a likely target. I feared for my father's safety because he now held a high-profile position with the Royal Commission on Prices and Incomes. Somehow, to be part of the country's political elite was no longer a matter of pride. People like my father had become the oppressors, the enemy, and I was suddenly confronted on a personal level by that vintage 1960s question: Which side are you on?

This was an especially difficult question for me. While most teenagers of my generation seemed to be in overt rebellion against their parents, I got along better with my parents than with most of my peers. They were loving, supportive, encouraging, generous, thoughtful, flexible, and altogether reasonable in their dealings with me. I did not feel at all constrained by them, except in not wanting to disappoint them, and I felt they had the utmost faith in me. Martha was the Achilles heel in our relationship, but most of the time she was out of sight and out of mind.

Then my body announced that I was a woman, just as my sense of what I should aspire to – in fact, the very notion of what a woman was – exploded around me amid the ringing cries of the women's liberation movement. This was the moment when all the political ferment around me became personal, when the cruelty and injustice of social prejudice became real to me, when my experience of sexism and misogyny became visceral. Now that I had breasts, men looked at me in ways that were both validating of my attractiveness yet also threatening, because they were asserting their dominance and authority, even over my body. This was the moment that it became apparent that in the world I knew, as Garland-Thomson so aptly put it, a "powerful woman" was as much of an oxymoron as a "disabled person."

A woman couldn't reason like a man, I was told; women were naturally interested in babies and housekeeping, ruled as they were by their wombs. They weren't biologically capable of great art or anything of genius. They couldn't be entrusted with any kind of governance since a woman might push the button and release the atomic bomb just because it was that time of the month. Women didn't have the physical stamina or strength of character to be explorers or scientists or astronauts or even bus drivers, and anyway, all those occupations were unnatural – for a woman was her biology. You were supposed to keep quiet and support your man, if you could get one, and you needed to put your energy into making yourself beautiful to make sure you did. Otherwise, you would be a loser, an old maid, a dried-up old spinster who had been left on the shelf, not really a woman at all, or you were one of those excessively masculine women – think of the bearded lady, repulsive, the butt of jokes – whom no one could love and certainly no man would desire.

Although my own parents had countered the more egregious attitudes towards women around me, I had nonetheless absorbed the message that men were superior, smarter, better, and nobler, and it certainly seemed like they had all the fun – all the freedom, all the adventure, all the intellectual achievement, all the glory. I wasn't even interested in most feminine occupations or activities.

I remember the revolutionary impact of the anthology *Sisterhood Is Powerful*, which I picked up off a rack in a bookstore in 1970: Why were men judged by their actions, women by their appearance? Why did so many women accept their second-class status? Now, feminists were questioning why men were deemed the norm and women were denigrated for their deviation from that norm, or as Aristotle expressed it, "the female is as it were a deformed male." At the time, I never made the connection to the way my sister Martha was defined, but my status, my worth, and my future were determined by my supposed physical inferiority, my genetic and biological lack – and this was compounded because I was barely above five feet in height in a world built for taller people, especially men. How strange it was that now that my form was clearly female rather than androgynous, its unmodified state would be regarded as unnatural, abnormal, and shameful unless I shaved my legs, applied makeup, and wore a bra (and even a girdle) and high heels. In fact, as Garland-Thomson has commented, it was only in relation to even more "abnormal" bodies, such as my sister's – or those of women of other "races" – that my white woman's body was deemed "normal."

I was learning, as Erving Goffman famously noted, that the supposedly normal person in North America, upon whom all social expectations and hierarchies were based, was a "young, married, white urban, northern, heterosexual, Protestant father of college education, fully employed, of good complexion, weight and height, and a recent record in sports." Only a tiny minority of individuals in North America actually fit this description; everyone else suffered some sort of stigma because they didn't. We tried in vain to fit the mould like "Cinderella's ugly stepsisters, [trying] to squeeze their feet into her glass slipper," in Garland-Thomson's memorable words.

I wanted the freedom that men had. As soon as girls were allowed to wear pants to school, I left skirts and heels behind. I stopped shaving my legs. I was one of the only declared and vocal feminists in my high school, though I soon discovered the loneliness of this position. Everywhere, "women's libbers" were ridiculed or dismissed as unfeminine, hysterical complainers; we were just a bunch of man haters and lezzies, going against what was natural and normal. What we needed, some men said ominously, was a good "you know what" to set us straight. My new found radicalism blazed through me like a white-hot current – but I was also exceptionally vulnerable, because to be labelled as abnormal or unnatural was especially threatening to me, sister of Martha.

And so I began to live a secret life. Inwardly, I rebelled and lived as I wanted, but there were many things I didn't share with my family or schoolmates. When I was fourteen, I became sexually involved with a boy from my high school, something that no girl of an upper-middle-class family was supposed to do. I knew that to be sexually active at such a young age and especially with someone from a different social class was to risk losing my so-called reputation, which in my mother's generation had meant certain social death, though in the new age of the birth control pill, this was less certain. All the same, I told no one what I was doing.

That silence, that surreptitiousness, increasingly marked my struggle to reconcile the rebellious me, the one who was inspired and exhilarated by the social ferment around me, with the me who was terrified of being socially ostracized or excluded and the me who felt threatened and confused by any kind of conflict. Above all, in spite of my actions, I did not want to be disloyal to my family. There was something so profound that tied me to them, some deep, dark tangle of love and pain. But there was something else I was even more loyal to, even if I couldn't express it, some kind of truth, some kind of belief in justice, maybe even the faintest whisper of outrage, something very, very deep in me.

Shame also lived its insidious life in my psyche, another whisper, another voice, a spirit, alive. Shame could change shape, but its shadow never left me; it was my twisted dark side, my devilish twin. My pride was the other face of that shame: I could not show others my vulnerability, my fear. I felt it whenever feminists were made fun of or when the other girls in my class shunned me because they said I was a flirt. Some said I was stuck up and had a swelled head. They were right: I did have to be superior to others, though I could never have explained why. Looking back, I can see that it was so I wouldn't be cast out, as my sister Martha had been.

I developed a certain anxiety, sometimes even a paranoia in some social situations: Were people talking about me, whispering behind my back, plotting to exclude me? *Keep her out. She doesn't belong. Don't let her in. She's not one of us.* Was my difference real if it wasn't visible like my sister's, or was it only in my imagination? That fear of social exclusion, of not fitting in, became a powerful narrative in my life.

I did feel different from many other girls my age, and it was not just because I was sexually active or a feminist. I didn't hold my body in the embarrassed, hunched over way so many other teenage girls did. I loved my body, almost defiantly. I had discovered modern dance at a summer arts camp when I was eight and had studied since then with the most original woman I had ever met, the dancer Elizabeth Langley. She was utterly unlike any other woman I had ever known – a completely committed artist who had studied with Martha Graham in New York, a strong, passionate, even fierce woman who ended up raising a child on her own, who was never defined by a man, and who seemed unafraid to speak her mind. She modelled female freedom to me, and she gave me the precious gift of improvisation – the freedom to move my female body in an entirely unscripted way, to explore my world and every inch of my body through movement, to listen for the unexpected, to dare and to take risks.

Dance changed me. When I danced, when I improvised, there was no right or wrong, and there were no secrets – dance encompassed everything, welcomed everything. Only in the physical did I feel whole. I could not articulate my complicated feelings about my life or about my sister, but I could dance them, and Elizabeth gave me permission to dance every feeling I had. I could dance abandonment, loss, and deformity, even if I did not know why I did so. I could dance hatred and isolation. I could dance revolution and hope. I could dance lust and sexiness and love. When I danced, I was male, female, and everything in between. I could dance shame, but when I danced, I had no shame. When I danced, I could move through complicated feelings into the sheer pleasure of the body, the joy of freedom and expression and creativity, my youthful energy and delight at being alive. Dance gave me access to my inner joyous core.

Remarkably, my mother also started taking dance classes with Elizabeth, as did a couple of her friends. I loved that my mother opened herself to those experiences and to so much of what Elizabeth offered – and that she was brave enough to dance with me, her teenage daughter. There were things we couldn't talk about, would never talk about, especially with regard to Martha, but there were also times we didn't have to.

Martha was also a joyous dancer, as her institutional file attests. In this we were alike, but I never truly knew her in this way. Sadly, apart from those first dances in her presence when she was a baby, I have no recollection of ever dancing with her.

It was the dancer in me who first noticed Esther, a young woman in my high school who could have been my double – or my sister. She was small, slight, funny, somewhat androgynous, a developing actor and mime artist, just as I was a dancer. I remember her wearing trim black pants and a long-sleeved black turtleneck. She had short, wavy brown hair and a funny button nose and impish face. She could mimic things: a pompous man, a prudish woman; there was something subversive in her wiry body, her wordless but sly look, a hint of power in the slight upturn of her lips. I loved the sense of surprise I felt with her, my curiosity about what she would do next, how she seemed to be so completely her own person.

There was an excitement in the air between us, and I know she felt it too. There were moments when it felt like we were on the verge of moving into a different world with each other, but we never did cross over. Yet in that time I spent with her a certain duality in me was confirmed; I was attracted to women as well as men. In those moments when I first felt it, I was not ashamed of it or even afraid of it. I did not dismiss or judge it;

rather, I filed it away for future reference. But I did not speak of it to anyone. I knew it was something that would have to remain private, that it existed in a very different part of me than the normal me who flirted excessively with boys. In fact, I was becoming a warren of secrets.

From then on, even if I appeared to do so outwardly, I always had a sense of not fitting in to the mainstream social structure that many other people seemed to comfortably and effortlessly live within. For years it would be other outsiders, rebels, and outliers who interested me, particularly as romantic and sexual partners, because with them I felt at home. Yet I was perpetually caught between "the rage of being unseen and the self-protective impulse for concealment" – another memorable Garland-Thomson phrase. Describing the tension between the desire for sameness and the longing for uniqueness that is "at the core of the equal respect that democracy promises," Garland-Thomson observes that "we need to be wholly ourselves and at the same time just like everyone else." Another disability scholar, Lennard Davis, notes how we are obliged to act, feel, look, and be normal – at almost any cost: "Passing is an intentional quest for civil inattention in a racist or sexist environment." I knew all too well that difference could be dangerous.

Passing was never an option for my sister. Down syndrome was always visible, physically manifest, seen almost as an ethnicity or racial difference – hence she would live "with her own kind." There was no way for Martha to escape the staring or the social marginalization and segregation that went with it.

In 1972, I graduated from high school in a blaze of glory, winning several awards and scholarships. I began to plan my move to Toronto, where I would start classes at the University of Toronto. Only later did I learn that my scholarship had only been made available to students who were white, Protestant, and showed promise in becoming leading citizens of the British Empire. The funder had stipulated that no more than one-quarter of the scholarship fund could be awarded to females.

Sometime in my last year of high school, in the midst of various deliberations about my future, I had a wonderful if mysterious dream. I was vacationing at a summer resort with my family when I stubbed my toe, and it started to bleed. After some searching, I found a doctor. He led me along a path leading away from the resort, which eventually narrowed and led uphill. The path became strenuous and rocky, and we passed fewer and fewer people, until we summited on a mountain top, alone.

The sky was a rainbow of colour, the peak majestic. There was a rushing river that I had to cross, and I did so in a moment of pure delight, jumping up and down in the sparkling, frothy rapids in the sun. On the other side, I found an entrance into the mountain and began to descend into it. The passageway led circuitously downward through various floors of a museum, and the doctor became a museum guide who showed me dinosaur bones, Roman coins, Anglo-Saxon pottery, and other relics of the past. I descended deeper and deeper into the mountain, fully absorbed in the displays, until suddenly I realized my guide had disappeared.

I was alone. I wasn't sure what to do, and I was afraid I was trapped inside the mountain and would never find a way out. Then, from a completely different direction, an ancient woman appeared, in a wheelchair, her face immensely wrinkled.

She looked at me without speaking for several minutes. "You've learned all you can here. It's time for you to leave," she finally said in a voice that was authoritative but also sympathetic. I descended a circular cast iron staircase, the sound of my footsteps clanging in the vast emptiness of that inner chamber. I opened a door and then stepped out into the great, wide world.

10

Normalization

The same social ferment that was spreading revolution across the planet also eventually reached my sister at the hospital school at Smiths Falls. In tandem with other struggles for civil and human rights, activists were now demanding that people with disabilities be seen as fully human and deserving of love, that they be welcomed into the human community and no longer shunned or shut away in huge institutions. This was a wonderful change for people like my sister but a very threatening one for my family, because we had made certain choices, and we had to justify them to ourselves and to others.

When Harold Frank, the long-time superintendent of Rideau Regional Hospital School, retired in 1969, it was the end of an era. Hundreds of parents came to say thank you to the "little grey-haired psychiatrist" who had been "a sort of foster-father to more than 2,300 retarded children," the *Ottawa Journal* reported. He had tried to be a reformer from within, the article stated; he had come close to "jeopardizing his job for his criticism of overcrowding and staff shortages" and had gone on record, saying that "no hospital of this type should ever exceed 1000 patients ... Our biggest problem is that we have to water down any intensification of individual attention." He had been outspoken, to be sure, but he was ultimately limited in his ability to make change.

His replacement, Claude Harpin, was an energetic reformer in tune with the spirit of the times, and the next couple of years saw many changes. A qualified physiotherapist was hired for the first time, and a Speech Therapy Department was established, which my sister so desperately needed. The aides and attendants were reclassified as residential counsellors and no longer wore uniforms. Even the residents started to wear everyday clothing. In the early 1970s, the institution finally began paying residents who worked in the wards, the laundry room, and the dining room, though the wages were still pitifully low.

Reflecting on his time at Rideau, Harpin wrote:

> When I first visited Rideau, I was concerned, if not dismayed, by some of the conditions that were being provided for the handicapped. With the full support of management and the care teams at the Centre, a two-year target goal was set to become an accredited facility by the Canadian Council on Hospital Accreditation.
>
> Through extreme diligence and hard work by our whole team, we had an initial survey that resulted in our becoming the first retardation facility in Canada to be accredited by the Canadian Council on Hospital Accreditation.
>
> In my total health career, my experience at Rideau was one which presented me with the most demanding challenges and yet the most personal satisfaction in view of what a strong team of staff and managers were able to accomplish.

The accreditation program stressed the quality of patient care and hospital facilities, safety measures, organizational patterns, and professional and technical procedures. Accreditation confirmed that a hospital was operating at an acceptable level of performance, and through accreditation Harpin hoped to reassure parents. It did not change the basic model of institutional care, however.

The institution was reorganized into five distinct units – Adult, Education, Progressive Activity A and B, and Nursing – an innovation supported by the ministry, which made similar changes at Huronia and Cedar Springs. The unit system aimed to provide a more personalized program for each resident, one geared to her or his particular needs. Residents were assigned to individual staff members so that the families and residents "could be in touch with specific staff members who knew exactly the status of their son or daughter, so that much more personalized communication could occur."

Meanwhile, the Smiths Falls newspaper, the *Record News*, reported additional improvements at Rideau, such as a new swimming program, hockey games against teams from the surrounding community, a new double gymnasium, and activities such as ping-pong, billiards, floor hockey, dances, card games, films, fastball, T-ball, picnics, and Cubs, Scouts, and Brownies. Residents received certificates and trophies for the year at Rally Day, and sports celebrities such as Bobby Hull of the Chicago Black Hawks or Ottawa Roughriders quarterback Russ Jackson visited. Residents even went on occasional trips beyond the institution to compete in the Special Olympics.

I was not aware of such changes, and they did not address the fundamental problems associated with institutional care. But that resident life improved significantly is suggested by a remarkable newspaper article published, unedited, in 1972 and written by an unnamed adult resident of the Ontario Hospital School at Cedar Springs. I hope my sister experienced similar improvements at her institution.

On July 12, 1963 when I first came to this place I thought I would never like it here at first but after a couple of months I sort of got used to it. When I was only 13 at the time. I always thought the staff were mean. And as I gradually grew up threw the years my thoughts had changed about the staff. And I didn't even like the rules but now even the rules have changed even the privileges were strict that that has changed to. The clothes were kinda a drag at first but now they are getting better all the time ... And on the wards we used to sit on hard chairs but now we are sitting chairs as soft as a feather. The TV? we were not a loud to touch it only the staff but now the kids are doing it. And when we went to work we never used to get paid but now we do. We used to stay up until 9 oclock but now we can stay up at any time we wanted to long as we didin't make any noise. Before we had to line up nice and straight but now we don't.

... We never went to a hockey game only once a year. We went to camps and picnics we never did this before. We were never aloud to have radios, watches, record players, we can have them now. The doors on the ward had to be locked at night. We never had a Unit Director we have now. If we got into trouble we had to wear a night gown plus we had to work on another ward. We were never aloud to have a razor we got them now ... Before we had all the boys on one side and all the girls on the other side we have it changed now. Now we have boys and girls mixed. The only time were were aloud to see our girlfriends was on Friday night at the dance. This place used to be runed by two or three nurses up front we don't have them anymore.

We never had instructors to teach us different jobs we have them now. We never had a sheltered work shop in which we have to-day. We never had good clothes unless it was given to us by are parents. We were never aloud to have a coffee pot or a toaster now we have. We were never aloud to have breakfast on the ward now we have. We were never aloud to sleep in on Sunday morning. We never had arts & crafts before. We never had good curtains before now we have ... We could never have a coffee break in the morning or afternoon but now were having them. We were never aloud to roam the halls but it is still being done.

... The wards were never aloud to have animals on them but now we have. We never had under arm Deodorant of our own we always had to line up and somebody would squirt us with it. Our beds had to be perfectly made or we practice making beds all day until we knew how to do it right. We were not aloud to sit or lay down on our beds.

Things are much better than they used to be to-day.

P.S. First time I ever wrote a story before.

From my sister's point of view, one of the best changes must have been the completion of the long-awaited $300,000 Olympic-size pool, hailed as a sign of Rideau's progressive model of care. Martha soon learned to swim, and it became her favourite activity. She began competing in the newly formed Special Olympics for disabled athletes and was even featured in a television ad for that groundbreaking athletic competition. I imagine her discovering a new freedom in that buoyant medium, pushing herself beyond her previous limits, learning for the first time that she, too, could excel.

Martha was placed in the Education Unit, and that "school within a school" gained new energy with an increasing push to prepare residents for discharge into the community. By 1972, it had twenty-nine classrooms, thirty teachers, and a principal, vice-principal, and two staff for three hundred pupils. There were never more than fifteen students in one classroom.

In April 1970, when my sister was almost twelve years old, an Education Unit case conference convened for the first time to discuss my sister's progress and potential. The report from this meeting contained the fateful words "She would probably fit into a trainable class in the community," and it recommended that the Social Work Department check into the home situation with a view to eventually releasing Martha from the institution.

In likely preparation for this case conference, a new photograph of my sister was added to her file, apparently the first photograph to be taken since July 1960 and the last before she was discharged. The eleven-year-old girl who stares so directly, even defiantly, into the camera takes my breath away. She does not look happy, but you can see her struggle to survive in that harsh environment and her incredible strength, determination, and resistance. This was a Martha that I never saw or recognized while she lived. Like me, she clearly had an inner rebel. Like me, she had some difficulty socializing with her peers and spent a lot of time alone.

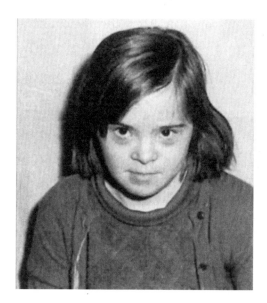

Institutional photo
of Martha, 1970.

In May 1970, my parents received a letter from a social worker that informed them of the results of the case meeting and the conclusion that Martha could succeed in the community: "In general, we are pleased with Martha's progress at the hospital school, and are anxious to know how she behaves while she is at home. We would also be interested in discussing with you any plans you might have for Martha's future."

Plans for Martha's future? What did that mean? My parents had always assumed that the hospital school was Martha's future. I can only imagine my parents' unsettlement after receiving this missive.

In August, the social worker noted in my sister's file: "Martha's parents were written on May 8, 1970. It was felt that she would fit into a trainable class in the community, but there has been no answer from the Freemans. A home visit might be worthwhile if only to find out what the home situation is like." Nothing came of this immediately – perhaps my parents found ways to avoid or delay the dreaded encounter. Meanwhile, Martha's schooling was switched to a half-day program that may have had a more

academic focus while a succession of social service students under-
went placements at Rideau and continued to monitor and record
Martha's progress at the institution:

Oct 31/70 S. Smith
    She is quiet but can be quite stubborn at times.

Jan. 71 G. White
    Martha is a quiet, neat clean mongoloid ... She makes a
    bed well and very cooperative when asked to do anything,
    and when cleaning does a good job. She talks well. She
    prefers to play alone with her toys, especially dolls,
    undressing them and dressing them, and will not bother
    anyone. She participates well in all activities. Goes to
    school half day in Group 18 with Mrs. Norstrom.

April 71, S. Smith
    Martha is a white female child age 12 years. She is able
    to set up in the dining room. She gets along well with
    other residents and the staff. Martha is usually quiet and
    you don't see her angry very often ... She likes sports
    and dancing.

Finally, a year after the first letter to my parents, a second
attempt was made to set up a home visit, and this time the letter
was harder to ignore.

May 14, 1971

From Miss J. Howard, Social Work Dept.
For J. McHugh, M.D., Director of Treatment and Training

We are at present reviewing Martha's progress and formulat-
ing plans for her future. We would appreciate it very much if
I could visit with you on the afternoon of May 21st, to discuss
Martha's progress and any plans you may have for her future.

Apparently, Ms. Howard, a summer hire, had a hard time when she visited my parents and tried to get them to take Martha home for an extended period in July or August. In her report, dated May 26, 1971, she noted that my parents resided in a "very spacious upper class home" with three other children and my grandmother, who she characterized as serving "as a house-keeper." Lack of space or help was obviously not the problem.

Right from the get-go, my parents were only superficially cooperative, Miss Howard noted. My father apparently cited the depth of the lake at what Howard referred to as our "summer home" (actually a rented cottage) as an obstacle to Martha spending the summer with us. He was, she noted, outwardly polite but "rigid and opinionated if the surface is scratched." He tried to maintain control of the conversation and keep it general by repeatedly questioning her about the institution's programs and staff ratio. My mother followed his lead in the conversation, Howard observed, speaking freely only when my father was out of the room about the great upset that Martha's birth had caused their families, a statement that my father denied when he returned. When Howard raised the issue of having Martha home more often, my father objected that communication with the other children would be a serious problem because of Martha's speech impediment and that all the children, but especially Eric, would be frustrated by Martha's inability to keep up with them in their activities.

Howard reported:

> I suggested that an interview could be arranged with the speech therapist and a home program planned. I also volunteered to come over to assist and give them a break, as Mr. Freeman expressed the view that Martha was a full-time job. They were most receptive to the home program but very noncommittal. Just before departing, Mr. Freeman dashed any hope of this by stating that there was just too much going on with the other children to have Martha home this summer.

The Freemans would seem to be a very interested and concerned couple, but I feel this is on a very polite, superficial level, as they offer the most minimal obstacles blocking Martha's visiting for more than a couple of days.

Were my parents only making excuses, as the social worker implied? Now that my father was one of three commissioners serving on the federal Royal Commission on Prices and Incomes, a highly stressful appointment, he travelled frequently, so part of his resistance might have been his worry about my mother's ability to manage, particularly with Eric and Martha at a cottage together. It was also true that my grandmother now lived with us – she had moved in after the death of her second husband – but in some ways this was an added stress since she liked to drink and could be unpredictable. This could have contributed to my parents' feeling that they just couldn't handle having Martha home as well. But, fundamentally, the social worker was right: my mother and father did not really want Martha home under any circumstances.

In any event, by this time both my parents knew they were fighting a rearguard action, as public opinion continued to mount to get people like my sister out of large institutions. The outcry caused by Pierre Berton's 1960 article about the school at Orillia had long since died down, but public outrage had been rekindled a few months before the social worker's visit to my parents, when a former resident of the Rideau Regional Hospital School committed suicide after being discharged from the school to work on a local farm as an indentured labourer. Frederick Elijah Sanderson, a Cree man from Kirkland Lake, was found hanging from a length of baling twine in the barn of Justin Dervin of Richmond, on March 5, 1971. His life was a terrible illustration of all the deficiencies of the system. He had become a ward of the Children's Aid in 1956, at the age of four, following the death of his parents, and had subsequently passed through thirteen foster homes in six years. After repeating Grade 1 three times, he was admitted to the institution at Smiths Falls in 1962. Various intelligence tests administered to him at the hospital school indicated that he was functioning at a "low moron level" of intelligence, with IQ scores in the 55 to 69 range, depending on the test, though it was unclear to what degree his traumatic childhood had been responsible for his learning difficulties.

Sanderson's death was followed by the near death of another former resident of the same institution, also an indentured farm worker, whose poor living and working conditions prompted him to run away in the depth of winter, resulting in him suffering from severe frostbite. Although he had technically been discharged from the hospital school, he, like Sanderson, was still under the supervision of the institution's social workers. The ensuing outcry led the Ontario Ministry of Health to appoint a Toronto lawyer, Walter Williston, to study the care and treatment of people with intellectual disabilities in the province.

Williston's 1971 report strongly criticized the whole system of care for people with developmental disabilities. It confirmed that the conditions that Berton had earlier described – few, if any, toys in the wards, lavatories without doors and often without toilet seats, locked wards, the entire staff in uniform, "while keys dangled from every waist" – had only eased somewhat in large institutions. Referring to the conditions Berton had uncovered in 1960, Williston confirmed that

> overcrowding was most apparent in wards where profoundly and seriously retarded adults, naked or near naked, sat rocking, or aimlessly walking or crawling, often dirty. There was little attempt at programming their activities. Conditions such as these prevailed in Orillia and Smith[s] Falls until the new systems were introduced beginning in 1964, and until three years ago at Aurora. Patients were organized into work gangs to perform many of the routine tasks necessary to the operation.

Reviewing the situation at the Rideau Regional Hospital School in Smiths Falls and other institutions in 1971, Williston reported that not much had changed. In April 1971, the resident population of Smiths Falls was 2,070, an improvement over the worst overcrowding of the early 1960s, but there were only 782 ward staff, 273 fewer (or 25 percent) than the minimum requirements demanded by professional standards. In addition, only three of the ten social workers were fully qualified.

The emphasis in all the institutions was still on custody, not training or rehabilitation, Williston wrote. Worse, children lived in isolation. The majority of residents did not receive regular visits from relatives, because the institutions were often hundreds of miles from their families' homes. The institutions rarely interacted with neighbouring communities. The residents were paid from four to eight cents an hour for their work (and any payment at all was a recent innovation). Williston also noted the "profound psychological effect upon both staff and residents when there are hundreds of helpless and hopeless cases in one institution."

Citing a "century of failure and inhumanity in the large multi-purpose residential hospitals for the retarded," he denounced the whole system as inherently dysfunctional: "I recommend that the large hospital institutions for the mentally retarded be phased down as quickly as is feasible." Instead, he advocated the adoption of the Scandinavian concept of normalization, in which people with disabilities are maintained in the community through a network of social services "to let the mentally retarded obtain an existence as close to the normal as possible."

> The needs of every child, be he normal or handicapped, are basically the same. They are: family ties, love, emotional warmth, understanding and acceptance. There must be growth of his social, physical and emotional resources to prepare him for the future. The best place for a child to receive such essentials is in a healthy home environment.

It sounded a lot like Pearl Buck.

Following Williston's report, the government began to move residents out of large hospital schools into community settings and offered more funding for day nurseries and other support services in the community. Williston did not advocate immediately abolishing all institutions, however: "Many parents who have become accustomed to having their problems stowed a long way away would now be shocked at the prospect of the return of their child," he commented. This was certainly the case with my parents.

For my mother in particular, these new attitudes and expectations were difficult to deal with. As both expert and public opinion shifted away from support for large institutions, my mother felt more and more vulnerable. She knew she was now being judged for not keeping Martha at home, even though institutionalization had been what her doctor had recommended at the time of Martha's birth and what most people had supported since there were no sheltered workshops, schooling, or other social services available in Ottawa at the time. She could see that all kinds of people now viewed her with the self-righteous presumption that they would have done things differently and behaved more nobly.

"How is Martha doing?" I remember Vera Bernstein asking my mother at a party at my parents' home, one summer in the early 1970s. Vera was a physiotherapist and socially progressive activist on many issues, especially health care.

"Oh, she's fine," my mother answered.

"Do you see her often?" The question seemed innocuous, but there was something in Vera's voice that rankled and caught my attention.

"Several times a year," my mother said evenly. Vera frowned and said nothing, and my mother continued, somewhat nervously, "When we can ... It's harder with the children's swimming lessons and Brownies and so on. We're always on the go."

"Did you read that article in the *Citizen* about those two boys from Smiths Falls?"

"They were no longer at Smiths Falls, actually ... "

"Yes, but the institution placed them at those farms."

"We've always been very grateful to the hospital school ... They've taken good care of Martha ... "

"But it's not the same as being in a family, is it?"

"They do the best they can."

Vera smiled a superior smile. "I don't think I would have had the strength to send my child away to one of those places."

"You don't know till you're in that situation, do you?"

"Oh, I know I couldn't. I think Down's children are so happy and cuddly ... I don't know how you can keep Martha in one of those places."

I saw the look on my mother's face as she stiffened and composed herself.

"Besides," Vera said, smiling sweetly and trying to recover, "I always wanted to meet Martha."

My mother glared at her.

"I'm just asking," Vera protested.

"Like hell you are."

And that was the end of their friendship.

My mother would seethe with rage for days after such exchanges. Her closest friends supported her and were understanding of her situation, but she was always vulnerable to other people's opinions and judgments, somehow more vulnerable than my father ever was. They had made the decision to institutionalize Martha together, but my father largely escaped such censure or at least didn't seem as affected by it. My mother was the caregiver, my father the wage earner. It was my mother who was tortured by other people's comments and her own guilt and rage. Was she only imagining that people scrutinized and judged her more? Or was she indeed being judged more harshly because sending her child away was somehow more of a violation of the still sacred ideal of motherly love, and fathers weren't judged to the same standard? That Victorian ideal of motherhood required her to be "self-abnegating, domestic, and preternaturally attuned to her children's needs," as Molly Ladd-Taylor and Lauri Umansky put it in *Bad Mothers: The Politics of Blame in*

Twentieth-Century America, or risk being judged inadequate, unnatural, or selfish.

How terribly hard it must have been to be seen as a deficient mother in the early 1970s, when for most women successful motherhood was still the single most important measure of their worth and success as a person. Not so for my father, who by then had moved on to a senior position at the Bank of Canada. Although my mother was now starting to work part-time for the Department of Manpower and Immigration, being a wife and mother was something she had prepared for all her life.

In my mother's case, however, there were additional reasons for her vulnerability to other people's opinions. She had been deeply shaped by the social censure and ostracism she had endured as a child, to the point that her mantra in life – something that annoyed me to no end as a teenager – sometimes seemed to be a fearful "What will the neighbours think?" I also believe that deep down she knew that she had harmed my sister, however she rationalized it, however limited her options or desperate her choice, however much she did it for the rest of us or told herself that because Martha had Down syndrome she didn't feel things as much as normal children would. My mother knew what parental abandonment felt like, and yet she had left her own daughter in the care of others at the incredibly vulnerable age of twenty months. She knew she had rejected Martha, and she openly acknowledged that she wished her daughter had never been born.

Looking back, I think one of the worst effects of Martha's institutionalization was its erosion of my mother's confidence in her own ability to love. In *The Normal One: Life with a Difficult or Damaged Sibling*, psychotherapist Jeanne Safer comments, "Wanting to abandon one's own flesh and blood, hoping they will die, wishing they had never been born, repulsion – and even hatred – are utterly antithetical to what good people are supposed to feel." Every time the talk of deinstitutionalization heated up and everyone said what a good thing it would be, my mother had to confront her fear that she would be forced to take

Martha back and her own vehement inner refusal to do so. Every time that happened, my mother's heart constricted, her sense of herself as a good person was shaken, and something in her became more brittle. She then had to find other ways to try to rationalize her feelings or assuage her guilt.

Sometimes, she would try to get us kids to sanction and approve of what she'd done. This left us in a horrible quandary: to implicate ourselves in her decision by validating it for her or to distance ourselves from her and judge her when we needed and wanted to love her. It is evident to me now that my mother was punished in innumerable ways for my parents' decision to put Martha in an institution. Only over time did it become apparent that it had truly been a devil's bargain and that we would all pay the price.

Despite the efforts at institutional change at Rideau, another tragic death occurred in the winter of 1972 when a seventeen-year-old resident, Joanne Martineau, somehow "wandered away" from the institution. Heavy snow covered her tracks, and her nude body was found curled up in a field a mile and a half from the centre, just north of Highway 43, at 2:40 a.m. by a team of snowmobile searchers who were among the fifty-five to a hundred people who searched all night for her in sub-zero (Fahrenheit) weather. There was no sign of violence on her body, and she apparently froze to death. The coroner, Dr. John Hogan, was quoted as saying the girl had the mentality of a three-year-old. "The coroner says there will be no inquest and the OPP have closed the case."

A similar tragedy had occurred in 1964, when a nine-year-old deaf boy, Mauro Uliana, ran away from the institution and was found dead eight days later in dense bush two miles from the school. The school and staff were publicly criticized, and a probe into the death was promised, though Dr. Frank commented,

"There is no way we can guarantee children will not run away. We can never stop it although we can take every reasonable precaution to prevent it ... But if public opinion is for a 20-foot wall to be built around the place like a prison, I would like to hear about it." Still, one wonders what prompted these children to flee.

In 1973, a new report by Robert Welch, the provincial secretary for social development, again criticized the lack of improvement in care for the eleven thousand developmentally disabled living in Ontario institutions and called for a new system of residential homes in the community. Following the Scandinavian and American examples, the Ontario government formally adopted the policy of normalization. It gradually closed its large institutions, including Rideau, and housed its former residents in smaller, more informal settings in the community.

That many of these changes were welcomed by the staff is indicated by an article written by Dr. McHugh, who became acting administrator in the wake of Halpin's 1973 departure. The article appeared in a 1974 issue of *VOX, The Voice of Staff and Friends of the Rideau Regional Hospital School,* a publication that began as a new initiative in 1969:

> The institutions will be needed for many years to come, but at least we can see in these new proposals a glimmering light which suggests to us that we will never see again the dreadful overcrowding of these institutions and the conditions that so many of our staff have endured for so many years. Much is owed to our staff who have had to tolerate these conditions and who have been subjected to the conditions imposed upon them by authorities, who until recently (since 1965) have had little or no understanding of the needs of the retarded.

But by the time McHugh wrote those words, Martha had already left Rideau.

In February 1973, the hospital had held another resident conference to review Martha's situation. The result was a recommen-
dation that she be placed in the community but not returned to
my parents:

BACKGROUND INFORMATION

Reason for admission: Institutional care and training

Martha is of a family of three other children, one of which is
adopted. She is of mongoloid characteristics but is happy
and contented. While at home she has considerate care from
her parents; although she is not destructive she has occasional
outbursts of temper. In a home visit the feeling is they prefer
not to have Martha for more than a couple of days at a time.

Communication:
Paper and Pencil Work:
Cannot draw recognizable "men" and "houses"
Cannot recognize 40 or more words of everyday
Cannot write her own name but can print her name.
Cannot read simple instructions.
Cannot address envelope in an acceptable manner.
Cannot read simple printed matter, eg. Radio and
TV times.

Personality: Martha keeps her temper most of the time. Is
helpful and cooperative and when given a little praise or
attention will do extra jobs on her own. When corrected appears to be unaffected. Martha likes to be by herself on the
ward, enjoys going to the gym, playing basketball, joins in
skipping and other group activities.

Her attitude is mostly satisfactory.

Emotional maturity easy and friendly, other residents take
little notice of her.

Can be relied on to speak the truth, respects others
property. Willing but needs constant prodding. Converses
readily – chatters even with a speech handicap.

Recommendations at programming conference: To explore possibility of community placement. Mrs. Jean Art (Liaison Officer) felt she would function well in a community school. Mrs. Jennie Ord (Counsellor) felt she could function well in a home.

Recommendations: To remain in present academic program.
I would like a program set up for socializing or occupational therapist for a future approved boarding home (ABH).

Signed Jennie Ord, Counsellor

Two months later, another social worker recorded that my family had been contacted by phone and that a home visit had been offered but that it had been turned down. Over the phone, the social worker discussed the institution's plans to place Martha in an Approved Boarding Home, with a placement in a community educational program, in the near future. It is apparent that my parents were worried that once Martha was out of the institution they would somehow be forced to take her back:

> They were outwardly more or less accepting of this idea, though it was entirely new to them, and they were quite cautious and questioning about all the details. Programmes and other aspects of Approved Boarding Homes were discussed at length. The question of actual parental permission or refusal came up indirectly, and I brought out that, for those families who were unable to have their children home and plan for them themselves, that RRHS was obligated to protect the child's rights, and place him or her in the setting felt most beneficial to growth, when institutionalization was no longer needed. This question may arise again; for the moment the parents are simply getting used to the idea.

My mother kept the letter she received a few weeks later informing her of Martha's placement.

May 7, 1973

Dear Mr. & Mrs. Freeman:

We are planning to place your daughter, Martha, in an Approved Boarding Home in Cornwall.

An Approved Boarding Home is a recognized extension of the Hospital School, approved by the local Health Department, Provincial Ministry of Health, Fire Department, two references plus three social workers of Rideau Regional Hospital School. The Hospital is responsible for medication, follow-up service provided by the Social Work Department and miscellaneous items. Clothing and pin money in most cases is expected to continue to come from the parents if it is now being provided. A community doctor and dentist is provided in the community for Martha.

While in this home, Martha will attend Kinsmen School for the Retarded in Cornwall, five days per week.

We plan to place Martha in the home on May 8th. She will reside in the home of Mr. and Mrs. Frank Zaretsky, 39 Donald Street, Cornwall. The phone number is: 822-3766. We would encourage you to visit the home at any time in order to view Martha's progress.

Miss Celia McAfee
Social Work Assistant

11

Becoming Human

My parents did not visit Martha right away after she moved to the Approved Boarding Home in Cornwall. They may have thought it was best not to visit at first to allow her time to settle in. It's also possible, given my parents' trepidation about her move into the community and the fact that the decision had been made by the institution, regardless of their wishes, that they may have needed time to become reconciled with it.

A month after Martha moved, the social worker from the hospital school sent a progress report to my parents:

> We have found quite a difference in Martha since going to the home. She is much more willing to join in group activities, she is talking more to everyone, she is more willing to be in a group rather than by herself, and her general attitude is much cheerier. I am very pleased with Martha's progress in the home and I know that Kinsmen School feels the same way.

This was all very good news, but it was distressing in its implication that she had been listless, depressed, and antisocial at the hospital school. In fact, the social worker recorded the following in my sister's file.

May 18, 1973 – My first visit was paid to the Zaretsky home on May 16th, to determine Martha's progress and adjustment in her new setting after one week's period. I am very pleased with the results. Martha no longer has to be coaxed to join in group activities, she no longer sits sullen and by herself, she is talking a great deal more and generally appears to be much happier as demonstrated by her lively smile.

Two weeks later, she visited Martha again. That the social worker saw the boarding home as a temporary placement and hoped that Martha would eventually return to our family is evident in her notes:

Speech therapy would prove to be a help to Martha as she talks too fast and when she does, it is unintelligible. Even though she has been away from home for such a long period of time this may serve to demonstrate to Mr. and Mrs. Freeman exactly what Martha is capable of. Presently she is attending Kinsmen School for the Retarded in Cornwall. Due to the short length of time for Martha in the home, it is difficult to assess what her future needs are. I would highly suggest a social worker work with the Freemans in Ottawa to improve Martha's chances of going home permanently.

The social worker noted disapprovingly that my parents still had not visited Martha or communicated with her two months after her move to Cornwall.

However, they finally paid a short visit in mid-July.

According to the feedback from Mrs. Zaretsky, the Freemans appeared to be afraid to show outward signs of affection towards Martha. Martha was taken out for a half day shopping and to supper by her parents. The Freemans were very happy with Martha's progress, e.g. her extroverted personality. Another visit is anticipated by the Freemans but we are unsure as to the date.

At the beginning of October, the social worker again noted that "Martha's extroverted behavior continues ... When you look at Martha you can see her own self-respect and the degree of self-confidence has improved vastly. Family contact is still minimal."

That fall, another letter arrived at my parents' home, this time from Mrs. Zaretsky, requesting funds to buy Martha a fall jacket and reporting that "Martha is fine and very happy at home and at school. She loves her teacher and the teachers are making great headway with her and here at home we are taking great care about her co-ordination problem."

In November, the social worker noted that my parents had visited Martha again and that "they were pleased with her placement but ... remained emotionally distant from her ... Martha continues to do well in the Zaretsky home. She appears to be a happy, interested, communicative young girl. The Zaretsky girls are teaching her to baton twirl which is developing her co-ordination and giving her a sense of pride."

I didn't accompany my parents on any of those early visits to Cornwall. Perhaps I missed them because I was working all summer. I then started attending the University of Toronto and came home infrequently, and my visits never coincided with visits to or from Cornwall. It might have been the following summer that I finally accompanied my mother to visit Martha in her new home, or it might even have been two years after her move, because when I went there the Zaretskys had moved their rapidly expanding caregiving services out of their own house and had opened a larger group home in a new building. Martha and another girl from Rideau had been the first two residents, but now there were many more.

My mother and I drove to Cornwall on a warm day in late spring and stopped at a large two-storey suburban house with a sign out front that said "Sunshine Home." We were welcomed by a large and generous woman in her late forties or early fifties. She had an ample bosom and grey hair in an untidy bun. My mother greeted Eva Zaretsky with a formality that surprised me, though Mrs. Zaretsky tried to put her at ease. I must have met her husband that first day, but I do not remember him at all. It was always Eva or her daughter Kathy who met with us.

The Zaretskys and their staff were taking care of thirty-three children by then, many of them with multiple disabilities. Mrs. Zaretsky showed us around the house, walking us by a row of cribs in the large room at the back of the building where the youngest children, some of them severely disabled, were housed. The rooms were airy and bright, and the overall atmosphere was cheerful and upbeat. It was certainly a huge improvement over the vast and impersonal hospital school.

Suddenly, there was Martha, running towards us and calling out excitedly, then running to Mrs. Zaretsky. I remember my surprise at the way Martha turned to her and started talking a blue streak and the way Mrs. Zaretsky laughed and responded, then hugged her impulsively. It was confusing seeing the bond between them, because our hugs with Martha had always been only at the beginning and end of her visits, never simply spontaneous expressions of affection.

"Martha loves to see her family!" Mrs. Zaretsky said, tussling Martha's hair. I must have stared: our own relationships with Martha were so thin and shabby in comparison. I could already see that this new arrangement was good for my sister, but I also felt a pang of guilt, for in all the years we had been visiting her we had never been able to give Martha such easy acceptance and affection. We hadn't been able to summon up the courage to love and enjoy her as Mrs. Zaretsky, a total stranger, so clearly did.

I soon had the sense that taking care of people like my sister was not simply a job for Mrs. Zaretsky but truly her vocation, that somehow she had copious amounts of love to give and that it truly satisfied her to give it. I don't know where that well of love came from or what had made her so accepting of people with disabilities in a world that viewed them so harshly. I felt severely humbled, glad for Martha but ashamed of myself and of my family for our emotional stinginess.

Did Mrs. Zaretsky judge my mother for sending Martha away? I never observed her doing so, and she certainly never said anything judgmental about my parents to me. But my mother was convinced she did, and Mrs. Zaretsky certainly commented on my parents' emotional distance from Martha to the social workers, though I don't know if she did so with compassion or judgment. So, although my mother was now able to say to those who asked that her daughter was no longer in an institution and had moved to a progressive, new group home, there was a new source of torment – Mrs. Zaretsky's maternal superiority. For my mother, it seemed there was still no way out of the devil's bargain she had entered into when she sent my sister away.

But Martha progressed in leaps and bounds in that nourishing environment. At her new school, she quickly learned to copy words and even to print her own name. The evidence for that appeared one day on the back of a letter Mrs. Zaretsky sent to my parents in the form of spidery printing in red ink.

G

CHRISTINAS

GIFTS

GIVE YOUR

FRIENDS

AND FAMILY

A WONDERFU

YEAROF

CHATELAINE

MARTHA

This was a disconcerting achievement, something we had never believed her capable of. Could someone with an IQ of 45 really do this?

In fact, some time after my sister came to live with the Zaretskys, a social worker writing to Martha's speech therapist asked much the same question. She noted the various assessments of my sister's intelligence and potential that had been made over the years. Upon her admission to the Rideau Regional Centre at twenty months, Martha had been diagnosed with severe mental retardation and an IQ of 27, according to the Slosson

Intelligence Test. In June 1967 she had been reassessed at Rideau using the Wechsler Intelligence Scale for Children and obtained a score of 43 on the verbal test, 35 on the performance test, and 33 on the full-scale IQ test. Now, however, the social worker noted: "In view of Martha's progress since her community placement, it is the worker's opinion that the above results were perhaps an under-estimation of her potential."

This comment haunts me. What more could Martha have achieved, what more could she have enjoyed, had she had speech therapy and real schooling from an early age? And who would she have become if she had grown up in a family situation where she was loved and encouraged and where the people around her were attentive to her needs? For thirteen years, Martha had not been in a situation of optimal care, and some of the damage and loss of potential from those years was likely permanent. Now it seemed, she was finally in a setting where she could learn and grow.

That same summer that Martha moved to the Approved Boarding Home in Cornwall and just before I set off for university, my slightly older cousin Louise, who had grown up in British Columbia, visited us on her way to France. I had only met her once or twice before, when the extended family had gathered for family reunions. Like most of my family on my father's side, Louise had grown up within the United Church and shared its sense of social responsibility and advocacy for social justice. She told me later that she had always wondered about Martha, the one cousin she had never met, the cousin who, as a small child, had been shut away somewhere in an institution and was rarely mentioned. That absence, that erasure haunted her. In 1973, she was heading to France to work with Jean Vanier, the founder of L'Arche, an international movement dedicated to creating intentional loving communities for people with intellectual disabilities. I'd never heard of him.

Jean Vanier was a French Canadian Catholic academic and son of the former governor general of Canada Georges Vanier and his wife, Pauline. Originally a philosopher, he left academia to follow a spiritual calling. His own personal decision in 1964 to live with two men with developmental disabilities in Trosly, France, sparked a movement advocating that people with intellectual disabilities and those who assisted them live together in ordinary housing, where they could build long-term communities founded on interdependent and loving relationships. Vanier's methods were simple and quickly spread around the world: he recommended "a regular rhythm of work and sharing the daily life of a group of people who cared" and the fewest possible distinctions between the core members (those with disabilities) and the assistants. The residents of each L'Arche community held weekly meetings at which everyone was present and where each person could have his or her own say. The results were astounding: people with disabilities who joined L'Arche made huge gains in their development and often felt loved for the first time in their lives.

Vanier disputed the widespread belief, which my family shared, that people like my sister would remain perpetual children. He believed that everyone had the capacity to grow and mature into adulthood, regardless of their physical or intellectual limitations, and that all could and needed to contribute meaningfully to society. He spoke of the profound gifts of people with intellectual disabilities and their capacity to teach others and enrich life for all; he called on caring people around the world to build communities guided by compassion, inclusion, and respect for diversity. He insisted that "a truly just and compassionate society was one which welcomed its most vulnerable citizens," asserting that all people were bound together in a common humanity, that everyone had the same dignity and the same rights, including the right to life, to a home, to work, to friendship, and to spiritual fulfillment. Thus, the L'Arche communities that he founded were open to people of different intellectual and physical capacities, social origins, races, religions, and cultures; in a word, they embraced difference of all kinds.

This was truly a radical message. So influential was Vanier that he had even visited the Rideau Regional Centre and met with the staff there the year before my sister had been moved to the Zaretskys' home. His two talks at Rideau were open to the public and were reported in the Smiths Falls newspaper under the headline "Dr. Vanier: Prejudice is a World Sickness." Speaking of "the joys and sorrows of deeply wounded people," he told the staff of the province's largest residential institution for those with intellectual disabilities that "the very size of our institutions is a symptom of a sickness not caused by the retarded."

Louise had spent the previous summer working at an institution for children with developmental disabilities in British Columbia, but it was run using behavioural modification methods she felt extremely uncomfortable with. By chance, soon after her job ended, she saw a film on TV about Jean Vanier, and the following February she had the opportunity to meet him in person, when he conducted a retreat in British Columbia. At that gathering, she told Vanier about her previous experience and her interest in his work; he immediately invited her to come to Trosly.

Louise was twenty years old when she visited us and, like any new convert, full of enthusiasm and idealism. I did not know what to make of her, and I listened to her with a sense of utter disbelief. I could not imagine why anybody would voluntarily choose to live in extremely modest circumstances with people who were intellectually impaired. In fact, I could not imagine anything less desirable. How could she possibly stand it? On the one hand, she seemed totally misguided and naive about the potential of people like my sister and the challenges of living with them (so I assumed), yet she also seemed to possess some kind of inner strength and moral heroism that were wholly outside my own experience and seemed totally beyond me.

I don't think Louise had any idea what sort of reception she would get from my mother. I think she genuinely wanted to share the good news of Jean Vanier's wonderful work. But as she spoke to us about the miraculous changes in people who had previously been institutionalized, a chill descended on the room, a sure sign of my mother's rage.

"I am not going to be Mrs. Retarded Mother of the Year!"

Louise stopped talking and looked at me in alarm. My mother turned to me for confirmation of her position. I felt impossibly torn.

I was certainly intrigued by Louise's idealism, by this philosophy of radical love. But I was also my mother's daughter. I saw how angry and defensive she was, how she was reacting to what she feared was judgment in my cousin's eyes. *You are an unnatural mother. You abandoned your own child. Your daughter deserves your loving care.* I didn't know what to say or do, so I tried to avoid both of them and simply stared at my plate through the uncomfortable silence that ensued and waited with both dread and a sickening, stomach-churning curiosity for whatever would come next.

To my surprise, nothing happened. Louise swallowed hard and changed the subject. My mother did the same. Nothing more was said, and for the rest of Louise's stay we all skated politely over the impossible rift between them.

Yet witnessing that moment of confrontation was eye-opening for me. It was different from my mother's encounter with Vera Bernstein: Louise's compassion was not theoretical. She was speaking from some kind of knowledge, not a position of presumed moral superiority, even if that was how my mother read it. There was something genuine in Louise and her experience, something true. For that reason, I was profoundly disappointed by my mother's reaction to her and to the teachings of Jean Vanier. Couldn't she acknowledge that this was a better way? Couldn't she begin to open her heart and truly love my sister as she loved me? Why did she have to disparage Louise and L'Arche? Why was she so convinced she could never love my sister, that she was at heart a selfish person?

I couldn't understand how she could reject Martha for who she wasn't when Martha herself was blameless. It was becoming harder and harder to make excuses for my mother's refusal to love Martha: under the facade my mother presented to the world was a heart that I in my teenage purity increasingly judged as empty, unfeeling, selfish. In my eyes, she became a monster because she couldn't love her own child.

Yet if my mother was a monster, there was also a monster in me. I criticized my mother intensely in my mind, but I could not talk to her about what I felt. I, too, maintained a polite and loving facade, but I was becoming more and more lonely and estranged from her. It seemed to me that she didn't want to hear my truth, that who I was and what I felt threatened her. Yet I also couldn't stand up to her and speak truthfully, and that made me ashamed of myself.

For the next several years, I saw Martha very rarely. I find it striking now, looking back, that I never once visited her on my own or even thought to do so. Perhaps it was because I did not have a car and Cornwall seemed so distant from both Ottawa and Toronto, although I could have taken the train. Or perhaps it was that like most young people attending university and living away from home for the first time, I was going through a period of disengagement from my family. It was clearly something other than physical distance that stopped me, since I had no difficulty making plans to travel to Europe on my own. The sad truth is that I never thought visiting my sister was worth the effort.

At that time, I did not have my own relationship with Martha. I had interacted with her only in the context of our family. I had no idea who she was and no real desire to know her. In fact, I would have to say that, despite my admiration of Louise, I did not believe that there was much in my sister to know. I saw her as the ruined shell of a human being, empty of significant content, defined only by her lack, deserving only of pity. I saw her as the detritus of a sad narrative, a tragedy that had befallen our family, but it was a tragedy I didn't feel except as anger at my mother over the apparent failure of her humanity.

Besides, I was soon immersed in my new, independent life in Toronto. Academia was a marvel and a puzzle at the same time. I revelled in such esoteric courses as the History of the Ancient Near East, Music History, Medieval Literature, and Symbolic Logic. I felt like I wanted to go to university forever and take every course in every discipline in the social sciences and humanities. The whole world of learning opened up to me ... but I was also dogged by nagging questions: What was I going to do? What did I want to be? Who was I, really, under the facade?

Living away from home was also challenging in ways I hadn't anticipated. I'd never realized just how sheltered my life had been. I discovered, for example, that political radicals on campus had no compunction denouncing people such as my father and his friends and colleagues as members of the ruling class; they talked cavalierly of lining such people up against a wall and shooting them. It was disconcerting, to say the least, to be perceived as one of the enemy. I knew that I had grown up within a network of social and economic privilege, but I had never really acknowledged that it was unjust or how that privilege had shaped me. Yet the more I thought about it the more I knew that accusations of unjust privilege were true – deeply true, in my case – and this realization made me feel guilty and unworthy and socially insecure. I felt in my bones that my privilege was much more than a matter of social class, though I could not have fully articulated its true source.

Meanwhile, the world of my childhood, my parents' world, seemed to be shrinking, fracturing, and fading into the past. Most of my parents' friends' marriages had gone belly up in the wake of the sexual revolution, women's liberation, and the general loosening of social strictures. My parents were still together, though when I went home to visit I observed that they seemed to be bored and unhappy with each other. Family dinners were excruciating.

In my second year of university, I began to feel increasingly anxious. I was interested in everything and nothing. Everyone was talking politics, but any career choice seemed to involve becoming part of the patriarchal, capitalist system that everyone was criticizing. Other people my age seemed to be finding their path in life, choosing careers or partners, but I somehow couldn't get any traction.

Meanwhile, as Martha approached the age of eighteen, the question of her future came up again. The Rideau Regional Centre still had ultimate responsibility for her, even though she lived in an Approved Boarding Home. Given her success in living in the community and following the new policy of normalization, the institution intended to formally discharge her once she reached the age of majority. But where would she live?

The Social Work Department hoped that Martha could finally live with my parents and planned another home visit "to encourage more frequent contact with Martha and to discuss their plans for her." But as is clear from the social worker's record of this meeting in my sister's file, my parents were not at all enthusiastic about this plan.

> Given the Freemans' negative attitude towards Martha, it could be that frequent contact between them would be more destructive to her than beneficial. Mrs. Zaretsky's reports confirm that the Freemans' brief, often off-hand visits are rather sad experiences for Martha. It would be inadvisable furthermore to consider returning to the home on a permanent basis, since her emotional needs are being adequately met in the Zaretsky home.

The social worker noted that Martha had spent a weekend with our family in Ottawa at the end of November. My parents had taken her home because they did not intend to have her home at Christmas. "Martha apparently spent the better part of the weekend watching television alone in her room and was consequently glad to return to the Zaretsky home."

Reading these words now is intensely painful. We always told ourselves that Martha was glad to see us and sad to leave or that she really didn't feel much one way or the other. It hurts to think that she actually felt lonely and miserable and unloved in our midst and that such visits were as painful and depressing for her as they were for us. There were good moments, to be sure, and I cling to those happier memories with determination. I know we tried to be a good family to her in our emotionally constricted way, but the social worker's comments speak to the essential brokenness of our relationship with her.

Mrs. Zaretsky had indicated that she was ready to keep Martha in her home indefinitely, and so after some financial negotiations between my parents and the Zaretskys, Martha was discharged from the Rideau Regional Centre into the care of the Zaretskys on August 1, 1978.

The words on the discharge papers do not convey the utter transformation in my sister's life that this change represented. Initially, when Martha was at the Sunshine Home, she lived there with the other children, but Mrs. Zaretsky soon started to take her back to her own home at night to keep one of her own daughters company. This daughter didn't have Down syndrome but had suffered brain damage at birth because of a lack of oxygen. She and Martha became good friends, and Martha spent more and more time with the Zaretskys as a family. Eventually, she moved out of the group home altogether (though she spent her days there when she was not at the Kinsmen School) and lived with the Zaretskys permanently.

This was a miraculous if incomprehensible development. Martha lived with the Zaretskys not because they were paid to take care of her (since they were paid in any event) but because they loved her and enjoyed her company. It was Mrs. Zaretsky in particular who bonded with Martha. She told my parents how good Martha was, how helpful, how much Martha enjoyed it when they took her to the movies, bowling, or for Kentucky

Fried Chicken. "Mama Thaweki" quickly became the most important person in my sister's life. She taught my sister the skills of daily living with infinite patience, and she truly delighted in Martha's growth and development. She could see Martha as my family never had, as both the person she was and also the person she could be.

This was doubly fortuitous because after several years the Zaretskys closed the group home. There were a number of reasons but one was that the marriage between Mr. and Mrs. Zaretsky had ended. Residents were moved to other locations, but Martha remained with Mrs. Zaretsky, even when she moved with her other daughter, Kathy, to Kingston. In all, my sister lived with Eva Zaretsky for twenty-nine years.

My parents were deeply grateful to Mrs. Zaretsky, and told her so on several occasions, but my mother always found interacting with her difficult. My mother felt so inadequate, so shown up, that she couldn't bear to have much contact with her maternal replacement, even though Mrs. Zaretsky had in a sense become part of our extended family; she was certainly never acknowledged as such. My parents kept their interactions with her to a friendly, circumspect, and business-like minimum, perhaps because they were afraid to jinx such a wonderful arrangement. They were grateful to Mrs. Zaretsky, but how could they ever explain to her why they had sent Martha away, something she would never have done? How could any of us ever explain our pain and shame? Whenever we visited Martha, we found ourselves so wanting; we could not escape our deficiency, our lack of generosity. It was as if we were stuck in two dimensions in our interactions with Martha, while Mrs. Zaretsky lived effortlessly in three. I don't mean to idealize her or her life, for she was an ordinary human being, but her heart was open to Martha as no one else's had been.

Martha was now allowed to phone us between visits, something that had never happened in all her years at the hospital school.

The phone would ring, and usually my father would answer. He would later relate and re-enact the conversations, often to humourous effect, for the rest of us.

"Hello?"

"Daee!" A stream of talk would follow in which the word "Kagua" (Santa Claus) would be prominent.

"Oh, it's you, Martha ... How are you, dear?"

Martha would answer with another voluble stream that usually included all of our names. She'd ask after Sparky, my sister's dog that had run away several years previously, and "Gwamma," my mother's mother, and then she would usually ask for me. Martha never forgot those she loved.

"Towee? Victoria's not here. She lives in Toronto now ... She goes to university. Maybe you'll see her next time she's here."

Sure, I wanted to see Martha – for a few minutes, maybe half an hour – but I didn't know how to be with her beyond that, other than watching *Mary Poppins* together. She would be so happy to see me, she would exclaim with delight, but I couldn't fully reciprocate. There was the constant horizontal movement of her eyes, a relentless rapid oscillation of her pupils, which signalled the medical condition known as nystagmus, which occurs frequently in people with Down syndrome, but which I found unnerving. That was just one of the physical signs of her difference that I dwelt on, along with what we called the "double-jointed" way she sat, which stemmed from the extreme flexibility of her joints. She had also developed epilepsy, which is more common in people with Down syndrome than in the general population and usually develops either in infancy or between the ages of twenty and thirty, as was the case for my sister. I never saw Martha have a seizure, though; she took anticonvulsive medication to control them.

At some point during this period, Mrs. Zaretsky sent us several copies of an eight-by-ten-inch school-type colour photo of Martha, and one copy was given to me. I considered it a rather embarrassing and sad imitation of the ones the rest of us had taken in high school – as if Martha could ever be a student! I thought she looked ridiculous, like she was pretending to be what she was not. To me, the photograph only highlighted her coarse features, her dull expression, her difference. I stuffed it in the back of my closet and didn't look at it again for years.

12

Into the Fire

One summer evening in 1977, when I was home for the summer after my third year of university, I was crossing a busy street in Ottawa with a friend. Three lanes of traffic were stopped, and the fourth lane was empty. Out of nowhere, a car veered into the empty fourth lane and accelerated, just as I began to traverse it. The driver didn't see me until it was too late – I never saw what hit me. I was struck from behind and must have fallen forward because my face hit the pavement, and I split my lower lip. The car screeched to a halt, but I didn't hear a thing.

I stood up, or someone helped me up – I can't remember those first few moments after the impact. I didn't know that I was injured. The driver of the car that hit me insisted on driving me to the hospital, despite my insistence that I was perfectly fine. Only after several minutes in the car did I notice the blood spilling down my chin onto my shirt. There were two young men in the car, and I remember that it smelled of marijuana. I kept telling them not to worry, that I was fine. My friend and I must have been in shock because we never thought to take their names as they let us off at the Emergency ward of the Ottawa General Hospital and drove away. Ellen phoned my mother, who rushed to the hospital but was quickly reassured by the nurses and doctors who examined me. After my split lip was stitched up and the rest of me declared more or less put back together, my mother drove me home.

Over the next few days, my lip got infected and became horribly swollen. It filled with pus and had to be drained, and then it didn't heal properly, leaving me with a permanent swelling and a faint zigzag scar. The imperfection in my lip gave me a crooked smile and a basic facial asymmetry, which became more pronounced when I was upset. After the initial healing of the wound, I was offered plastic surgery to get rid of the scar, but I refused it. That imperfect healing, that disfigurement – maybe even that ugliness – was the truest thing about me. It needed to be known.

I wonder now if I was suffering from a mild concussion, though it wasn't diagnosed at the time. Certainly, there were a few minutes that were unaccounted for. By the time my consciousness returned, I was on my feet again, but something had been lost. Somehow, I couldn't put everything back together again. Like Humpty Dumpty, I had been sitting on a wall, waiting to fall; I had not known that I was as fragile as an egg.

There was something so strange about being hit from behind, about being knocked off my feet by something that I never saw coming at me. Whatever it was had emerged without warning from some other reality to strike me down in an instant, with utter indifference to who I was or what I might wish for myself. I relived that moment of impact over and over, imagining it really, since I had no memory of it. I looked at myself in the mirror, and I was not the same person. Who I was now I did not know. Where that other me had gone I could not fathom.

In the strange and tangled summer that followed, I met Paul, or, rather, I re-encountered him, since I had known him slightly in high school. All I knew about him was that he was very, very smart – but he was also a bit of an oddball. He wore baggy pants of an uncertain colour, shirts with ink stains on the breast pocket from the leaky ballpoint pens he kept there, and old, scuffed, misshapen shoes with heels that sloped outwards from constant wear. His dark hair was wild and unkempt and surprisingly curly, a sign of his mixed English and Chinese ancestry, and he wore ugly black-framed glasses, behind which his dark almond-shaped eyes looked out at the world with sarcastic amusement. You always had the feeling he was laughing at your stupidity, if he noticed you at all between cogitations on mathematics or chess. In fact, he looked the way I imagined a Chinese Albert Einstein might have looked as a teenager – a stereotype, I know – but that is how he appeared to me at the time, and it was an image he himself perpetuated. He did not hang out with the other Chinese kids at school, who usually remained aloof from the white kids, for good reason. And although he sometimes seemed to be on the fringes of my social group, during high school I had never exchanged more than a few words with him. I was impressed and intimidated, but there was also something almost comically pompous about his displays of intellectualism. He seemed too weird to be boyfriend material, though I was curious about him and his tastes. But I never talked to him because I assumed he despised me.

I ran into Paul and his friend Jamie at a movie theatre a few weeks after I had been hit by the car. My lip was pretty well healed, but I looked different, and I certainly felt different. In a way, I felt that *something* had finally happened to me. I was between boyfriends and hoping to get together with Jamie, so I invited both him and Paul to go for coffee after the film. Jamie demurred, elusive as ever, so I ended up with Paul.

To my surprise, he started to flirt with me. He said he had always admired me and wanted to know me. He said he was envious of my university entrance scholarship, but he said it in such a self-deprecating way that he made me laugh and feel flattered at the same time. He insisted on walking me home even though it was miles out of his way. The night air was warm and heavy, but I felt giddy, and I think he did too. Halfway to my parents' house, he pulled me to him and kissed me.

I knew things were moving rather quickly and that I should have been more cautious, but it felt good to feel wanted and desired, particularly in my new, changed state, even if I felt a bit ungrounded. I was astounded that this person who had always intimidated me now seemed to want to be with me. What had just seemed weird about him before now seemed interesting. He was funny, in a sardonic sort of way, and surprisingly frank, if also endearingly awkward around me.

Recklessly, I slept with him the next night, and after that it seemed we were a couple. Everything was heightened those first few weeks I spent with him. I had just turned twenty and felt that I was finally my own person; he was twenty-one. I had always known my previous relationships with boyfriends would be temporary for one reason or another, and I always withheld some part of myself from full commitment even as I enjoyed male company. But with Paul there was something that caught me and held me fast.

He was the most intelligent person I had ever known, though at times he was also insufferably arrogant. He beat my father at chess – playing the game entirely in his head in a bravura gesture, not looking once at the chess board – and my father was a very good chess player. Paul had already read most of the Western literary canon, all the major thinkers and writers and had laboriously worked out his opinions about each work. It flattered me that such a smart person would be interested in me. I hoped that meant that I was smart, too, for deep down I wasn't so sure, in spite of my high marks and scholarships. I hoped that somehow some of his intellectualism would rub off on me, or at least that others would assume that I was equally intelligent for such a man to be interested in me. I knew a little about a lot of things, but I wanted to be an intellectual with his kind of detached, critical mind.

He said he wanted to support my intellectual development and suggested books I should read and how I should summarize and critique the assumptions of everything I read. I did not mind his slightly paternalistic approach to my improvement, since it was evident to both of us that I lacked intellectual discipline. I was taken aback by his criticism at times, but he could always justify his reasoning, and I felt uncertain and uncritical by contrast, if also motivated to learn more, to think harder, to become a true intellectual as he was. I liked that he challenged the conventional wisdom I'd grown up with and forced me to examine my assumptions, as if in doing so I could root out what I didn't like about myself, that feeling I had of not being a good person, of being overprivileged, that sense of something wrong with me that perhaps I could change if I could only understand it.

But it was not just his intelligence that hooked me. When he took off his rumpled clothes and his geek glasses, I was astonished by his physical beauty. He was young and perfect and full of energy for lovemaking.

It seemed inconceivable to me that such a richly talented person should be debilitated by insecurities and resentments, but it soon became apparent that he was.

"Tell me something about your parents," I said one day, because he had never spoken of them.

"There's nothing to say," he insisted.

"There must be something you can tell me."

"What, that they're pathetic?"

"I'm sure they're not pathetic."

"My dad is in a dead-end, low-paying job. He's an engineer and should be making lots of money like all the other people with his qualifications, but he's never received a promotion or even asked for one. Why not? He never complains or looks for another job. He just passively accepts that everyone treats him as inferior because he's Chinese."

I didn't know what to say to this. I had read about prejudice and racism in the newspapers, but hearing Paul speak I realized that I was woefully ignorant.

Paul's voice began to shake as he continued.

"My mum is British and has a master's degree but can't get a decent job either. Her family and friends rejected her because she married an 'Oriental.' All she has to show for marrying my dad is a stiff upper lip."

"It's not their fault people are prejudiced," I began.

"They've been married twenty-two years! They have no friends. What did they fucking think would happen?"

"But they can't be the only mixed marriage in all of Ottawa ... "

"They probably wouldn't want to be seen with other mixed-race couples. On top of that, they're so afraid of going into debt that they have lived in this tiny two-bedroom basement apartment for the last fifteen years. They've never taken a real vacation. They're terrified that people might stare at them. So all the time that you and your family and friends were going to cottages and on trips to Florida or the Maritimes we never went anywhere. We never did anything we couldn't do in our rabbit hole."

I didn't dare tell him that earlier in high school I had been part of a group of friends who had made fun of Chinese people. We had used our index fingers to push up the corners of our eyes to make them look slanted, and we imitated the way Chinese people spoke, substituting *r*'s for *l*'s as my math teacher did: "Dees is a parabara" (This is a parabola). We had sometimes shouted things at Chinese people from car windows as we drove by. It had been an unthinking and naive racism – a joke we thought – completely oblivious to the humiliation and hurt and fear we had undoubtedly caused. I had been part of the prejudice that had so wounded him.

"I don't know if anything can ever make up for that," he said. "Everyone else is getting ahead, all these assholes with privileges and memberships at the tennis club, but I'll never be able to compete with them."

There was something whiny in his voice that disturbed me, a note of self-pity and helplessness.

"But isn't there any upside to your parents' marriage? I mean you have access to two cultures, not just boring, old white-bread Canadian ... Aren't you interested in your Chinese heritage?"

"Are you kidding? It's embarrassing."

"Don't you want to learn Chinese?"

"No. Then I'd have to talk with my stupid relatives."

He turned away from me and put his head in his hands. I could see he was upset.

"Take off your glasses."

"Why?"

"Let me see your eyes."

"What is this, some kind of weird fetish?"

"I love your eyes."

"I hate them. Stupid fucking Chink eyes."

"They're beautiful."

"You never got beat up for them."

It was true. I had not lived with such a mark of difference. I had never been laughed at for my appearance, except perhaps for my peculiar fashion sense. I had every advantage, had never thought about anything, really, and had enjoyed social prestige and success without really trying. I had everything he hadn't, and I hadn't deserved any of it. I hadn't even used it to good advantage.

But one thing puzzled me. I knew why I found him attractive, but I really wasn't sure what attracted him to me.

"Why do you like me?" I asked, hating the note of insecurity that crept into my voice.

He gave a funny smirk. "You're sexy," he said, and then he stroked his chin thoughtfully, "and I want to know your secrets of success," he added almost coyly.

"What do you mean?"

"I want to know how you get your good grades and scholarships," he said. "I don't seem to be able to do it." He smirked. "Maybe it's because I always end up criticizing the teacher for intellectual laziness, and they don't like being shown up!"

But that wasn't really the reason he was with me. Or it was only part of it. He had suffered intense humiliation and shame all through high school and university because women had ignored him. Only gradually did I learn that during my final year of high school he had followed me furtively around the school, spying on me with my boyfriend, resenting me, even hating me, because I was pretty, popular, had good grades, was from a well-to-do white family, and was completely oblivious to his interest in me. And now he did have me. I was the first woman who would give him the time of day, and he both loved and hated me for that.

"You are the best thing that ever happened to me," he would say, but there was a sullen edge to his compliment.

It frightened me a little, the way his anger flared up so easily, but it also intrigued me, perhaps even attracted me. I had never allowed myself to feel such bitterness or rage, whereas with him it seemed to be a chronic condition. I thought I could help him feel better, and perhaps I felt I owed it to him to do so. Looking back, I see that I was the moth, and he was the flame.

For a brief time that summer he felt encouraged and happy, not only because he had finally put his humiliating virginity behind him and acquired a girlfriend, but also because he had been hired by the university to conduct experiments for his clinical psychology professor. At work, he wore the white lab coat of an expert, and no one treated him as an outsider. He loved the scientific aspect of clinical psychology, and it appealed to the part of him that believed himself to be discerning, rational, and objective.

I was curious about his job and went to see him at work in the psychology lab one day.

He took me into the windowless room where he worked. There were rows of small cages with wire mesh fronts. I peered inside and saw that each one contained a white rat. There was something wrong with them: a little round plate of pink plastic stuck out of the top of each head.

"Those are implants for electrodes," Paul explained. "We're testing a theory about the development of epilepsy."

"Oh," I said weakly. "How do you do that?"

"Here," he said, "I'll show you."

He took the first rat out of its cage and held it firmly with one hand while he attached wires to the electrode in its head with the other. Then he set the rat down in a tray and flicked a switch. The rat jerked as the current moved through it. He turned a dial and flicked the switch again. He did this repeatedly, administering shocks of varying intensities and recording the rat's jerking responses on a printed form on a clipboard. Then he removed the wires, put the rat back in the cage, pulled out another one, and repeated the procedure.

"I administer electric shocks at varying levels of current to their brains so that they have convulsions. We are testing to see if they will eventually learn to have convulsions when they see the same signal even without the current."

I stared in horror at the poor rat.

"Do you think it's gross?" he asked.

I nodded in dismay.

"You can't be squeamish if you're going to do science."

"But what about the rat?"

"You have to get over that."

I said nothing. I knew I would lose the argument. But the image of the helpless rat's convulsive spasms wouldn't stop replaying in my mind. I tried to put it out of my mind, to think of those experiments objectively, in scientific terms, to try not to think of Martha, but I couldn't.

From then on, some part of me was repulsed by Paul, and afraid of him, though not in any way I could articulate.

"What's going on?" he'd ask if I pulled away from him, and then he'd get angry when I couldn't say. He said that I had no reason to withdraw, that it was irrational, and that after all he had gone through, I should be willing to comfort him when he needed it, if I truly loved him.

But the visit to the lab had altered me. Increasingly, I felt stupid that I could not defend myself against Paul's cold logic. I could not draw out my feelings and thoughts into clear lines of argument; they were as fuzzy and indefinable as clouds. Perhaps I was still lost in the nowhere land where the jolt of the car had left me, struggling to discern recognizable features of the landscape around me. I had always been talkative, articulate, and socially adept, even bossy, with my friends and even with previous boyfriends, but the random violence of the car accident and now the sight of the rats' seizures had knocked the wind out of me and taken away my confidence. The protective armour that had shielded me from others had been cracked open as surely as the impact of the car had sheared in two some of the muscle of my right buttock, leaving a permanent dent.

To Paul, my increasing inarticulateness was evidence of my intellectual laziness, or what he increasingly called my dishonesty. As I pulled back from him, he became irritable and critical of me, especially for my bourgeois attitudes. He wanted to know everything about my past, particularly my sexual past, and then he became wildly jealous of my previous boyfriends. Increasingly, he demanded that I compensate him, usually sexually, for his woundedness and the deprivations he had suffered. I was resentful of his demands, but I couldn't justify my feelings or explain myself.

News came that I had been awarded three additional scholarships based on my past year's marks, and recklessly I shared the good news with Paul. That just fanned the flames of his envy and, inevitably, of my guilt and shame. As he pointed out repeatedly, these awards were merely the fruits of my unearned privilege.

"What would it take for you to live in the real world for a change? Are you going to spend your whole life writing essays about ancient Mesopotamia while the world burns? Do you have any idea how privileged that is?"

I had a brief respite from Paul when I spent several weeks working on an archaeological excavation in England, but even thousands of miles away, there was no real safety. One night, I dreamt it was me who was being given electric shocks in Paul's scientific experiment. Little by little and then with greater and greater intensity, the jolts of electricity began shooting through my body, convulsing me in seizures, filling me with indescribable panic because I was powerless to stop the current. My speech became slurred. I heard my own words blur and melt until I could not make myself understood, until people reacted with horror and disgust and turned away from me, just as they did from Martha. I tried to hold onto my thoughts, tried to think of how I could get out of this, but the current was erasing my mind, obliterating who I was, turning me into my sister. I knew Paul would reject me utterly. Then the men in white coats would take me away and lock me up, in a straitjacket, at the hospital school in Smiths Falls.

The morning after that dream, I could not wake up. I could not find solid ground. I felt like my eyes were unfocused, and I could not get them to work together. Everything seemed unreal. I stumbled around, terrified that I was losing my mind, becoming stupider and stupider, more and more like my sister. I was terrified of going crazy, but now I also wanted to, because I did not know how else to escape the situation I was returning to, how not to fly back through the clouds to my tormenter.

From then on, I lived in an alternative reality, a strange and sometimes beautiful netherworld that I travelled through alone, cut off from others. I could see other people, but somehow they couldn't see me. They thought I was one of them, that I was with them, the same person they had always known, but I wasn't.

When I returned to university in Toronto, Paul followed me and moved in with me, against my better judgment. He planned to take a year off, he said, maybe to work for a bit, then travel, to try to somehow make up for all he had missed out on in his life. Once he moved in, the campaign for my improvement and his compensation intensified. He disapproved of my friends, so I stopped seeing them. He outlined my faults with what he claimed was dispassionate honesty and rigour, for my own good, of course, and I, fool that I was, agreed with his assessments.

I returned to school, but I couldn't seem to engage. I had been able to succeed academically in the past through a certain cleverness and ability to memorize, but now in third year something more was required. I could not think for myself. I had no real insights into the literature I was studying, because I had no access to a deeper self that might have responded to it – I could only parrot what I thought the professor wanted me to know. I felt like I had been swept out to sea and could no longer touch bottom, and I didn't know how to swim. As my marks plummeted, I came to the conclusion that studying English literature and ancient history was frivolous anyway and that I should study something practical, like economics. I drew up new goals for myself, which I shared with Paul in a bid for his approval.

Day by day, his unremitting criticism undermined everything I knew about myself, and my response was always a resolve to do better, to try harder to become the person he could love. He accused me of always telling lies and said that I couldn't be honest if I tried – which I knew was true in a way, but in the world I had grown up in, one never spoke the unvarnished truth; we all had secrets and were always polite and didn't rock the boat, for better or worse. Paul said he wasn't fooled by the social self I presented to the world. In fact, he rightly saw that I needed the truth to be real, but he was also merciless, because he wanted revenge.

"Why are you always trying to get people to like you? Why are you always wanting my approval? Don't you know how infantile that is?"

It was one thing to know that I shouldn't need someone's approval so desperately, to know that I shouldn't be so vulnerable to criticism, so insecure or self-hating. It was another thing entirely to rid myself of such needs when the roots of the need were very, very deep and entirely unconscious. I knew he was right, and yet I couldn't change any of it, because I didn't know how. And so I just felt more stupid, more wrong. I couldn't defend myself – because I knew I did not deserve to be defended. But I also despised myself for not standing up to him.

The more I felt phony, unreal, worthless, empty, and disconnected from others, the harder it was to tell anyone what I felt. I was cut off from my life, and yet I couldn't leave. I couldn't contact my friends or family, and I couldn't explain to anyone what was happening. I feared Paul, but I also needed him because I knew I was imploding, and I was afraid that if my false self disintegrated there would be nothing left.

Then Paul left for a trip through South America. As soon as the door shut behind him, I began to come apart. I couldn't eat. I couldn't sleep. I alternated between a state of restless agitation and a trance-like stupor, the outside world, my university classes, a distant dream. Day by day, everything I knew fell away. I could no longer understand the rules of everyday life. Sometimes I observed this process with detachment, sometimes with morbid fascination, sometimes with terrifying panic. I was a child who would never grow up, who would never attain adulthood, maturity, self-sufficiency. I dropped out of school and gave up my scholarships, because I couldn't see the point of university anymore.

I could no longer discern any meaning in the jumble of stimuli that reached my brain. Words and thoughts took me to strange places, away from others, away from my family. Sometimes there were harassing phone calls from someone claiming to be my boyfriend; I dreaded his return. I retreated further into a place beyond knowing, beyond connection, into the back of beyond, my thoughts like molasses, indistinct like Martha's speech, words melting and mutating until they were unrecognizable. I wanted to go where no one could reach me, so Paul couldn't torment me, yet it was profoundly unsafe there, particularly when I left the house: strange men sensed my vulnerability, followed me with their menace.

In that dark time, I became aware of an energy inhabiting me, but not "me" in the sense of the person I knew myself to be but rather an alien, perhaps hostile, force. Then I was ruled by fear, utterly transformed and transported by it. Every day I felt the urge to kill myself, just to be free of this madness, this terror.

One day, a strange calm came over me, and I accepted my changed state, the strange, the distorted, the weird. I accepted my own abnormality, even my insanity. You could say I crossed the boundary between worlds and visited my lost sister in the fairy mound. Or I became the weird sister of my former self. I would know the world as she did, be outside, be other, be alien. It was in that other world that I finally discovered my power over Paul. When he returned from South America, my irrationality terrified him. That pleased me, because he then kept his distance.

It was an awful time, but I was also lucky. A friend recommended a counselling referral service, and through it I found a good therapist, and my family agreed to pay for her. It was only my parents' financial status, my privilege, that saved me from dying as a mad woman wandering alone and unmoored on the streets, running before a car or murdered. I did not know if the therapist could help me, but I clung to her desperately because with her I didn't have to pretend I was sane. Because of her, I did not end up institutionalized, locked up in the mental hospital of my nightmares.

I finally saw that it had been me who had been the changeling, not Martha; she had always been herself. Paul had demolished my false self, and in some unconscious way I had even wanted him to do it. It was Paul, not my mother, who threw the imposter into the fire.

13

Breakthroughs

$\mathbf{M}$y therapist was very skilled. She showed me breathing techniques and certain movements or positions to break through my body's physical armouring – the habitual ways I held myself to avoid feeling certain emotions. Gradually, she helped me bring the various split-off parts of myself back into relationship with one another.

But it was a simple question that changed my life.

One day, after about six months of therapy, she casually asked, "Did you blame yourself for Martha?"

"No," I said. "Of course, I knew it wasn't my fault she had Down syndrome."

"But did you think it was your fault that she was sent away?"

The question hung in the air for a moment. I watched it as if from a great distance and then a part of me witnessed from completely outside of myself the earthquake of my response: my whole body convulsing, uncontrollable shaking and crying, deep moans emanating from my gut, a storm of feeling so deep and profound I felt a sense of wonder after it had passed. It was the deepest pain I had ever experienced, but it was also the moment of coming to consciousness, of reconnecting mind and body.

I thought it was my fault that she was sent away, that I was responsible!

I blamed myself ... but I was only four years old!
I didn't do it! It wasn't my choice or decision.
I thought I was a bad person.
That's why I let Paul abuse me, why I thought I deserved it,
why I had no right to defend myself.

It is a strange feeling when all of a sudden your life starts
to make sense, when all your inexplicable and seemingly random experiences suddenly snap into place and form a coherent
pattern. My mind began to race. So much of it went back to
my sister – my fear of being different, my fear of not being
understood, my terror of insanity and being locked away, my
epilepsy dream, the feeling that I did not deserve to live, the
fear that I did not deserve everything I had enjoyed: love, parents, family, home, education, or happiness. I had no right to
be angry or to defend myself against any accusation because
I had everything my sister didn't. Why had I not recognized
that I suffered from survivor guilt? Why had I never even considered the effects of our family "tragedy" on me? Why had no
one else recognized this?

As it began to sink in that I truly was not responsible for my
sister's institutionalization or my parents' decisions, I began to
peel back the many layers of guilt I carried, especially my guilt
that my parents had "gotten rid of" Martha to concentrate on
me, that they had rejected her for me. No wonder I felt so overprivileged and had been vulnerable to Paul's criticisms. It was
true that I had benefitted from so many kinds of privilege that
others didn't have – as an able-bodied, white woman living in a
well-to-do family at the centre of political power in Canada –
and I needed to understand how all that had shaped me and
how I could live ethically and responsibly given that inheritance,
but I had not asked for any of it. It was not my fault. It was not
my doing.

Then my long-suppressed rage at my parents exploded. They
had robbed me of my sister! I had never let myself fully feel
this. They had not recognized my pain, my grief, my anger, or
my guilt. They had said it was for my own good, forcing me to
hide my true emotions so they would see me as the good girl,

the smart girl, and not send me away as they had my "defective" sister. That was the genesis of the false self, the split. They had shaken my fundamental sense of security, broken my trust that they would take care of me. I had not wanted to feel any of that because I truly loved my parents but also because I had been only four years old at the time and I had absolutely needed them.

The realization that I was not responsible for Martha's institutionalization was a life-changing moment, perhaps the most important realization of my life. I remember the strange sensation that a huge weight had been lifted from my shoulders, a clichéd metaphor suddenly revealed to be an accurate description of this experience of release. Waves of relief and wonder washed over me, and all through the night I repeatedly wept in gratitude. By morning, my whole body felt rearranged, cleansed, released and restored. I truly felt reborn.

That was the day I began to emerge from my private hell, where I'd been held captive and silent for many years while my simulacrum walked the earth in my place. That was the day I became real.

It was such a relief to know that there had been a reason for becoming so unhinged, that it wasn't just a character defect or inherent weakness, that it stemmed from a child's response to something terribly confusing. I felt for the first time that I could begin to have compassion for that bereaved, bewildered child who feared she might also be sent away if she complained or misbehaved or even mentioned how she felt. I felt that perhaps now I could finally love myself – or at least stop hating myself – and also love my mother and father from a more honest and authentic place. Maybe I could even love Martha.

I did intensive therapy for two years. I went back to university and finished my undergraduate degree. I started writing, for in the dark inner world I had escaped to, I had also discovered the importance of articulating my own truth and the power of my imagination. It did not have to be the terrifying place I had careened through as a madwoman, a nightmare world of self-torture and hatred, a hermetic alternative universe where I might become trapped and die. It could also be a nourishing inner sanctuary where, in the utmost privacy, I could rest and restore myself and discern my own meanings and direction – through dream and image, through sight and sound and movement, through emotion, or through utter stillness and silence. Looking back on it, I think that in some ways "going crazy" was the best thing I ever did – though I can only say that because I survived. I returned from the fairy hill an older and wiser person who knew first-hand that transformation was possible. I know many are not so fortunate.

Through that psychic passage, I managed to find the strength to end my relationship with Paul and to begin rebuilding my life with a new kind of personal resolve and inner strength. I hope Paul found his own healing, as he was clearly suffering from his own trauma, much of it a consequence of the racism that had so permeated his life. I hope he recovered from all that hurt him in his relationship with me.

The revelation that I had blamed myself for my sister's institutionalization was a momentous step in my recovery, but it was only a beginning. I did not yet understand that the trauma of her departure, and the attitudes that had precipitated it, had affected me – indeed, shaped me – in countless other ways. It would be decades before I would fully understand how these dynamics affected all my significant relationships, even with people I would meet years after those formative events. And it did not yet occur to me to wonder how institutionalization had affected Martha.

As I put my life back together, I also came to see that something else had contributed to my mental confusion, self-loathing, and runaway fear, something that seemed at first only peripherally connected to Martha. I gradually acknowledged another secret, split-off part of myself that I had kept hidden for years but that threatened to reveal itself or be exposed. I feared not fitting in and ran away from myself because I did not know how to live with my own difference, a difference I felt deep down but which, unlike Martha's difference, was not immediately visible to others. Ever since meeting Esther in high school I had known that I was attracted to women as well as men. I accepted that intellectually, but given my traumatic experience of my sister's exclusion and marginalization for being different, I lived in terror of leaving or being banished from the heterosexual norm for some marginal, undefined place.

It was no accident that the "undesirables" that the Nazis had sought to exterminate included both those deemed mentally defective and those labelled "homosexual." Western cultures have long vilified both queers and disabled people as abnormal and unnatural, as abominations or mistakes, as threats to the healthy continuity and survival of the "race" or nation. We have been ridiculed, hated, marginalized, and persecuted as so-called normal people have shrunk from us in horror, for fear of contamination. For me, sister of Martha, the similarities were all too real.

During my childhood, I had learned that there were two mutually exclusive classes of people – normal straight people and homosexual perverts. If you had any feelings of same-sex attraction, you were really homosexual. Until 1969, homosexuality – or at least the male variety – was a criminal offence in Canada, and even after its legalization it was still classified as a mental illness. That's certainly what I believed. I did not know it at the time, but while I was a child in Ottawa in the late 1950s and '60s, the RCMP had kept homosexuals under surveillance. They were tasked with identifying "character flaws" in government employees, even producing a map of Ottawa showing all alleged residences and places frequented by homosexuals. Doctors were also busy experimenting with many kinds of therapies and treatments – including electroshock and lobotomies – in misguided attempts to cure queers, while the general public considered us to be hopelessly and incurably defective.

As a developing sexual being, I was not aware of these particulars, but I certainly was exposed to the attitudes behind them, even in my own family. I remember vividly that my grandmother evicted a gay man – my acting teacher – from the winterized cottage she had rented to him when she found out he was gay and that his lover was living with him. I still remember her shouting in a raised and outraged voice in my parents' kitchen: "I will not have perverts doing their disgusting business on my property!" In those days, my grandmother had a legal right to kick him out, as homosexuals were completely unprotected by any kind of law. As I had already learned with my sister, to be different was to be cast out, to lose your home, even to deserve none.

It was not until 1973, when I was in my first year of university, that the American Psychiatric Association finally removed homosexuality from its list of psychiatric disorders in the *Diagnostic and Statistical Manual of Mental Disorders*, or DSM-II; by then, attitudes towards homosexuality, like those towards people with intellectual disabilities, were beginning to change. In countless demonstrations and marches following New York's Stonewall riots in 1969, gay men called for an end to discrimination and described their sexual orientation as a natural genetic variation. They were born that way, they said, and could not change. For me, sister of Martha, that was a scary argument.

Intellectually, I supported gay rights, but deep down I suffered from the same internalized homophobia that prompted some closeted queers to kill themselves. I was convinced that my attraction to women meant that there was something essentially wrong with me, that, like my sister, I was defective, abnormal, a misfit or freak, or that others would think I was. But even more than my fears of exclusion and persecution, what I could not bear was the thought of disappointing my parents. It wasn't even that I feared they would reject me outright. I didn't think they would, though my mother would likely never forgive me for the social embarrassment I would cause her, and my father would likely pity me for my misfortune. They would certainly "tolerate" me, as they tolerated Martha, even if my unfortunate sexuality diminished their love for me and certainly their understanding of me. I feared there would always be an unfathomable chasm between us if I revealed myself to them: I would have dashed their hopes and dreams, just as Martha had. I profoundly believed that they needed me to be normal, and I could not bear to hurt them, even if it meant disowning a part of myself.

The worst thing, though, was that it wasn't even clear to me what I was – sometimes I was attracted to women, sometimes to men. And there was more: sometimes, when dressing in feminine clothes, I experienced the disturbing, ungrounded feeling that I was in drag, a feeling so upsetting that it made me feel "crazy" again. I didn't consider myself "a male trapped in a woman's body" – the dominant understanding of gender dysphoria at the time – nor did I aspire to be "butch." Was my desire to dress androgynously merely my inability to "accept" my own femininity – the popular analysis of so-called masculine women? I had no words to describe the uneasy, inchoate mix of male and female that I experienced in myself. I did not know that gender fluidity could be a distinct gender orientation and that gender orientation was distinct from sexual orientation (who you experienced yourself to be versus who you were at-tracted to) – but then no one did in those days.

Meanwhile, while gay men were arguing that they should not be discriminated against because homosexuality was in their genes many feminists did not see lesbianism as a congenital condition but as a superior political choice. As one slogan put it: "Feminism is the theory; lesbianism is the practice." If my bisexuality was merely me clinging to heterosexual privilege and thus reinforcing patriarchy in a world where the personal was political, it was yet another cowardly moral failure on my part.

What I finally recognized through therapy was that I could not go through the rest of my life being ruled by fear about who or what I was and the reaction of others, that such fear was literally depriving me of my sanity. I knew I had to explore my sexuality, even if I risked being cast out.

During those years of my breakdown and healing and my intense confusion about my sexual and gender identity, I did not see Martha often. Certainly, I was far too preoccupied with my own emotional survival to pay much attention to my sister or her situation. I knew she had left the Rideau Regional Centre and was in a far better situation with the Zaretskys, and that was good enough for me.

However, she now came to stay with my parents for an extended one- or two-week visit twice a year – once in December and once in the summer – instead of the few weekends a year that had been the norm during her institutionalization. The goal was to give Mrs. Zaretsky vacation time, and these visits marked my family's first sustained contact with Martha since her departure for Smiths Falls at the age of twenty months. When my visits home coincided with hers, I got to spend time with her.

In many ways, Martha was now a stranger to me. She had certainly become more animated since her departure from the institution at Smiths Falls – even a chatterbox – but I struggled to catch her drift from the few recognizable words that bobbed like corks in a river of largely indecipherable commentary. Mrs. Zaretsky seemed to be far more fluent in her language; I'm sure if my family and I had spent more time with her we would have come to understand her better too.

The sullen child who had kept to herself at Smiths Falls now loved company and would get so excited when our family friends came over that she would become boisterous and loud, until my mother remonstrated with her to calm down. All of us except my brother were basically introverts who liked to spend a lot of time reading (and Eric was usually out with friends), but Martha just kept talking, loudly, even if to herself, and she asked the same questions over and over, especially if she wanted something

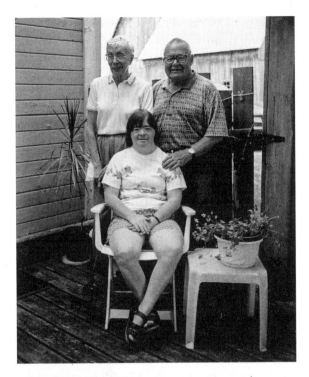

Martha, my mother, and father at the farm, 2002.

Martha, my uncle, and I playing dominoes after Christmas dinner, c. 1995.

to happen, like Christmas, or dinner. Really, she just needed company and something to do.

She now printed obsessively, endlessly copying words wherever she found them. In spite of how little contact she had had with our family over the years, when she was with us, she always wanted to print our names – she would badger me endlessly about how to spell them. She wrote on old envelopes, the margins of book pages, photographs:

> VICTOR
>
> KATE
>
> JUNE
>
> ERI
>
> Fre
>
> Jun
>
> Geo
>
> VICTORIAS
>
> MARTHA FREEMAN

She especially liked copying out recipes. She filled scrapbooks with photos of food from women's magazines, copied out the recipes, and then added her name at the end. She loved glossy photos of cakes and cookies and fruit bars and would contemplate them longingly, showing them to me and exclaiming over them. She also loved to help my dad make pies or muffins. Two words in her specialized vocabulary we all got to know were "anuts" (eggnog) and "punkin pie."

Unlike the rest of us, who generally did the minimum whenever we were asked to help out around my parents' house, Martha enjoyed being useful. She always made her bed and liked to clear the table, sweep the floor, fold clothes, and help to prepare food. The only catch was that she approached these tasks as an inviolable sequence of activities that could not be altered or rushed. At night, she took off each item of clothing in the same order, folding each one meticulously and then laying it in the drawer. Then she rearranged everything on the bedside table just so, and she got very disturbed if the routine was changed or interrupted.

While it was largely through such rituals that we knew her, we did learn that Martha also loved to dance and sing. She did both when she watched her two favourite videos, *Grease* and *Mary Poppins*, which she did repeatedly whenever she visited, since there was not much else for her to do. She knew the words to every song.

Martha was twenty years old when *Grease* came out, and as far as I knew she had never had a boyfriend. She was excited by John Travolta and would talk back to him on the screen and dance provocatively at him during the dance numbers. Sometimes, she would also bump and grind in the direction of my brother or try to sit on his lap, to his intense discomfort, and once she did that to a male friend of mine. My brother remembers my mother crying on one occasion, because, she said, it was evident Martha had sexual feelings like anyone else, and it made her sad that Martha would never get married and have children and know love in the ways that my mother hoped her other children would. When I think of that now, I am touched that my mother cried for what she believed Martha would not have. It shows that she did care about Martha – more than I realized at the time. But why did we assume that Martha could never have at least some of these experiences, just because she had Down syndrome? Why were we so embarrassed by these intimations of her sexuality? We were much more comfortable with what we had originally been told – that Martha would remain a child forever.

I do know that Martha was put on birth control pills, partly to help with her epilepsy, which was tied to hormonal variations, but also to prevent the unthinkable. Sexuality was something we could not imagine in a positive light when it came to people with intellectual disabilities. I think very differently now.

As far as I know, Martha never did get to explore her sexuality, but the first moments when I took off my clothes and lay naked with a woman are indelibly etched in my memory, their intensity and wonder undiminished even after four decades. Yet, truthfully, my first sexual experience with a woman was a bit of a bust, rather like my first sexual experience with a man, because I was too apprehensive to really relax. Afterwards, however, I was exultant. I had stepped, however tentatively, into that other reality that had so terrified me – and nothing bad had happened. Why in the world did people make such a fuss about same-sex relationships? I knew that the next time we touched I would not be so afraid.

But that was the only sexual experience my first female lover and I would have together. It was also her first time with a woman, and she decided the next day that she could not handle the social ramifications of being in a lesbian relationship. She was a single mother on mother's allowance, seeking employment in a rarified, male-dominated field already overtly hostile to women, let alone lesbians, and she feared losing her family's critical support in raising her child. I was devastated. But at least I had discovered what I most needed to know: that I liked the part of me that had moved towards her and the way she had responded to that part of me. I now knew, indisputably, that love between women was as healthy and beautiful as love between women and men.

After that relationship, I sought out other female partners, but nobody attracted me as she had. Confusingly, it seemed I was sexually and romantically attracted to particular people more than to people of a particular gender or with particular body parts. Where to find a place in the world? I was never treated as badly as my sister, but I also experienced exclusion and isolation on account of my difference, since people like me were rejected and excluded by both heterosexuals and gay people. While Martha had been treated as if she shouldn't exist and had been made to disappear, I was told that as a person with homosexual desires I shouldn't exist and as a bisexual or gender-fluid person that I didn't exist.

One thing I still did not do, as I made these discoveries about myself, was discuss my sexuality with my parents. It was bad enough that my mother still fell into a depression whenever Martha visited. It was always the same: as the week wore on, my mother became more and more desperate; she'd drink several glasses of wine at dinner and make the usual bitter, self-deprecating comments, even muttering that it was only after Martha's birth that she'd realized she was fully capable of murder. My father also became increasingly short with Martha, partly because of my mother's tension and unhappiness, until finally, finally, finally, he was able to take Martha back to Mrs. Zaretsky's, and they could go back to their normal lives.

I could not understand why my mother couldn't heal, why she couldn't get over Martha's birth, especially now that I was in therapy and going through so many changes. Why didn't she see a therapist? But to most people of my mother's generation and upbringing, you only went to a "shrink" if you were certifiably crazy; otherwise, you just soldiered on as best you could. The stigma associated with seeking help with mental health was just too great – for her, it was an insurmountable barrier.

Even as Martha moved through her twenties and into her thirties, my mother said she could never stop thinking about the child Martha might have been, and I would think to myself, *Why not? What's the point of holding onto that? Why can't you love Martha as she is? If I can heal, why can't you?*

14

Echoes

Was it only a coincidence that the person I would connect with most deeply as an adult was someone who had also been institutionalized? At the time I didn't make the connection to my sister's experience, yet the person who became my life partner had also been sent far away as a child, exiled from his home and family in Vancouver to boarding schools in England, from the age of eleven to sixteen. Like my sister, he had been essentially held captive, forced to live in a highly regimented situation not of his choosing but supposedly for his own good, his liberty and childhood stolen from him.

I certainly didn't understand any of this when I first met Mark in 1980; the more salient points of connection were that we were both developing writers attending the Banff School of Fine Arts summer writing program, and we initially became friends because we both differed from what seemed to be the unquestioned heterosexuality of the people around us. I was not looking for a male lover at all – and he was just leaving an intense eight-year relationship with a man. His gender doubleness intrigued me and resonated with a similar duality in me: like the famous image of the vase that can also be seen as the profile of two people, he appeared masculine or feminine depending on how you looked at him or even on the quality of light. But then one day when we were alone, there was a moment

when everything slowed down, when the air between us became pulsating, vibrant energy, and neither of us could move.
We weren't touching; it wasn't anything I could identify as
lust or even sexual attraction, but we were alive to each other's
feelings in a way I had experienced with no one else. He was the
most exquisitely sensitive, empathic being of either sex that I
had ever encountered. He understood things about me that
I couldn't even begin to articulate but that had always needed
to be known.

His fluid and sensitive energy reminded me in some ways
of my mother at her best, the beautiful, nurturing loving energy
that had sheltered and taken care of me in the first years of
my life, before Martha's birth, and even sometimes after –
though my security in my mother's love had been shattered
when Martha had been sent away. Mark appreciated my strength
and creativity but also recognized the wounded and fragile me
that had almost self-destructed, that so strongly identified
with Martha, and that Paul had refused to see. Like Martha, I
had finally found a haven, a place where I was given what my
parents had been unable to give me after her arrival, despite
their best efforts: the deepest listening, compassionate understanding, and a primal safety.

Yet Mark, like me, was also a deeply wounded person. He
had paid the price for not being a conventional male, beginning with the noncomprehension and judgment of his father
and later the institutionalized cruelty and enforced masculine
conformity of his second boarding school. There, he had endured a world where there were no loving relationships or even
people who he could be safely angry with, where he experienced
daily an overwhelming powerlessness. His relationship with his
family – the people he loved most – had been irrevocably broken
by prolonged separation; ever since, he had felt displaced, up-
rooted, homeless, never knowing where he belonged.

Marriage was a surprising development given our histories,
but it was our vision of being parents together that cemented
our bond. Somehow, whatever our other uncertainties and con-
fusions, we had both always wanted to have children, and now

we sought familial and community support to sustain us and help us do so. We arranged a lovely outdoor wedding and were married by my cousin Louise, who had become a United Church minister and was still involved with L'Arche. That it was Mark's former partner who served as our wedding photographer and my former lover who provided the music was known only to a few – our bisexuality was invisible to most of those who attended.

At least by then my parents knew that I was bisexual, and they had even met Mark's former partner and now best friend. But the fact that we were getting married publicly as what appeared to be a heterosexual couple is what made these private inclinations tolerable to them. My father had gamely read Nigel Nicholson's memoir, *Portrait of a Marriage*, about the unusual marriage of his bisexual parents Vita Sackville-West and Harold Nicholson, when I offered it to him. He was clearly willing to accept me, and I felt no overt judgment from him, though it is perhaps telling that we also never referred to it again. What I find striking now is that I have no memory of ever discussing my sexuality with my mother, though I think she may have been sitting in the same room, silently withholding comment, as my father and I discussed the book. Somehow, talking directly with my mother was just too difficult.

Our wedding took place at the beautiful farm my parents had moved to the year that Mark and I met, and after the ceremony, Mark, my father and mother and I, and many other members of the wedding party changed into our swimsuits and jumped into the above-ground pool beside the farmhouse. We frolicked in the water on that beautiful July day just as Martha did when she stayed at the farm for two weeks every summer.

Looking back, I wonder why I did not invite her.

Some of my fondest memories of Martha are in that pool: she swam like an otter, sleek and confident, her skin glistening. She floated, she dove and surfaced, she sputtered and blew out, water streaming from her hair and darkening it so that it looked almost brown like mine. She would float on an air mattress or recline on a plastic inflated tube, staring up at the clouds, laughing and talking to no one in particular. Sometimes, one of us siblings or my mother would swim with her, but most often it was my father who jumped in and played all the same games with her that he had played with us as children and that he would later play with his grandchildren. Long after he headed back to the house, she would still be swimming, her lips blue, chattering from cold – but she still wouldn't leave her element. I think of it as her ultimate pleasure.

Sadly, though, she wasn't there with us the day Mark and I married. If I have any regret about my wedding day, it's that I didn't include her in my circle of family, that I didn't share my happiness with her.

A few months later, I became pregnant. Mark and I were elated, as were all our family and friends. Lurking in the shadows, however, was the question of whether I should be tested to see if our child had Down syndrome, particularly since the incidence rises with maternal age, and I was already thirty-two – and then there was the question of what I would do if it did. Would I terminate the pregnancy as most women now choose to do? As a feminist, I had long supported the right to abortion, and I absolutely dreaded feeling as my mother did about Martha. I wanted the free and autonomous life that feminism had seemingly promised me and feared being "encumbered" and held back by a child with disabilities, just as my mother had, though I knew there were a lot more services and supports now. But ... did I really believe that Martha should not have lived, should never have existed ... even if my mother sometimes felt that way? Could I really deprive my child of life simply because she had Down syndrome? That was the stark question I had to ask myself, my moment of truth. I thought of my sister's joy in *Mary Poppins*, her jokes and laughter, her love of wildflowers, her swimming, her happiness when she first saw us when she came to visit us, even her painful experiences. Should she not have a life? I absolutely could not say that. My sister loved life. Scared as I was, I realized I could not have an abortion for this reason.

As it turned out, there was nothing unusual about my pregnancy. After a long and difficult labour, our daughter, Claire, was born, and my mother was ecstatic at the birth of her first grandchild. When Claire was three months old, we brought her to my parents' farm for Christmas, and Martha met her for the first time. I have a beautiful photograph of Martha holding Claire, Martha's face radiant with tenderness and pride, as if Claire were her own child. Five years later, after the grief and disappointment of two miscarriages, we joyfully welcomed our son, Ariel, into the world. Martha was thrilled to hold him too. She loved babies and children, and they responded to her as to any other loving relative. In those early days, my children's exploring fingers reached out to her, and she touched them tenderly with equal wonder.

Like his sister, Ariel had golden-red hair, and everyone asked Mark and me how it was that we had two red-headed children when neither of us had red hair ourselves. In truth, it was our children's clearest link with Martha; I always answered, with a certain poignant acknowledgment, "My sister has red hair." Yet once I became a mother, I was busy with work and family; I rarely thought of Martha except when we visited my parents. She had her life, and I had mine.

Yet was it again only a coincidence that in the writerly and activist life that I undertook over the next period of my life that I was drawn to bear witness to the experiences of another group of people who had been forcibly institutionalized, namely, Indigenous peoples? They had also experienced profound marginalization and had been told repeatedly that they were inferior, less intelligent, unworthy, that they had nothing to contribute to modern Canadian society; many had been deprived of their

Martha meets my
daughter Claire, 1988.

families and communities and struggled daily to survive generations of trauma and loss. I heard residential school survivors
tell terrible stories of being neglected and deprived of food and
love as children, subjected to horrific physical, emotional, and
sexual abuse, deliberately separated from their families, their
cultures, their communities, punished and shamed for speaking
the only language they knew. I did not want to believe that those
who ran the schools – supposed Christians – would engage in
such cruelty and brutality; surely the survivors were exaggerating? Over time, however, I heard too many similar stories
and witnessed too much pain to sustain my disbelief. I was horrified to realize that Canada was founded on the twin injustices
of racism and colonialism, but I think it was the trauma of
Indigenous people that resonated most with me, in a visceral,
not fully understood way. I had direct experience of how trauma
was held in the body and at least some understanding of what
healing entailed, and the Indigenous healing methods I was

increasingly exposed to paralleled in some ways my own experience with therapy. There were also issues of entanglement, complicity, guilt, and privilege, which discomfited me: my revered grandfather had been involved in overseeing the running of Cecilia Jeffrey Indian Residential School at Shoal Lake in the 1920s. I began to research my own family's history of involvement with colonialism, which eventually led to the publication in 2000 of my first book, *Distant Relations: How My Ancestors Colonized North America*. It was an Indigenous friend of mine, Mary Alice Smith, who first made the connection between my interest in Indigenous issues and my experience of my sister's exclusion.

But there were limits and perils to this identification. It was confusing to feel these resonances but also to be confronted with the differences. Indigenous people's experiences were the same and not the same as my family's experience. Residential schools were part of a much larger coordinated assault, over generations, on the existence of Indigenous peoples as peoples, as communities, as cultures, as collectivities, all of which furthered the goal of assuming control over their land and resources. There were limits to how much I understood, and even to how much we could be friends. I risked overstepping, conflating, speaking for others, not recognizing my own privilege and social position as a white, middle-class person who had benefitted from the very assaults I deplored. It was never easy to navigate these dynamics. But these were truths I also somehow could not turn my back on, could not walk away from, even when I wanted to. I've worked on addressing Canadian colonialism for more than thirty years now, in my own limited way, and I recognize that has had everything to do with my sister and my loss of her.

Those years of intensive child rearing and activism were mainly happy years, yet sometimes, even in spite of my partner and children and this very meaningful work, I experienced that same strange sensation of being split in two or having two parts of myself working at cross-purposes that I had experienced during my earlier breakdown. I experienced this physically, as a difference in sensation on the left and right sides of my body, with the split sensation most pronounced in my face, head, and upper body. When it happened, it felt as if my eyes would not work together, as if I could not focus; I felt strangely uncoordinated. I knew that something was still not right with me, and I feared I would become mentally ill again. Sometimes, when upset, I would feel the split quite keenly, and one spot just above my left elbow would ache and ache. I would hold it and massage it to try to relieve the pain. Sometimes, Mark would massage it, and various feelings would emerge, and the ache would go away for a while. But eventually it always returned.

I felt I still carried some kind of secret, something in my body that affected my ability to be fully myself and to enjoy my life. I began to wonder if I had been sexually abused as a child, as this was just beginning to be talked about. I did not have any kind of conscious memory, but my body was full of feelings of trauma. Had someone touched me inappropriately, and if so, who? I went to various therapists and tried all kinds of techniques to "recover" the memory, but nothing worked.

Then one day, when I was once again bothered by this left-right split, a friend suggested that I try writing with my left hand to give voice to that side of my body. So I took a pen in my left hand and began to write. It was difficult, because my left hand was much less coordinated than my right, and it was hard to form the letters, but immediately, as I began writing, another voice came out through my hand, a completely distinctive voice that I did not know, speaking through this spidery handwriting:

You bitch. You cunt. You nothing.

It was a voice of pure hatred – but it was almost a relief to hear it. It was not Paul's or anyone else's that I recognized.

You shit. You loser. You moron.

I stared at the words with horror. Where was this coming from? It didn't feel like my voice. Who hated me this much?

"Why don't you just kill me if you hate me so much?" I wrote with my right hand, and the anger in my response surprised me too.

No.

I became bolder. "Who are you?" I wrote.

And the voice gave me an answer in its spidery scrawl: *Idiot.*

"What are you doing in my body?"

Need you.

"Why do you hate me so much?"

I love you.

The answer surprised me, confused me. I stopped fighting the voice and began to truly pay attention.

Again, the question came into my mind: Who are you?

And then the answer appeared: *More than your body, more than your mind.*

OK, I thought, feeling a bit spooked but trying not to be. I need to know you. And then that other self began writing, again with the left hand, and the words spilled out in the shaky, unfamiliar scrawl:

I love you. I need your love. I need your help, your understanding.

"What do you need me to understand?" I wrote.

I want your intelligence, your beauty, your normalness.

The hair rose on the back of my neck. I knew who it was.

"Why do you hate me?" I wrote.

You betrayed me.

I had never believed in ghosts or spirits, but suddenly I knew that I was haunted – or possessed – by what seemed to be Martha's spirit or soul. Which was strange because my sister was very much alive and living in Kingston with Mrs. Zaretsky. And yet it was unmistakably her or some simulacrum of her. Somehow, she, the "freak" that nobody loved, had come to inhabit me. "She" was separate from "me" but inside of me, and I had no idea what to do.

It was a relief, in a way, to know that I was haunted by my sister, but it was strange and unnerving too.

"I love you too," I wrote, the tears suddenly coursing down my face, and then deep sobs wracked my body. I had not known that she had been right there with me all those years.

And then she spoke again through my left-hand writing with an intensity that was almost unbearable.

I want you to be with me always. Never leave me. There is no one else who loves me as much as you do.

It was strange to think that she thought I loved her, when I felt endless guilt for not doing so. I could reason that she was a figment of my imagination, but I didn't experience her that way. She was speaking to me and through me in the only way that was possible for her, and I had to listen and treat her with respect, not say she didn't or shouldn't exist.

So we talked. Or mostly she did.

"How did I betray you?"

There was nothing you could choose that wouldn't hurt someone terribly: Mum, Dad, me, you. But you sacrificed me. You sacrificed me for them. I understand, but it will hurt forever. There are things that hurt forever. You have to live with it. I can't help torturing you with that choice.

"You torture Mum too."

Yes. But she will never believe I am with her too. She would never accept that. Or want that.

I felt the power of this secret conversation that only we shared.

I'm sorry. I'm sorry I hurt you. I didn't mean it. I couldn't help it. I'm bad.

"Who told you that?"

Mummy and Daddy and the people at Smiths Falls. People who stared at me. You.

It was strange to think about the real Martha, whom I almost never saw, whose life I knew almost nothing about. Or maybe this was the real Martha: her spirit was not retarded or delayed or challenged or in any way incomplete. Only her bodily incarnation was different from that of most people.

I did not want to stay in this split state, but I knew that I did not want to see a psychiatrist or psychologist who might treat this Martha only as an aspect of myself, even if that is what she was. That felt far too disrespectful of my sister. So, instead, I visited a spiritual healer, because that's how I experienced this inner voice, as an energy or consciousness different from my own, housed in my body. The healer said I must send her soul back to her, that she had come to me for safety when there were no other options, but now that she was loved and safe with Mrs. Zaretsky, she needed to leave and return to her own body so that I could live my own life and she could live hers. This felt right somehow, even if it was a strange thought, even if I didn't really believe spirits existed independently of bodies. Even if she was just an aspect of myself, it seemed I had to go through some kind of ritual of acknowledgment to set us both free and heal. I knew I couldn't force this Martha voice to leave, and I also knew I couldn't abandon her; I could only invite her to leave and gently encourage her.

"Martha," I wrote, "I don't think I should have an ongoing relationship with you like this, with you in my body. I don't know if I can commit to that."

Don't send me away.

"Martha, I can't keep doing this. I don't think it's good for me."

Don't send me away.

"I need to make a relationship with you in some other way. I don't want to be guilted and used or judged or told I'm stupid by this inner you."

I need you!

"All I can do is go and see the real you with an open mind and see what happens. I'll try to see you as clearly as I can, without the family baggage."

I don't want to go. I'm afraid of being on my own. I like it here.

I suddenly knew that I could never send her away. I could not abandon her.

"Martha," I wrote, and again I was surprised at what I suddenly needed to say, "you are as good a soul as anyone else's. You will always be free. You will come back again to another body that won't have Down syndrome. You are not in that body forever. And even with Down syndrome, you will be loved. You will feel many beautiful things. Life is still beautiful."

Why did I say that? Why did it feel so true? I didn't even believe in reincarnation or souls, but that was the only language that felt right, the language of souls and a self that is distinct from one's physical manifestation. There was, indeed, a Martha that was more than her body and more than her mind – her feeling, energetic self, her spirit, a part of her that had always been there but that I had never before recognized.

I had so terribly wronged her. I finally understood how.

"I promise I will keep talking to you," I wrote. "That I can do, wherever you are."

And I knew that all of this was my own imagining, and I had no idea who my sister was to herself or to others who did not experience her as I did. But I also made a promise to carry that part of her with me always, to protect her, even if that meant that I would never just be me.

15
Crossing Over

For years, the split feeling would come and go. Different things would trigger it, and I would sometimes try the left-hand writing, but mostly I just lived with the uncomfortableness of it, accepting that my childhood loss of my sister had profoundly affected me and that in some weird way I was still haunted.

Meanwhile, there was the other Martha, whom I saw occasionally at my parents' farm when we came to visit. I was freer and more affectionate with her, but somehow I still never truly relaxed with her or visited her on my own – the damage to our relationship had been done. My siblings lived closer to my parents and spent more time with Martha over those years and got to know her better, but whenever I saw her I felt suffocated by those oppressive family dynamics that never seemed to change.

As the years passed, as my mother approached and then moved into her seventies, she became ever harsher and more brittle with Martha and also with Eric, increasingly excluding him from family gatherings or rejecting his partner. It was true he was struggling with addictions, and he had let down my parents many times, but my mother seemed to have turned him out of her heart.

To me, her behaviour was inexplicable. It seemed like her heart was shrivelling; her ability to love or be empathic was shrinking, constricting. It was painful to witness and to have to deal with. She forced Kate and me into making difficult choices between her and my brother, and often we were afraid to challenge her. In my own mind, she still had that terrible power to withdraw love and to turn away or banish me, as she had done with Martha and now seemed to be doing to Eric. I might have been in my mid-forties, but I still viewed her from the perspective of a bewildered and terrified child. If I truly stood up to her, would she banish me from the family? Then my children would have no grandparents, because Mark's parents had already died. Would she poison my relationship with my father and force my siblings to choose between him and me? I did not know why she was this way now, so different from the loving mother she had been to me as a child.

Martha had also begun to change in worrying ways. As she entered her forties, she seemed to get upset more frequently, sometimes about seemingly trivial things, and there would be scenes of prolonged crying or refusing to do things or running off unexpectedly, which triggered even bigger negative reactions from my parents. Even Mrs. Zaretsky admitted she was having difficulty with her, and my parents attributed her changed behaviour to the premature aging that often begins for people with Down syndrome in their forties, including the onset of dementia.

Then Mrs. Zaretsky developed her own serious health problems and finally, and with great sorrow, had to admit she could no longer care for Martha. She and my parents began to discuss the necessity for alternative care and began exploring the possibilities. Once again, my parents were in that precarious position of not knowing if they would be able to find care for her or if they would be forced to take her back into their own home. But now, because of their advancing age, they were less equipped than ever to do that. We discussed whether Kate or I would assume responsibility for Martha should that be required, and we decided it would be Kate, since she was not raising children of her own.

However, after a couple of months of searching, Mrs. Zaretsky found a place for Martha in another group home in Kingston, this one run by Christian Horizons. This was not my parents' first choice of placement, given that they were nonbelievers, but we were all relieved when Martha made the move and seemed to settle into her new living arrangements.

Soon, a letter arrived from the director of the group home:

> Hi Mr. & Mrs. Freeman. I hope all is well with you. I have met your daughter Martha and she is a lovely woman. I have also had the opportunity to meet with Kathy and Eva Zaretsky. They have been very helpful in getting to know Martha ... and have both indicated that they will remain active in Martha's life.

Then there was a letter from her new support worker at the home: "Martha wanted to write to you and let you know she is doing well." She was busy with church on Sundays, "Friendship Group" at the church on Mondays, swimming on Tuesdays and Saturdays, helping to sort and fold clothing and serve refreshments at a local Christian sharing centre two mornings a week, and a day program with residents from other Christian Horizons group homes and community outings. She liked to get out and socialize with others, the worker said, and she also enjoyed helping out around the house, eagerly folding laundry, doing dishes, and sweeping the floors. "Martha has fit in very well with the other ladies living at Christian Horizons, and they are all very fond of her." Martha was so happy when my parents and Kate visited, the worker wrote, and talked about it frequently. "Take care & God Bless," she concluded and signed her name. Then, in Martha's large printing, were the words

MARTHA FREEMAN
THANK-YOU GOD

A month later, another letter arrived in response to one my mother had written. "Martha was very happy to hear from you again. All is well here and we have been very busy! Martha enjoyed a wonderful Thanksgiving with turkey, pumpkin pie, & all the fixings." Martha was now looking forward to Halloween,

Kate, Mum, Martha, and Dad in Kingston, 2002.

the worker wrote, and had already attended a Halloween party. She included a photograph of Martha in her clown costume, bending over to help another costumed resident in a wheelchair.

> She is still keeping in touch with Kathy Zaretsky and her family and she often calls her on the phone, and as well Kathy came to take her out for lunch last week. She also sometimes asks to make a phone call to you – would it be okay for her to do this once in a while?
>
> Well, we hope you and your family are all doing well and I know Martha would be very happy to have you visit again whenever it works out for you.

We all breathed a sigh of relief that the move had gone so well and that Martha seemed to be happy in her new home.

One day, Martha complained of a headache to one of the personal care workers at the group home, and then a few hours later she collapsed. The worker accompanied her in the ambulance as she was rushed to hospital. My parents received a phone call later that evening from a doctor at the hospital. My sister was in a coma. A scan showed an aneurysm, a broken blood vessel in her brain. Should he operate? There was a 50 percent chance Martha would survive the operation, but even if she did, there would be massive brain damage. If nothing was done, she would die within twenty-four hours. She would never regain consciousness.

It wasn't a difficult decision for my parents, though it was a momentous one. It was not nearly as agonizing as the decision to bring her home from the hospital after her birth or to send her to Smiths Falls. She had already begun suffering from dementia, and that was only going to worsen, so the likelihood of massive brain damage on top of that meant that her quality of life, if she survived an operation, would likely be very poor.

My parents chose to let her die.

"We'll let nature take its course," they said to me on the phone when they informed me of the situation.

"I think that's the right decision," I told them. I did not want my sister to live a miserable life in a hospital, in a vegetative state. But I've asked myself since, if it had been my other sister, would I have so easily supported their choice to let her die, or would I have fought for the chance that somehow she might survive the surgery and continue in a life that although diminished might still have been worth living?

"How long does she have? Can I see her?" I asked.

"We're going to go down to Kingston in the morning. You can meet us at the hospital. Get there as early as you can, because the doctor says she won't last long."

The next day, Mark and I arrived at the hospital later than we'd hoped since we'd got caught up in bad traffic on the 401.

When we finally rushed into her room, she was still alive – miraculously, it seemed – though comatose. She looked so small in the bed, more like a child than a forty-four-year-old woman. Her lank auburn hair fell against the pillow. Her right hand was curled, her fingers stubby and the nails cut short.

My mother and father, Kate, Mrs. Zaretsky, and her daughter Kathy were all gathered around her bed. There was also a worker from the group home where she had lived for the past four months. Only Eric was not there; his partner, Lisa, had just given birth five days previously to their first child, but little Michael was still in hospital because he, like his father, had been more than a month premature. In any event, Eric had no car to get to Kingston and had not been able to coordinate a ride with my parents. My own children must have been left behind with friends; I have no memory of why we didn't bring them.

"Thank God you arrived in time!" Mrs. Zaretsky called out when she saw me and enfolded me in her arms, the first time she had ever done so. "She always asked for you; she loved you so much. It's so good you came!"

Overwhelmed by her effusiveness, I hugged each and every person in the room then took the empty chair beside my sister's bed. Kate sat on her other side and bent over Martha, stroking her forehead, telling her, whether or not she could hear, that all of us were with her. I took Martha's hand and held it gingerly. Her skin felt warm, soft, and very much alive. "I love you, Martha," I murmured, but I doubted she could hear me. I stroked her cheek, not really knowing what to do and feeling self-conscious because I was aware of everyone watching me. My father kept mournfully repeating, "She won't last long," as if he couldn't quite believe what was happening. None of us could, really. I looked over at my mother, but she was talking in a low voice with Mark, her eyes glancing only occasionally, fleetingly, towards the bed.

It was strange to be there, in that hospital room, with almost all the most important people in Martha's life, yet fitting too. There was no outward sign of the catastrophic bleeding in her brain, just her mild and steady breathing, as if she were asleep.

Mrs. Zaretsky had been keeping vigil all night, praying, massaging Martha's hands and feet, telling Martha she loved her, making sure that if she could hear or feel anything at all, she would know that she was loved.

For a while we sat in silence, watching Martha's silent form. There was nothing to do but wait for her passing. I kept hold of one of her hands, and Kate held the other. As we sat and waited for her last breath to leave her body, I thought about the word "expiration," how it is the opposite of "inspiration" – breathing out and breathing in, all to do with spirit. Now she was "giving up the ghost," but she had haunted my family, had haunted me, even when alive. And I thought about how strange it was that my sister was dying just as my new nephew was entering the world, which was sad, because Martha really loved babies.

Mrs. Zaretsky's words were echoing in my brain. Had Martha really missed me, loved me? Why had I assumed it was only my parents she really wanted to see? I felt stupid, unbelievably stupid. And now it was too late.

I sat by my dying sister, feeling strangely detached. I had hardly known her, and now she was dying. I'd been so uninvolved in her life; now here I was playing the role of the grieving sister. Maybe all of us were playing the role, waiting for her to die, and then we would be free.

The silence was getting to us, so we began reminiscing.

"Remember how Martha would always ask after Grandma?" Kate began. "No matter how often you told her she had died?"

"And Sparky?" I added. Sparky had been Kate's dog, but he had run away about fifteen years previously. "She really loved that dog."

"It's true – once she gets an idea, you can't get it out," Mrs. Zaretsky agreed, and it was strange to ponder her use of the present tense. "She always asks after you and Mark," she said, pointing in my direction, "sometimes twenty times in an hour! I'd say, 'Victoria is in Toronto,' and that would last for about five minutes and then, 'Where's Towee?' That used to drive me crazy! But you know, she loves you so much she even sang hymns to you at church."

That was something else I hadn't known.

Then Kate said, "Remember how she always used to take all the family photos and hide them in her suitcase and try to take them back with her ..."

"Even when I'd already given her copies!" my mother added. "I always had to check her suitcase ..."

We all started laughing, but it was sad, too, how tenaciously she had clung to us, her birth family, in spite of everything. We were laughing and crying at the same time.

"Remember how much she loved 'punkin' pie?" my father began. She had often helped my father make it and always asked for second helpings.

"And don't forget 'anuts,'" Kate added, and we all laughed again, because Martha's word for eggnog always sounded like "anus."

"She really flummoxed the waitress at the coffee shop when she asked for it," my father continued.

Suddenly, Mrs. Zaretsky said, "Is she still breathing?" and we stopped laughing and looked at her.

She wasn't.

"She waited for you," Mrs. Zaretsky insisted, turning to me. "She couldn't leave until everyone she loved was here."

Was that true? It felt good to hear her say that, but then what about my brother? He should also have been there for the circle to be complete.

We sat with Martha as her body slowly settled into death. Everything had happened so fast that we needed time to know she was really gone, that the drama of her life that had so shaped each one of us was so unexpectedly over. She still looked as if she were sleeping peacefully.

I didn't feel anything – perhaps it was the shock. I didn't even feel sad that she was dead. I told myself I should feel sad that she was gone, but I didn't, not for her or for me or for my family. Rather, I felt a guilty relief. I felt released. I felt all of us had been released from the terrible dynamics that had imprisoned us, and then I felt awful for feeling that. But I felt that she was also finally free of something, her limitations, I suppose, or maybe those that we imposed on her.

"I can't believe it! I can't believe you're gone!" Mrs. Zaretsky cried out suddenly. "Martha, I'm so sorry I couldn't take care of you. I'm so sorry. I couldn't do it anymore. I'm so sorry," she sobbed, in an alarming display of emotion. She kissed Martha's face many times and hugged her dead body, tears streaming down her cheeks. "I'll miss you! I'll miss you so much. Every day, I'll miss you!" and her uncomplicated grief put the rest of us to shame. Kate put her arm around the grieving woman, and they wept together.

"She was so loving," my sister said. It was strange to hear the past tense. It felt much too soon.

"If only I'd known there was so little time left, I would have kept her at home!" Mrs. Zaretsky cried. "I shouldn't have put her in the group home ... I'm sorry, Martha. I'm so sorry!"

Although Mrs. Zaretsky had visited her several times and Martha had been settling in well in her new home, none of us wanted to think about what it must have been like for Martha to leave her second family and start afresh with new people. She likely had not understood it, especially with her developing dementia.

"You took such great care of her. We'll always be so grateful to you," my father told Mrs. Zaretsky. She began to sob again, and my father started to cry too.

There was a bewildering pain in my chest. We all had tears in our eyes, except my mother, who sat rigidly, her eyes on the floor. Even as a welcome grief washed over me, there was a detached part of me that observed her.

Mrs. Zaretsky's daughter put her arm around her mother and said, "Mama, it's time to go. We need to leave her with her family so they have a chance to say goodbye."

Mrs. Zaretsky struggled to compose herself. She got up from Martha's bed and gathered up her coat and bag. "It's so hard to leave her," she cried. "She loved you all so much!"

She hugged each one of us, even my mother, who stiffly shook her hand. "Thank you, Eva," my mother whispered hoarsely.

After their departure, the room settled into silence, as if someone had just switched off a radio. We sat quietly by Martha's body, not really saying anything, not really looking at one another. I stared at the silent form on the bed and thought of all that Martha had gone through.

By now, the blood was draining from her face, and she no longer looked asleep. There was a waxiness to her, the mask of death that I'd heard people speak of. She was gone, and we were left only with her corpse.

My father was suddenly restless and stood up. "We better get to the funeral home and make the arrangements."

"Wait," I said. It was too soon to leave, to abandon her.

Reluctantly, he sat down again, and we sat for a few minutes more, but soon I could again feel his impatience.

"We really should get to the funeral home before it closes," my mother said. It was only 2 p.m., but I knew I couldn't fight them over this.

The time had come to say goodbye, to leave. To go on.

We each took our turn to say farewell. Kate went first and held Martha's hand to her cheek and then hurriedly left the room. Then it was my turn. I stared at Martha's body, trying to take it all in, but she no longer looked quite like herself. I didn't know where she'd gone, but she wasn't there. I felt only her absence in that room. I wanted to sit there for hours with what was left of her, but I knew I couldn't; my parents wouldn't let me, and they would never understand why I might want to.

There was an awful pain in my chest, and I felt terribly confused. Part of me wanted to stay, and part of me wanted to leave. I reached over and touched her cooling cheek. I didn't know what else to do. I started to leave. I stood for a moment at the doorway and looked at her for one last time, and then I walked slowly out into the hall, out into a world without Martha.

To my surprise, my mother joined me. I thought she would want to stay behind to say her own private goodbye to Martha, but she left Martha's chilling body without a backward glance. And I suddenly realized she had not touched her once the whole time I had been in that room. Shock spread through my body, and I was suddenly in an altered state, untethered, disconnected, swimming through a strange miasma, as if drugged.

It was my father who was the last to leave, despite his earlier impatience, and he came out openly weeping.

Once out of the room, both my parents seemed to collapse in on themselves, suddenly helpless and much older. We drove them to the funeral home, and Mark took charge, helping my parents through the paperwork, the newspaper death notice, the arrangements for the memorial service and cremation. What would we do with Martha's ashes? Maybe we should bury them, plant a tree, and invite Mrs. Zaretsky and her daughter, I suggested. But my mother was noncommittal. Later, in the spring, we'll figure it out, she said. Not now.

Proof of Death Certificate
Deceased: Miss Martha Ann Freeman
Female, Never Married, Age 44
Place of death: Kingston General Hospital, Kingston
Date of death: November 16, 2002

Cremation Certificate
Name of Deceased: Martha Ann Freeman
Date of Cremation: November 19, 2002
Registration Number: D04065

At the memorial service four days later, we were surprised at how many people were there, most of whom we did not know. Who were these people? How could there be sixty people who cared enough to attend my sister's memorial, all these people with tears in their eyes? Young people, workers from the group home, came up to me or my parents to tell us how much they would miss Martha, how kind she had been, how generous, how she always made them smile. They told me how thoughtfully Martha had cared for another member of the group home who was severely disabled, and there she was, Martha's friend, slumped over in a wheelchair but still present to say goodbye to her. They said how funny Martha could be, how sad they were that she was gone, how sorry they were for our loss.

But I didn't know what I had lost.

I still have the program for Martha's memorial service, a single folded sheet with a blurry photo of a single red rose and a spray of baby's breath. In large white curlicue writing, the words: "Remembered in Love." Below, in smaller letters: "I have loved thee with an everlasting love, Jeremiah 31:3." Inside it said: "IN REMEMBRANCE OF MARTHA ANN FREEMAN." A minister I had never met before officiated, though she apparently had a connection with the group home. We sang "Jesus Loves Me" because Martha had loved that song.

Kate and I gave the eulogy. I struggled hard to find a way to speak about my sister's life without judgment of my parents and without speaking only of my pain.

> The most difficult decision of my parents' lives was to put Martha into an institution when she was two, just before the birth of my sister Kate, a decision that our family doctor encouraged and supported. There were few if any support services for parents who kept their children at home; there were no local schools for mentally disabled children or group homes in the community. There was one volunteer support group, the Retarded Children's Association of Ottawa, which my parents got involved with and which introduced them to other parents of children with Down's ... My dad became vice president of this association.
>
> Martha went to the Rideau Regional Hospital School in Smiths Falls when she was almost two years old and she stayed there until she was in her mid-teens. Over the years, we went to

visit her or she came home to visit us many times, but there was always that terrible moment when it was time for her to leave. She never wanted to leave, she never wanted to be separated from us, and we relived the pain of that choice to send her away over and over and over. In some ways, it would have been easier to just give up Martha completely, but my parents did not choose the easy course. They wanted to make sure she was well cared for and they wanted to ensure that we knew our sister and that she knew us.

Then Kate and I told a few stories about my sister. Kate said that what had struck her about Martha was that as a kid she never cried; even when she fell down the stairs to the basement and got a bloody nose, she never cried. And Kate said that Martha had no fear: "I brought her out to the riding stable to see the horses when I was fifteen and she was seventeen; she walked right up to Icarus, and when I helped her into the saddle, she immediately started heading off towards the jumps! She wanted to trot and canter right away, and luckily the horse seemed to know not to act up with her on board." She spoke of how Martha loved animals and how, when she took her to a petting zoo, Martha had talked to them, patted them, and even tried to climb into their pen to be closer to them.

I related humorous stories that my mother, father, brother, and aunt had told me because I had no stories of my own to tell. I said what my aunt had told me, that Martha had been kind and very sensitive to the feelings of others. When my uncle was terminally ill, and Martha hadn't seen him for a while, she immediately saw how much he had changed. She was concerned and kept asking, "What's wrong? What's wrong?" and then told him, "It's OK," and took a cloth and wiped his forehead.

What could I possibly say about my own sorry relationship with Martha? "My relationship with Martha was not an easy one," I admitted,

since it was shaped as much by her absence as her presence, and by my own attempts as a young child to come to terms with her difference and my loss of her. In our later relationship, sometimes she taught me about my shortcomings, my impatience, my judgement or insensitivity, my lack of love or tolerance; other times she taught me what was really essential: relationship, loyalty, kindness.

I've carried away this image of all of us around her bedside, watching, waiting, caring for her. And I think what both her life and her death have taught me was the truth of that African proverb: it takes a village to raise a child.

We said the Lord's Prayer and gave our ceremonial farewells. We ended with a benediction and "Let's Go Fly a Kite," from the musical *Mary Poppins*, which Martha had loved so much. The final words of my eulogy were still ringing in my head: "Go well, Martha. I hope your time on earth was a good one. If anyone deserves to become an angel, it is you."

At the reception, Mrs. Zaretsky was still wracked with grief and told me over and over how loving my sister was, how many good times they shared, how she didn't know how she would survive without her. Other people were similarly grief-stricken, and my family was forced to confront the fact that in many ways we had not known my sister at all. Especially me. I'd thought I had known her, but I hadn't known anything about her life or all the people she had touched. I had not known she lived a full, rich life that was obviously worth living. It seemed everyone else had loved her and treasured her, and I had not. She had been the nexus of pain in our family, yet she was innocent and oblivious to all the pain her birth had caused. It was only when she was dead that I realized what I had missed, and what I had lost.

After the funeral, we said our goodbyes, and my mother took the box containing Martha's ashes back to the farm. She said she wanted to wait until spring to scatter them, so that would give us some time to decide what to do with them, and also the weather would be better then.

I went back to Toronto and fell apart.

Where is Martha? Where is my sister? I don't know where she is. She had disappeared from my life all over again. I couldn't find her, and I didn't know where to look. *Who would take care of her now that she was dead?* The question was irrational, but it haunted me. I needed someone to take care of her, to let me know that she was all right. I didn't even believe in life after death, but now I needed to know what would happen to her spirit and what I should do so that she didn't just disappear, so that she wouldn't be lonely.

My mother had put away all the pictures of Martha, as if by simply removing her image, she could avoid the pain. Rage at my mother overwhelmed me, devoured me, ate away at me. I knew it was about the past, a four-year-old's rage. I would never forgive her. I didn't know what to do with these feelings. I felt she had robbed me of my sister and then insisted she had done it for my sake, so that I became a participant in my own victimization. I couldn't forgive her for that, for not protecting me, for confusing a four-year-old so terribly. And I was angry at my father, too, for not standing up to my mother, for abandoning me to protect her. I was so terribly angry. I couldn't forgive, and I couldn't let go.

The rage became loss again, and I grieved the loss of my love for my mother as much as my loss of Martha. I grieved her inability to truly love my sister, her emotional brittleness. I felt sick at heart, because so little was left to me. And I felt she didn't love me either; if she had, she would have taken better care of me. Finally, I was mad at Martha, too, because Martha had come between me and my mother; she didn't mean to, and it wasn't her fault, but she had certainly done so.

But most of all I hated my mother for her frozen grief.

I want to love you, and I can't. I want you to heal so that we can love each other again. Why can't you heal?

It didn't occur to me that this might also be a projection – that I was also a frozen person who had never healed.

16

Ashes

Over the winter, I began imagining a ceremony for the disposing of Martha's ashes. It would be a ceremony of healing, of laying painful things to rest. I didn't fully understand it, but I felt guided through pain along a certain path. It had to do with releasing the dead. I felt I should be with my mother, and we would help each other through. In the spring or summer, we would bury Martha's ashes and maybe plant a tree, with Martha's two mothers, Mrs. Zaretsky and my mother, together. Then we would always have a place to be with her. Perhaps if we as a family faced Martha's passing, there could be a healing. Perhaps my mother would finally be able to put that whole long and painful episode of her life behind her.

But spring and summer came and went and nothing happened.

A year and a half after my sister's death, my mother finally phoned me to tell me that she and my father were ready to scatter Martha's ashes. My mother set a date for this final ceremony. My own process of imagining an appropriate ceremony then began in earnest, because my parents had indicated that we would conduct this ceremony on our own, without outside help; it was really up to us how we said goodbye to my sister. It was a momentous thing to finally let her go, an opportunity for a potential opening to one another as well as an ending. Martha's life had had such a particular meaning for each of us that no outsider could ever understand, but perhaps we could understand who she had been to one another.

More than anything, I wanted that healing to happen. I needed it to happen. Martha's life had affected me so deeply that I was still taking stock of my relationship with her. If her institutionalization had been the most traumatic event of my childhood, her death had shaken something loose in me: a desire and need to connect with her, even though she was dead.

Images came to me in waking reverie or in sleep of various elements that I wanted to contribute to the ceremony. I imagined we would each speak of what Martha had meant to us and how we had been affected by her birth and life. We would honour Mrs. Zaretsky's extraordinary care and love and her own particular loss. We would acknowledge above all my mother's pain, since we had all felt it and absorbed it and carried it in different ways, and we would find some way to release it. We wouldn't give it back to my mother. We would bury it there, with Martha's ashes, and then we would each scatter some wildflower seeds over her ashes, and maybe something beautiful would grow from all that pain and misery, because beautiful things could be born of such pain. I wanted to write a poem or song, do something expressive that would speak to our spirits, just as I had offered the words of John Keat's "Faery Bird's Song" at my grandmother's funeral and sung them in a clear and loving voice when her ashes were interred beside my grandfather's in the beautiful hillside cemetery where he rested.

That was how I wanted to let go of my sister, with beauty, with song. I imagined we would scatter her earthly remains in the leafy woodlot on my parents' farm, where the deer lived, where her spirit would remain in the privacy and solace of the wild. I dreamed that we would not turn away from one another in our pain. We would be together with our tears, because the pain we were all feeling was a human pain. It was the pain of the mysterious and unanswerable and awful in life, and it would be a little bit less if we could be together in feeling it, in spite of all our differences. Perhaps it would be as I remembered when my mother's beloved father had died, my mother and father and I hugging one another all at once and crying together. We would pray that the flowers that grew up among her ashes would have something of Martha's radiance, her happiness, her joy. That would be her final gift to us, and not all that pain. We would bury the pain with her because it had been born when she was born, but it was not her pain, and she did not cause it; it was already there, life's pain in all its ignorance and brutality, waiting for the moment to be felt.

I also imagined that I would forgive my mother for being so wounded for so long. I would forgive her for the times her woundedness had made it hard for her to see me or respond to my grief and confusion. In her death, Martha could be the guardian of all the pain that her disability – no, not her disability, the attitudes towards her disability – had caused. I didn't think she would mind if it brought her closer to us and us to her. We would also recognize the many gifts that Martha had given us: the knowledge that life can be lived in many registers, for example, and that love is necessary for human flourishing; a certain skepticism about the heady claims of experts; and even our fears of social exclusion, which connected us to the experience of so many others. Without Martha, my brother Eric would likely not have been in our lives at all, and certainly not Lisa or little Michael. There were many gifts.

I was still planning how to talk to my mother and father about this, how I would convey my hopes and suggestions, when my mother phoned and told me she had talked it over with my father and that they had decided what would happen. We would scatter Martha's ashes in the depression in the hayfield by the farmhouse where the above-ground swimming pool used to be (by this time the pool lining had worn out and the pool had been removed and never replaced). Only our immediate family would be invited. We would each say something about Martha and then scatter her ashes.

I listened with growing dismay. My parents' plan made sense in a way because Martha had loved that swimming pool and had spent so many happy hours there, and that was how they wanted to remember her. The swimming pool was gone now, just like Martha was. But to me it felt wrong, completely wrong, disrespectful even, to dump Martha there among the scraggly bushes and unkempt weeds that had grown up in that location, to leave her there in that hollowed-out nowhere place, that eyesore, with the rotting wooden pool deck orphaned beside it, with so little ceremony as if she did not deserve a more dignified and beautiful resting place. And then it dawned on me with growing horror what my mother had meant when she had said, "It will be just our family." She meant that Mrs. Zaretsky would not be invited. My stomach began to tighten, and I could hardly breathe.

"But Mrs. Zaretsky took care of Martha for almost thirty years! How can you leave her out of this when she loved Martha so much?" I said.

"I don't want anyone else watching us or judging us," my mother said in a cold, hard voice, and I knew from her tone of finality that I would not be able to budge her.

I can't describe the chaos of my emotions then. I could not breathe. How could my mother be so cruel? How could she see Mrs. Zaretsky only as someone who shamed and judged her? I was appalled, mortified, enraged.

And then she added, "I told Eric that it was just for immediate family. Lisa can stay home and take care of Michael – we don't want a baby crying in the middle of the ceremony." So Eric's partner and their child, one-and-a-half-year-old Michael, born four days before Martha's death, were also not welcome. I had to marvel: even after forty years, Eric was still only provisional family, and his family was even more tenuously accepted. She had never excluded my children from anything.

"How can you tell Eric his partner and child can't come?"

"That's what we've decided, and I don't want to talk about it any further," my mother said. And that was the end of the conversation.

She hadn't even asked me for my ideas about the ceremony or what I wanted or needed. She wouldn't even allow me to be part of the conversation! I couldn't believe she would not invite Mrs. Zaretsky or Eric's partner, the mother of her grandchild.

How could I even go to the ceremony without being implicated in her exclusions? How could Eric go if his partner was excluded? What would I do?

That brittleness, that rigidity that had perhaps originated in my mother's original rejection of Martha, had worsened over time, but I had never dreamed it would come to this. Why had my mother never sought professional help for dealing with her feelings about Martha? Why couldn't she love Martha or even my brother? It seemed she still wanted to kick all the supposedly defective ones out of the family. Where was her compassion? And my quisling father would support her in whatever she wanted. "Martha was not just your child!" I wanted to scream at her, at them. "She was my sister, a huge presence in my life, and Eva Zaretsky's child, even more than yours!" But I didn't.

That was when the stomach cramps began, terrible stomach cramps that left me in such pain I could barely breathe. They continued for hours, and I was completely incapacitated. Should I refuse to go? Demand that Mrs. Zaretsky and Lisa and Michael be invited? But if I challenged my mother too much, she would exclude me too – and more than anything I had to say my final goodbye to my sister. My mother had me there. I needed to say goodbye; I could not leave her. I could not abandon her, unburied. I had to take care of her. I was too viscerally connected to her to stay away. These were old, old patterns and old, old wounds.

But it felt so disrespectful to Martha to dump her in that ugly place. There was nothing else to mark her life, no children, no work she did in the world. The more I thought about it, the more I realized that I wanted to keep what was left of Martha together. I needed her ashes to be buried with ceremony, perhaps with a marker to say who she was, that she existed, that her life mattered. I didn't want to be part of what felt to me like an attempt to obliterate her once and for all, as if she had never been. She still existed for me. She would always exist. She mustn't be forgotten. But it seemed to me that my mother still had no true place for her in her heart. I still could not trust her to take care of Martha, which meant that I also could not trust her to take care of me. I could not even trust her to respect the dead.

I did not know what to do. Whenever I spoke to my mother on the phone or thought of the upcoming ceremony the cramps started again and continued for days; they came and went at different times of the day or night, and I couldn't work or sleep or eat. I lived through spasms of pain so intense all else was blotted out except finding a way to survive them; painkillers were useless and, unfortunately, my own doctor was away. Finally, in desperation, I went to Emergency, thinking I must have appendicitis or ulcers or some other serious illness, but nothing showed up in the tests. Phantom pains for my phantom sister twisted my entrails, torqued my gut. If I had ever doubted the mind-body connection, here was the proof – my feelings about my sister, my mother, my father, and the scattering of my sister's ashes were literally gut-wrenching. I went to Emergency a second time, but to no avail. Finally, I found a doctor who diagnosed irritable bowel syndrome, brought on by stress, and she gave me antispasmodic pills that relaxed my smooth intestinal muscle. They worked most of the time if I took them soon enough after the first twinges began.

What was I to do? I'd been dreaming of a healing that could never happen. I wasn't my parents' healer, and it was hubris to think I could be. I had no responsibility for their well-being. But I didn't have to put up with the way they were treating Eric and his partner. Looking back on it now, I recognize that there were good reasons for their negative feelings towards him; I had not been there to see the anguish and pain he had caused them over the years, especially as his addictions took hold. What I did see was that since the birth of his own child, Eric had made a new start, for the sake of Michael's well-being and future. I saw the transformative power of that love and his own deep need for healing and connection.

The stomach cramps were turning my life upside down, striking at all hours of the day or night, doubling me over in excruciating pain. I didn't even want to go to the ceremony for Martha anymore. I didn't want to deal with my mother. I didn't want to deal with Mrs. Zaretsky being excluded. It seemed like our two pains, my mother's and my own, our two needs, were so incompatible that one or the other or both of us would not survive; in our pain we might destroy each other. I pictured my mother as Kali, the Hindu goddess who would eat her own children.

But my mother was not doing well either. As the day for the ceremony approached, her anxiety increased. She had her first panic attack a week before the ceremony. She had buried Martha's ashes so deeply in her own psyche that she had forgotten where she had actually put them. She searched the farmhouse for two days but still couldn't find them. It was glaringly symptomatic of her whole relationship with Martha, and she knew it. She had to turn the house upside down before she finally found the container wrapped up in some old blankets in a top shelf of an armoire in the upstairs backroom that had become a storeroom for all the detritus of thirty years of raising children and living on the farm.

In the end, it was my imagination that saved me, in the form of a dream. A great blue serpent emerged from the shadows and wound its way slowly, protectively, towards us. I felt its breath as it passed over the sleeping form of my mother, enveloping her in healing blue snake energy, then over my father, then over me, gently encircling me but never constricting, enfolding me in a beautiful blue light, then finally circling my parents' house counter-clockwise, circling, circling, circling, undoing. There was a healing, a loosening, an end to the terrible constriction. Everything breathed.

I thought about that dream for some time. Slowly, painfully, I came to the decision that if I had to choose sides, I would. If my mother wanted to scatter Martha's ashes without my brother's family, she would do so by herself. I had to choose the living over the dead. I would stop caring what she did with my sister's remains. Martha was already dead anyway. If my mother forced me to choose sides, I would choose my brother because he and his young child needed me the most, and I would do all I could to ensure they got what they needed. I resolved to be strong for him and for them. They were the future; my sister was the past.

Besides, I knew Martha would have wanted all of us to be there.

"I'm not going unless Lisa can come," I said to my mother. "I don't want to be party to excluding her." It had taken me weeks – no it had taken me decades – to find the courage to stand up to her.

The words hung in the air, shimmering, with that same calm blue snake energy. I felt my mother hesitate.

"Well, as long as she keeps Michael quiet," she said, in a hard, tight voice. It was a small victory but an important one for me. I felt giddy, triumphant.

"But there won't be anyone else," she said, and then I lost my nerve. I'm ashamed to admit I did not fight for Mrs. Zaretsky. I did not have the courage to challenge my mother over that. It was just too huge. It's something I still feel guilty about. I hate to think of what that exclusion must have felt like to her, when she of all people most deserved to put my sister to rest.

Right until the day of the ceremony, I wasn't sure I was going to be well enough to participate because the stomach pains were continuing. Mark, Ariel, Claire, and I drove up to my parents' farm the day before, and the night before the ceremony I was horribly agitated and went to my room early. The cramps were back with a vengeance. I knew I wouldn't sleep. I spent a lot of time in the bathroom and could not settle.

My mother must have heard me, because after a while she came to my room. Mark was still downstairs talking with my father. My mother was obviously agitated as well, but she was also concerned for me, because she could finally see I was in pain.

"Do you think you should go to the doctor?" she asked.

"I've been to the doctor. I've got pills ... sometimes they even work." I said. "I'll probably be a lot better after tomorrow."

"Yeah, well, I feel like cancelling the whole thing."

"We can't. We've got to go through with it. You know we do."

"Yeah. But I can't say I'm looking forward to it."

"I am, Mum ... I want to say goodbye in a good way."

"We all do."

I looked at my mother then, at her worn face, her slender body in her pale blue nightgown. She had lost weight recently and seemed thin, almost gaunt. Did she actually love Martha somewhere? Or was she just saying that because it was what she was supposed to feel?

There was a terrible ache in my chest again.

"This is so important to me ..." I began, and the tears ran down my cheeks.

"I know, dear," my mother said. Did she? She put her arm around me, and for a moment I leaned my head on her shoulder. It felt so good to be comforted by her. I shut my eyes and just rested there, letting the tears come.

That night I eventually slept, and I had another dream. I was mothered by a great big she-bear in a cave. She was big and fierce but enormously protective. It felt so good to be sheltered by her. In the early morning, I got up and went out to the wood-lot. I had to tramp over a couple of fields and climb over a couple of fences then cross the ditch to get there. It was rainy and cold, and I didn't really know what I was doing, but I had to do something for Martha, and for my mother, and for myself. I wandered around among the spruces and birch trees and left blueberries in the hollowed-out knot of a stump – for the mother bear of my dream, for Martha, for my mother. I listened to the cawing crows. I smelled the damp earth and rotting wood and let my spirit be soothed by the brilliant green ferns and wet-black tree trunks. I was soaked, but I didn't care. I needed that cleansing.

I would do a ceremony, even if I didn't have access to my sister's remains. I had to honour my mother and my sister, and I had to let go of both of them. Who would my sister have been if she had not had Down syndrome? What would my life have been like if I'd had another sister like Kate, with different interests and capabilities, instead of this person who had been more like an absence to me? What would my life had been like if Martha's disability, if Martha herself, had been accepted and she had stayed at home?

I release you. I release that pain.

I love and honour you both. I forgive you.

I acknowledge all that happened, Mum, and how it hurt us both, how that hurt affected our ability to love Martha. A hurt came with it that no one else will understand. I don't even understand your hurt. It's the pain of a parent whose child dies at birth; she died for you then, even though a different child was alive.

I honour you.

I honour that perfect daughter you dreamed of, my sister who was snatched away and who never came back to this world except to haunt you. Perhaps she is still alive in some other dimension, perhaps she could help you if you asked her, even if you can't see her or really know her. She can live in your heart forever; you don't have to give her up ever. But Martha was alive, too, and also deserved our love. She was also a gift.

Would I find a way to talk to my mother, at the right moment, with the right words? All I could do was pray and wait and watch for signs. It was probably not the best day, I realized; it would likely be easier when the others weren't there. I would wait until we were alone together, until I had a gift for her and could give it wholeheartedly. I would conduct my own little ceremony. It would maybe help her, and it would certainly help me. I prayed that my mother would heal that injury before she died so that she could die in peace and so we would not be haunted by her pain.

I headed back towards the farmhouse to have breakfast and prepare for the ceremony with my family. I felt calmer, more grounded and accepting. But on the way back, I unthinkingly put my wet hand on the wire of the electric fence, having forgotten about the current. A white-hot jolt coursed through my body, a searing spasm of pain, the worst shock I had ever received in my life. It knocked me out of my prayerful reverie and left me sore and ill at ease, wondering what other nasty surprises were in store for me and if I really could take care of myself. I felt disjointed, unsettled, and the left-right split in my body returned.

A few hours later, we finally stood in a circle on the rotting deck beside where the pool used to be. The sky had cleared. It was time for our ceremony, time for each of us to tell a story about Martha. My father started first. Ever the comic, his story was anything but funereal.

"I remember how I'd take Martha out to the mall or to a restaurant, and then she'd tell me she needed to use the washroom. So I'd walk with her to the door of the 'Ladies,' and in she'd go, and I'd wait. Ten minutes would go by, and I'd be watching the women going in and out, in and out, and there'd still be no Martha! And then I'd start asking women on their way in if they saw Martha to please tell her to hurry up. But it looks kind of funny, you know, this man approaching all these women going into the washroom. And anyway, they'd say, 'Yeah, I told her,' and then I'd wait some more, and she still wouldn't come out. I'd have been waiting fifteen or twenty minutes by then, and I'd be getting desperate, and finally I would accost some woman and beg and plead with her to go and lasso Martha and haul her out. A total stranger! Sometimes they took pity on me, but I could never convince Martha to be any quicker."

We all laughed.

Kate recalled how Martha liked to explore the farm, sometimes giving my parents some worried moments when they realized that she was missing again. Once, they saw her three-quarters of the way down my parents' very long laneway, in one of my mother's old bathing suits that didn't quite fit, leaving her breasts exposed. Unconcerned, she waved in her usual gregarious fashion at the cars that drove by. She returned clutching a huge mass of wildflowers that she had picked on her way.

"I remember driving with Martha in my car on White Lake Road," she continued, "and I purposely sped up the hill so we would get that momentary feeling of weightlessness that Martha loved so much as we hurtled over the top ... And I tuned in to Oldies 1310 on the radio, and we both sang along to old Beatles songs, terribly, terribly out of tune. She looked over at me with such joy in those hazel brown eyes of hers, and I felt totally present with her." Kate struggled to hold back her tears.

"And she loved to tease," she continued. "The last time I was at the farm, she kept saying to me, 'OK, Daddy,' and then, saying to Dad, 'OK Mummy,' with this twinkle in her eye – she knew full well who was who!"

Then Eric spoke as Lisa stood beside him, holding Michael. In later years, he had gotten along quite well with Martha. "Man, she was adventurous and game for anything. I remember when I took her to the Arnprior Fair; she went on every ride there. She loved being bounced up and down and upside down, and she had such an iron stomach that she could eat a huge lunch of hamburgers and ice cream and then go right back for more rides. She had a blast!"

Then it was my mother's turn. "Do you remember how she'd get ready to go swimming?" We all groaned.

"First she'd go to the change room (a corner of the shed maybe twenty paces from the above-ground pool) and spend literally an hour changing into her bathing suit. Then she'd come out with not only her bathing suit on, but a bathrobe, flip-flops, a sun hat, water wings, sunglasses, and anything else she could think of, and she'd be carrying her towel. She'd walk twenty paces to the pool, then take everything but the bathing suit off and arrange it all neatly on a deck chair. Then she would swim and swim, and you could never get her out – no matter how blue she turned! I had to threaten her with no dinner to get her out. And when she was finally persuaded to get out, she would put everything back on – the sunglasses, the sun hat, the flip-flops, the bathrobe – then walk the twenty paces to the change room and spend another hour taking it all off again."

She did love swimming, we all agreed. "That's why we wanted to scatter her ashes here," my mother began ...

They talked, and we all laughed, but they seemed so short, so pathetic, so unsatisfying, these little stories ... the same ones we'd all heard before, the same old anecdotes, as if our knowledge of Martha was thin and threadbare. That was it? Was there really nothing more to say? Could no one speak from the heart, from his or her deepest self? Would none of us speak about the pain?

Then it was my turn to speak. I could not be so light-hearted. How could I even begin to say what Martha had meant to me and the pain I had gone through? How could I begin to explain my loss of her?

"I don't know what to say," I began. I was shaking and began to weep. The others did not know what to do – I could see my sister struggling not to cry as well. I tried to compose myself so that I could say something honest, but my father didn't wait for me. He was already impatiently taking off the lid of the box of ashes and shaking it into the void below, where the old pool had been, just like that, without any ceremony whatsoever, before I had even spoken.

He hadn't noticed that the wind had come up, and it blew my sister's ashes back over him and onto the deck. "Oops!" he said, and there was nervous laughter. He brushed himself off. And that was that. That was the end of our ceremony and my sister.

It was done before I'd even had a chance to say a word. And now I was lost in the void.

I went straight to bed, and I couldn't get up. Everything hurt. I saw that we had just re-enacted the original trauma – my parents had decided how they would "dispose" of Martha without consulting me, in spite of my feelings. The reasons sounded like they made sense, but they did not take me into account. I had tried to express my reservations, but their minds had been made up. They had already decided, and nothing I felt mattered, yet I was called on to participate, to give my sanction to their actions and not make a fuss. I had no power. I had no voice. I had always assumed that my parents had carefully prepared me for Martha's departure, but for the first time I wondered exactly what my parents had told me and whether they had told me anything at all before they acted. I wondered if Martha had been simply taken away without my knowledge and things were then explained to me after the fact, so as to avoid a scene. Martha had "gone" to the hospital, and we would "visit" her.

Nothing felt real to me, least of all my parents; they had become as insubstantial as ghosts. I couldn't believe what they had just done. It seemed nothing and no one could help me.

After that day a door closed, not on Martha, but on certain aspects of my relationship with my parents. I was so angry that they didn't listen to or respect that bereaved child in me. My father hadn't even tried. At least my mother had, a little, the night before. But nothing I said had really mattered. I would never trust them with my deep feelings again.

At the same time, I was not going to fight them. I still loved my parents very much, and I knew they loved me, but I also knew now that it was impossible for them to be there for me in my pain. Because they couldn't attend to themselves at that deep psychic level, they couldn't attend to me. Perhaps they knew I was in pain, but they dealt with my feelings in the same way their parents had probably ignored or rejected their own. My vision of a communal healing had been unrealistic, given that it was so foreign to our family culture to express strong emotions in front of one another. While therapy had freed up emotional expressiveness in me, as a family we almost never shared negative emotions – they were something to deal with quickly and in private.

I felt again that four-year-old's distress in all its intensity. Back then, I hadn't been able to protect myself because I loved and needed my parents and wanted to please them. I had been caught, unable to act without further hurting myself. My parents had been wonderful parents in so many other ways, but then (as now) they had been unable to acknowledge my grief, because they didn't know what to do with their own. No one had known how to help me – or how to help my mother, or even my father. My mother had done her best, for all those forty-four years of my sister's life, but she still carried that wound, a deep wound that would never heal by itself.

I felt alone and forlorn and that I had lost my parents even more than I had lost Martha. I would never again look to them for certain kinds of understanding. I would never again go back there with them to that pain they had caused me. I would deal with it alone or with others I could trust.

That day, thinking especially about my parents, I realized that every one of us is born with or acquires handicaps or disabilities – none of us is born whole and perfect – and every one of us acquires more handicaps along the way. Dad's memory was going, and he had been deeply wounded by his own mother's rejection of him. Mom's stomach gave her a lot of trouble, and self-hate crippled her ability to love. Kate had suffered from several major depressions. Eric we almost lost to alcohol and cocaine. I had had a breakdown when I was twenty and narrowly survived, and I was still struggling. Mark had had trouble knowing his purpose in life or believing in himself. We were all handicapped in real and painful ways.

Our parents are our original universe, and the universe contains all things. That's why we can't expect to feel only love for our parents and why it hurts to admit the universe into our love for them – pain, terror, horror, joy, admiration, pity, weakness, frailty. Perhaps every relationship reflects all that there is eventually.

So that was how I said goodbye to Martha and also in some way to my parents. The only good thing was that I would never again have to deal with my parents' reactions to her; anything more that had to do with Martha was my own business, and I was finished with having to take them into account. That was a good but also a sad feeling – I didn't need my parents' love and recognition any more. Where I went, they could not follow. Martha would be present for me, unencumbered by their feelings about her. I was finally free to love her as I wanted to.

But there was a part of me still looking for Martha, still trying to connect with her. A part of me was at loose ends, flapping about in confusion. On top of everything else, I was still trying to come to terms with the finality of her death; there was nothing left really – how shocking that was. *What now?* I thought. *There is nothing more to do. Life goes on in its relentless flow, stopping for no one.*

I looked in the mirror, and I had aged ten years in a couple of months. I looked awful, run down, worn out. There was a sadness visible in my face that I hadn't carried before. I was grieving over my poor dead sister and this pitiful send-off.

Sorry, Martha. I did my best to honour you.

I collapsed in utter exhaustion, as I had after my sister had died, simply overwhelmed with too much feeling. I didn't really know how to help myself, but I knew it was up to me to find the help I needed. I knew my imagination and my intuition could help me. I knew I needed a place to put the pain. I felt that a part of me had died and I would now become someone else.

In the end, I did give my mother a gift, and I told her I loved her because I could not bear to leave her with relations between us in such a raw, primal state. Later, she invited me to come shopping with her, and I agreed, wanting to spend time with her. We drove to a little gift shop in the town near the farm. She bought five small stained-glass chickadees that you could hang in your window. She said they reminded her of Martha, and she wanted each of us to have one. There was one for me, one for her and Dad, one for Kate, and one for Eric. There was one left over. She wrapped it up and signed a card then popped it in the mail. It was for Mrs. Zaretsky.

August 30, 2004

Dear Eva,

We have hung a little chickadee like this in a window at the farm as an everyday memento of Martha. Something about it reminds us of her cheeky cheerfulness. We thought you might like to have one too,

Best wishes.
June

It was too little, too late, but it was better than nothing.

You did your best. So did she.

Several days later, on our way back to Toronto after the scattering of my sister's ashes, Mark and I decided to take Claire and Ariel whitewater rafting on the Madawaska River. We thought of it as something fun, something completely escapist. Usually we couldn't afford things like that, but my parents had given us a gift of some money, and we decided to splurge. We showed up at the excursion headquarters, paid up, got our paddles and our life jackets and had an orientation from our guide, and then we headed down to the water.

It was a beautiful day: hot, clear, perfect for swimming or barbecues. The inflatable Kodiaks were large, and we were told that there would be several going down the river at once. More people joined the orientation, and we were all waiting, a few of us making jokes, when a new group arrived: incredibly, unbelievably, it was a group of people with Down syndrome – they had been driven over from a nearby group home. I stared at them in utter disbelief. I had just scattered my sister's ashes. I thought I was done with Down syndrome. And here they were, getting right into our boat! I tried to be cheerful and not show my discomfort in front of my children; I pretended that everything was fine, but I did not want to be with them. I did not want to share this adventure with them. I wanted them to stay in their own boat, or at least get into someone else's boat, anyone's but mine. I hated myself for these feelings. I was not a good person. I was my mother's daughter, never Jean Vanier's. I was incredibly angry. My adventure was ruined.

Somehow, we got through the rafting and disembarked. We got into our car and drove off, home to Toronto, away from all of them. I was utterly exhausted and bewildered. It wasn't until later that I made the connection with the dream I'd had so many years ago of playing in the frothy water on top of the mountain, that moment of sublime beauty and sheer joy. But it had been this group of people with Down syndrome who had been laughing and playing in the water and sparkling sunshine, and I had begrudged them every second of it for intruding into my life.

So it seemed that although my sister was dead and gone, I was still not finished with Down syndrome – or it was not finished with me.

17

Remembering

It was almost eight years to the day after my sister's death. I arrived at my parents' farmhouse one evening in November 2010, after the sun had set. As I stepped out of the car, I saw that the light was still on in the kitchen; my parents had stayed up for me. There they were rising from their chairs at the kitchen table, illuminated by the warm glow of candlelight. I felt at once the intimacy of my relationship with them, the sense of home, the warmth and love, the laughter. They served me a late dinner of chicken stew and offered me a glass of wine.

My eighty-nine-year-old father was still remarkably vigorous, alert, and fully independent, driving off to town each morning to have a coffee and buy the *Globe and Mail* before doing the shopping and then returning to prepare lunch and dinner. He cooked all the meals now, because he loved to cook, and my mother was tired of it. It was true he was slowly losing his memory, but he was still only in the early stages of that.

My mother seemed healthy and happy, still involved in her book club, puttering in the garden, enjoying her favourite shows on TV, and laughing at my father's jokes. Every single day of their fifty-five-year marriage, my father had brought my mother breakfast in bed, and he still did that religiously every morning. Life was good. These last years had been rewarding and peaceful for both of them – and also good for my relationship with them.

$\mathcal{L}\!\mathcal{D}$

"I really thought of Martha at convocation."

"Did you?" my mother looked surprised, and suddenly wary. I knew it was dangerous territory to bring up Martha's name, since we rarely mentioned her now, but I wanted to share something with them.

A week previously I had been awarded my PhD in history at the University of Toronto. I had started it in 2002, at the age of forty-six, and Martha had died in the third month of my first year of studies. Now, eight years later, I had finally reached the end of the process. I hadn't asked my parents to attend my graduation because they found visiting Toronto too difficult now, but I had sent them photos of me in my gown and cap rubbing the head of the carved wooden gryphon in University College for good luck.

I had not had an easy time in the PhD program. After my first dissertation committee meeting, in which I had been unable to fully explain how I envisaged the project I wished to undertake, I had reacted with a fear so profound I had hidden myself in my own bedroom closet and wept in terror. With dismay, I realized I still had a fear of rejection grounded in the social ostracism of my sister. Although I knew it made no sense, I was still terrified of not being smart enough, of being judged by "experts," of "being left to starve outside the boundaries of humankind," as scholar Elizabeth Probyn describes fear of exclusion in *Blush: Faces of Shame*. Even before I had returned to university, when *Distant Relations* was first published, I had experienced the same terror at talks and readings, terror sparked by fear that my audience would find me so completely off base, so "crazy," that they would apprehend me, put me in a straitjacket, and cart me off to Smiths Falls.

I managed to research and write my dissertation, on the historical memory of the Indigenous and colonial past of Toronto, but I always felt wary and vulnerable in academia. Once, hurt by someone's misperception of me, I found myself crying out desperately to my husband, "I'm not an idiot! I'm not an idiot!" the words welling up from the deepest places in me, sobs shaking me to the core. I might have been studying for my PhD at one of Canada's most prestigious universities, but inside I was still a frightened four-year-old. And yet I passed, I surmounted my fears in academia, I survived. I dedicated my dissertation to Martha, and I conducted the defence of my dissertation in her honour, on her birthday.

But on the day of convocation, I was surprised to wake up in that confused, split, altered state that was always a sign that something had triggered me into my old feelings about my sister. Once again, my left side ached, my left arm in particular. I was angry with myself and puzzled because I thought I had worked through that pain years before. Hadn't Martha been dead for eight years? Surely I didn't need to deal with that same old history again – it was really so tiresome – especially since I had truly been looking forward to the convocation ceremony. But there was no ignoring or denying my emotional state, and I knew I had to sit with those feelings and allow them to come to the surface.

Why was I thinking of her now?

And then I knew why. Martha could never have gone to university; she could never have completed a PhD. Had I abandoned her by going where she could not have gone? Had I betrayed her again by graduating and accepting a PhD, something that she could never have done? It was that same old survivor's guilt.

That I should feel all these things so strongly eight years after her death stunned and disappointed me. How could I still be so affected, so haunted, after all this time? It seemed that she was still part of me, that I still carried her around with me. Somehow my identity was still fused with hers, so much so that I couldn't even distinguish what was her and what was me.

As I puzzled over this, it occurred to me that as a child I had believed that if I forgot about Martha, if I abandoned her as everyone else had apparently done, she would die. I had therefore accepted the huge responsibility of keeping her alive, and I had done so by becoming one with her in some way. And our identities were still fused, it seemed: I had to remind myself that she was dead, that she didn't need me anymore and couldn't care less if I earned a PhD or not. Besides, as my daughter reminded me, when she discovered me weeping in my room, if Martha could have understood what a university was, or the questions I was considering in my research, she would probably have been proud of me. I took those words to heart. I lit a candle for my sister, honouring her memory. Then I was able to put on my gown and hood and walk across the stage at Convocation Hall with my head held high, for her as well as for me. It was a good day in the end, and I felt a true sense of accomplishment.

A week later, when I visited my parents, I tried to convey some of this experience of survivor's guilt to them. I felt that old desire to have them understand, to have them fully know me and how deeply I had been shaped by Martha's birth and institutionalization, but somehow it was not as pressing, not as emotionally critical to me that they fully understand. Perhaps I had finally accepted that they couldn't. Over the years, others had come to understand how deeply I had been affected – Mark, my friends Athina and Margaret, my therapist, even my children to some extent. That night, to my parents, I said only, "I dedicated my dissertation to her," and smiled. It was a declaration of love, something my mother couldn't touch, even if she'd wanted to.

But this time my mother was listening as best she could and trying to understand what I was saying.

"I sometimes wonder if we did the right thing you know, in keeping her at home those two years ... Maybe it would have been better just to send her off right after birth the way other people did," she said. I could feel the vulnerability creeping into her voice and her desire for me to affirm that she'd done the right thing.

"I don't know what you should have done, Mum," I said gently. "I don't know what I would have done. You did your best with what you knew at the time."

And that was all either of us could bear to say. Martha was still part of who we all were together and what had shaped us, and she always would be. My fused identity was my burden, not theirs. It was not their fault or business. But I was glad to share that I still thought of Martha with love. I felt at peace with them. We hugged one another and went to bed.

Later that night, my father got up to go to the bathroom and took a wrong turn in the dark. I was awakened by my mother calling me.

"Vic! Come quick! Your father has fallen down the stairs!"

I had no idea what time it was. I stumbled out of bed and came into my parents' bedroom, which was over the kitchen, in the newer part of the farmhouse. I looked down the steep stairway that led to the kitchen, and there was my father crumpled in a heap against the bottom stair, lying in a pool of urine. His eyes were eerily open, but he was completely unresponsive. His body was twisted in an unnatural position.

I hurried down the stairs.

"Dad? Dad? Can you hear me?"

He didn't answer, but he was still breathing.

By the time the ambulance pulled up to the farmhouse fifteen minutes later, my father had come to. He was exceedingly confused but did what the paramedics told him as they loaded him into the ambulance and drove away. My mother and I followed in my parents' car, first to the Emergency room at the small hospital nearby and then to a bigger hospital in Ottawa. My sister and brother arrived, and we sat with him while the doctors conducted tests. My father's heart was in atrial fibrillation – beating irregularly. Had this perhaps precipitated his fall? An X-ray confirmed that he had three broken ribs, but it was his head we were most worried about. He seemed completely befuddled, speaking to us in a disjointed, confused way, trying to get up off the gurney, trying to undo the straps that held him there. Was there brain damage as well as a concussion?

After a while, we noticed that my mother wasn't doing any of the things we would have expected her to do, such as caress or reassure him or simply hold his hand. As my sister and I gradually realized, she was talking to us but not to him, in fact, avoiding him. It seemed strange because they had always seemed very loving together.

Eventually, he was transferred back to the hospital in Arnprior, where he would be for some time. I had planned to stay with my parents for the weekend, but it was now clear that my sister and I would need to stay longer to help my mother and keep an eye on my father's care and progress. I drove my mother to the hospital every day, cooked for her, and generally kept her company.

At first, my sister and I attributed my mother's befuddlement, her inability to make any decision, to shock; she said she had a fog in her brain and needed to lie down. Then we noticed that she didn't seem to remember where the hospital was some of the time, or even the liquor store. She would start reorganizing things in the house but never finish the task, leaving piles of things everywhere – she who had always been so organized. What was most strange was that she still would not touch my father and spent only a few minutes with him each day, as if she had somehow written him off. When she talked about future plans, it was as if he didn't exist. How could their loving relationship of the past fifty-odd years have evaporated overnight? If anything, she seemed angry at him because he had always been there to take care of her, and now he wasn't.

"I'm not going to be his nurse," she kept saying. "I didn't sign up for that."

What had happened to her? It was as if her caring self had contracted even more and there was no love left, even for my father, despite all their years together, now that he was disabled. Or perhaps it was her way of saying she simply couldn't manage it.

That was when, slowly, painfully, we realized that she was suffering not just from shock but also from dementia. She had fooled all of us, perhaps for a long time. Kate, who had worked as a geriatric assessor, had noticed some of these changes, but the extent of my mother's impairments only became apparent once my father was no longer there to cover for her. He had taken over many day-to-day activities, largely because he needed to keep busy, so my mother's multiple losses of function had not been apparent, perhaps even to him. Now, she angrily insisted that she could drive, that she could cook. But she did not, in fact, do either. Because I had to return to my family and work in Toronto, my sister then made the difficult decision to leave her home and business in Ottawa to stay for several months at the farm to help with my father's lengthy convalescence. I wondered if the dementia was responsible for the gradual hollowing out of my mother's heart as well as her mind, if it had contributed to her lack of compassion and excluding behaviour towards Eric and Martha, which had definitely worsened over time.

When my father was finally released from hospital, he was much changed. He slept most of the day and had lost his exuberant energy and interest in life. He answered questions in the fewest words possible; his short-term memory was almost completely gone. Although he was able to walk, he was unsteady on his feet, and it was clearly dangerous for him to attempt walking unassisted, without a walker. Yet my mother kept insisting that he use a cane rather than a walker, even though that was clearly less safe; sometimes, in public, she refused to walk beside him, as if embarrassed to be seen with someone with a disability. Perhaps it was too much like going out with Martha.

Over the next months of my father's convalescence, he did not get much better. It was hard to accept that my dad was not coming back, that the vital, energetic life of the party was gone forever. This much-diminished person was who he was now ... and the dad we had known would continue to leak away as his dementia progressed.

Although both my parents were still physically present, who they had been to me and even to themselves disappeared day by day. Just as my mother had found it so difficult to let go of the child she had expected Martha to be, so my siblings and I struggled to come to terms with my parents' terribly altered condition. Even as I mourned the loss of their old selves – such wonderful parents, such interesting people in their prime – I knew I could not hold on to that to deem them unworthy of my love in the present. I had to accept, know, and value who they were now, even as the scope of their lives diminished.

As my parents' need for daily care increased, my sister and I began to contemplate their possible need for institutionalization, with all the complicated feelings that accompany such choices. With my parents' permission, Kate sold my parent's farm, and we spent an entire summer sorting through their belongings. The old pool deck was still visible out the kitchen window as we packed, even more rotten, covered in lichen, and there was now a tangle of brambles in the depression below where Martha's ashes had been scattered. We were leaving it all behind.

Luckily, my father improved enough that my parents were able to move into a retirement residence rather than a nursing home, and he and my mother were able to enjoy a couple of years there, with meals provided and the assistance of personal support workers. Later, when my father's medical condition deteriorated and he was no longer capable of living there, my sister, a registered nurse, made the tough decision to care for my father in her own home so that he would not have to be institutionalized.

If we hadn't realized it before, we were learning now what my mother in particular had always refused to acknowledge: that all of us are only temporarily able-bodied, that aging itself is a gradual process of losing function, and that disability is the normal fate of most human bodies – even if not all elderly people develop dementia. Far from being an exceptional individual tragedy, as my family had once believed, disability of one sort or another was a "normal" part of human life and human experience. Now, looking ahead, I saw that in all probability, I would also spend part of my life disabled in some way. We had grown up thinking that to be disabled was to be less of a person, but now my sister and I were learning what Jean Vanier, the trailblazer of the deinstitutionalization movement, had realized and insisted upon: that to live with physical or mental impairment, our own or someone else's, was to become truly and fully human.

"Dementia" is a Latin word meaning "away from" or "out of mind or reason"; it is a cognitive impairment that many people regard as their worst possible fate – certainly my parents did. As dementia progresses, individuals lose their ability to understand themselves and represent themselves and eventually to communicate with others at all. Yet, as disability scholars note, dementia is not simply a biomedical impairment; like all disabilities, it is also a sociopolitical construction, often signifying weakness, dependency, and failure, particularly in a capitalist culture that idealizes the autonomous individual and denigrates what is deemed unproductive. As with old age generally, dementia is marked by stigma. Yet my experience of this phase of my parents' lives was that while it was challenging to care for them, particularly for my sister, there were also wonderful moments of tenderness and sharing that brought us closer. What dementia and even simply my parents' aging revealed to me is that the ultimate truth of our lives is our interdependence.

As Kate and I mourned our parents' losses of function and discussed options for the present and future, we became closer. Inevitably, we discussed the past, and I came to understand that she had also been deeply affected by the family dynamics that arose after Martha's birth and institutionalization. As a young child, she had suffered emotional abandonment by a severely depressed mother, but she had also been abandoned by me, the older sister who abruptly turned all her attention to our newly arrived baby brother. Kate's realization that her imminent birth was the reason for the timing of Martha's institutionalization had weighed on her all her life, and she had relived that scene of guilt every time Martha pleaded to stay with us when it was time for her to return to Smiths Falls.

For so many years after I left home for university, Kate had been the mediator between Mom and Dad and Martha as well as between Mom and Dad and Eric, trying to protect our siblings from being rejected and excluded by my mother, trying to protect them from the knowledge that they were not loved in the same way that Kate and I were. Kate had never felt comfortable or safe enough to share her pain, grief, and distress about these dynamics with my parents or with me. Only now did we move past those early experiences that had so painfully separated us.

My brother was still struggling with his addictions during this whole period of moving my parents from the farm, so he was far less present in the decision making and in their actual care. But I came to see that the dynamics surrounding Martha's life and institutionalization had profoundly affected him as well.

One day, several months after my parents' move to the retirement residence, I was helping my sister sort through the many boxes of my parents' leftover possessions. In one of these boxes we discovered a collection of mementos my mother had kept from Martha's life: the cards from Martha's birth, the cards following her death, old newspaper clippings about Down syndrome, and Martha's report cards.

"Did you see this, Vic?" Kate said, handing me a newspaper clipping.

It was an article from the front page of the *Globe and Mail* dated Saturday, May 5, 2007, with the headline "Doomed from Birth to Death" and a smaller subhead: "Medical Research: The Tragic Link between Down Syndrome and Alzheimer's."

The facts are dismal: more than ¾ of people who reach their 60s with Downs will also be afflicted with dementia; most people with Down syndrome are afflicted with Alzheimer's in middle age, and their final years are marked by a profound intellectual, emotional and physical decline ... Some get it in their 40s, others not till their 60s.

In 1920, the article continued, a baby with Down syndrome had been expected to live only nine years. Now, they lived to fifty-five or more, but by their forties their brains usually became clogged with the plaques and tangles of Alzheimer's. Their parents were often elderly and couldn't look after adult children who needed help dressing, bathing, and eating and who sometimes became aggressive and violent. They could have seizures, personality changes, apathy, loss of daily living skills, visual and speech deficits, disorientation, and other neurological problems.

Martha had definitely been displaying some of these symptoms. There were group homes now – new institutions – specifically for people with Down syndrome and dementia. At least my sister had been spared that.

And then, further down in the article: "Mothers of Down syndrome children who were under 35 when they gave birth to them are five times more likely to be afflicted with Alzheimer's." My mother had been twenty-seven when she gave birth to Martha. She had never told us about that link.

Then, gingerly, I lifted an unsealed envelope out from a pile of papers and examined it. On the outside, in my mother's familiar handwriting, were the words "Martha – baby hair." I opened up the flap and looked inside.

A single curl of golden-red hair.

Shock jolted through me like an electric current. Here was the only part of Martha's physical being still in existence, the rest of her incinerated ten years previously. It was so strange to see a part of her body when she no longer existed. I felt confused. Perhaps it was wrong to hold onto this; perhaps it was preventing her from becoming pure spirit, from moving on. I wondered if it would be better to burn it. But I also had another impulse, and after some moments of conflicting emotion, I reached into the white envelope and gently touched the soft red hair, so similar in colour to that of my own children. I was closer to Martha than I'd been in years.

A few minutes later, I came across the tiny hospital birth bracelet that had once encircled Martha's wrist. It was made of pink beads and had seven white beads with black letters that spelled "FREEMAN." It looked just as it must have on the day she was born.

I couldn't stop crying – there was just too much love and too much loss. But my living sister was there for me, and I was there for her as we sorted through all our family memories.

18

Not Ending

You think you are finished. You think it is over and done with. You assume you can leave it all behind, or that you *should* leave it all behind, or that you *have* left it all behind, and then you discover that it's not so simple. Nothing is forever; everything changes, yet everything also travels with you. Some people will always be with you. All you can do is rewrite the story of your entwinement – or discover the patterns that were there all along.

And so another retelling.

Surely the saddest, most heartbreaking failure of my life was the ending of my intimate connection with Mark, despite our devotion to shared parenting, our empathic communication, and our compassionate care for each other. Perhaps if we had understood more about the impact of boarding school on Mark, of Martha's institutionalization on me, and of gender- and sexual-identity confusion and homophobia on both of us, perhaps if we had had the language that is available today to describe these things, we could have resolved the impasse that came to characterize our sexual life. Or maybe we were both just too damn sensitive.

He and I went on for years, seeing therapists singly and together but unable to requicken our desire for each other, increasingly frustrated with each other, sad, yet somehow, mysteriously, also unable to leave each other. Maybe it was because we had been together so long and shared so much – the bond between us was bone deep. Or maybe it was because the promises we had made to care for each other until death parted us were somehow not empty words we could easily leave behind. Maybe it was because we still hoped against hope that somehow, with time, therapy, luck, or changing circumstances, we would rediscover each other. Above all, there was the concern for our children and the feeling that since other aspects of our relationship were still relatively good, it was better not to rupture their world. Maybe we were also simply afraid of admitting failure, of starting over, of being alone.

I think there was a deeper reason, however. Mark's years of prolonged separation, isolation, loss, bullying, and emotional stress at boarding school had resulted in a cluster of learned behaviours and emotional states that neither of us understood but that resonated with me in unconscious ways. For me, rejecting my husband, telling him he wasn't a good enough partner for me, and abandoning our relationship or disowning him as family were things that I, the sister of abandoned, rejected Martha, simply could not do. Perhaps what I responded to most deeply in Mark was his profound need not to be abandoned. Perhaps what I needed most for my own sense of self-worth – even more than a satisfying sexual relationship – was to never abandon someone I loved, so long as that person also needed me.

As the years passed without resolution, however, I felt increasingly that there was some way I needed to know myself, some way I needed to be loved, that I could not experience with Mark. Although I continued to share a home with him, one of the most challenging times of our life together was when I had an intense and passionate love affair with another man, which Mark never accepted and which we fought over bitterly. I moved into my own room and largely lived my own life, and I thought I would leave Mark altogether – or he would leave me – but that did not happen. Eventually, that other relationship ended, and while Mark and I did not resume our sexual relationship, we continued to share a life together.

Then I met Margot – and it was in the context of that relationship that I was finally able to separate my identity from my sister's and heal from the trauma of my loss of her.

There was something so steady about Margot, so trustworthy – and yet something unusual and quirky and light, too, a kind of playfulness – that attracted me. She had been married for a few years once but had lived as a lesbian for about thirty years, in fact, for as long as I had been with Mark, and she lived within and celebrated a queer culture that I'd never felt at home in, though I didn't know if that was my own homophobia or if I just didn't feel fully accepted as a bisexual person. Surprisingly, Mark was accepting of this new relationship and never begrudged the time I spent with Margot. He had always wondered if I would end up with a woman and sensed that there was something in my relationships with women that I needed to work out. He was right about that: what I did not foresee was that in this first sustained romantic and sexual relationship with a woman, Martha would be all over it.

I was a different person with Margot than I'd been in any other relationship. Partly it was being with a woman for the first time in many years, finding my way in unfamiliar sexual and emotional territory, not being wholly sure it was right for me, dealing with my own homophobia and fear of being ostracized. Margot certainly saw me differently than anyone else had, with a deeper understanding of my experience as a woman. Yet it was puzzling how inarticulate I was with her; in my previous relationships I had had little difficulty discerning and articulating my emotions. But with Margot I had to feel my way forward without words to help me, and I often felt terribly stupid – or at least "dumb," in the old sense of "mute." It seemed that the me that was drawn to her and that needed her could not speak in words or perhaps had never been allowed to have a voice.

When we both acknowledged that this was a potentially serious relationship, I suddenly became anxious. The vertical split reappeared in my body, and my left side ached. I couldn't get grounded and suddenly didn't feel comfortable getting physically close to her, although we had already been sexually intimate.

"I have the strangest sensation," I finally told her. "Somehow I have to ask Martha's permission to get involved with you." I felt utterly ridiculous in saying this.

"I need her to know that I'm not abandoning her ... or being disloyal to her." Tears were streaming down my face. "I've got to go and tell her that ... which is kind of strange since she's been dead for ten years," I continued, not daring to look at Margot, just wanting to get away and hide somewhere. I'd never needed to ask Martha's permission to be with anyone else, not even Mark.

Margot said nothing for a few moments. She took my hand and looked into my eyes, her face full of concern. Then she took me in her arms and held me close. I told her that I needed time to understand these feelings, to untangle them, that I couldn't really be involved with her until I did.

"That makes sense," Margot said quietly, and let me go.

But how was I to ask my sister's permission or reassure her – or at least ask the Martha in me? I wrote to her in my notebooks. I told her I loved her and would never abandon her and that Margot would always respect her. But the split feeling in my body persisted. So I went back to the therapist to try to get to the root of it.

It was discouraging to have to go back into therapy. So many times I had thought I was finally healed from this long ago trauma about my sister ... and yet here I was again, having to go back, discovering new ways that it continued to affect me. How could this thing still have a hold on me, fifty years later?

I went to the therapy session not expecting very much ... a discussion, maybe some tears and sober reflection. But that's not what happened. I don't really know how it started, but suddenly I felt an urgent need to call out Martha's name, to call her back from wherever she had gone when she died. Then I was yelling and screaming "Martha!" with every ounce of my strength, with every cell of my being, literally demanding that she return from the dead. I would not take no for an answer. I screamed at her to listen to me. I had never done anything remotely like that before. It was so eerie to call to her like that when I knew she was dead, but I needed to do it. I so needed to do it. But, of course, she didn't answer. And I was full of rage at her that she wouldn't come back. But at least I had called for her with every particle of my being.

I was exhausted afterwards and terribly confused. It seemed that I was still dealing with Martha's disappearance when I was four years old as well as her death. My therapist said that young children can deal with death, but a disappearance is much more confusing.

It was after that session that I began researching and writing this memoir. I knew that I had to conduct a deep inner excavation, to try to understand who Martha had been to me and how she had come to affect me so deeply in all aspects of my life: my work, my social interactions, even my love life. I needed to understand why it was that with Margot she came up the most. Perhaps, I thought, it was because my first and foremost female relationship (other than with my mother) had been with my sister. Then, in a quiet moment of epiphany, it came to me that, in spite of Down syndrome and everything else, Martha had been my first love.

And I had so berated myself for not loving her.

Did Margot stand in for my sister in some way? It seemed incontrovertible that in some way she did, though I knew that this was a level of emotional complexity most intimate partners don't want to hear about or deal with and that it really wasn't fair to her. Margot listened with love and attention, but it was difficult for her, especially because she had been alone for a number of years and was more than ready for an intimate relationship – in fact, for a life partner. She needed to know I was there for her, but I didn't know where any of this was taking me.

One day I was going through old boxes at home, trying to make more room in my closet, when I found the large eight-by-ten framed photograph of Martha that Mrs. Zaretsky had given me so long ago, the one I had previously dismissed as an embarrassing, pathetic imitation of a school photo. It must have been taken when Martha was in her twenties, though it was hard to tell, because she never really showed her age. She was wearing a beautiful blue and violet flowered dress, with lace around the collar and two narrow white ribbons down the bodice to her waist. I noticed for the first time her tasteful gold wristwatch and her string of pearls. Her hair was a beautiful, rich chestnut red and neatly cut to frame her face.

Perhaps because I had been so struck by Margot's attention to women's energies and body language, I now looked more closely at Martha's face. For the first time I noticed that she had big thick eyebrows like I did, and like mine, they had never been shaped and tweezed in the feminine style. In fact, when I looked at the photograph I saw a strong family resemblance – something I had never seen or acknowledged before – in the shape of her face and her nose and lips, in the lines from the sides of her nose to the corners of her mouth, even in the shape of her smile. If I covered her eyes, it could have been me. I had never, ever noticed the resemblance before. I had never looked closely, never wanted to see it.

But what struck me even more forcefully was her expression, which I had never previously considered. In the photograph, Martha looked calm, content, and completely at ease with herself. In fact, if I had to describe how she presented herself, I would have to say with dignity – not an assumed or pretended dignity but rather inner strength and self-acceptance. I saw

Martha's "school photo" from the late 1970s, after she left Rideau
and was living with the Zaretskys.

self-possession, even pride, in her face and an unmistakable
sense of humour and intelligence. The person in the photograph
had a strong presence; she commanded your attention. At the
same time, there was a sparkle in her eyes, as if she was looking
out on the world and was just about to laugh or smile, as if she
loved and laughingly appreciated who or what she was seeing.

This was a Martha I had never seen in real life, though she
was unmistakably there in the photograph. And although she

still had Down syndrome – you could see it in her eyes, and the flatness of her face, and the twist of her mouth – for the first time that is not what I dwelt on. It was there but only part of the picture. For the first time in my life, I saw my sister's character; I saw Martha, the person, for the first time in fifty years. And what moved me to tears was the realization that she was beautiful. Not ugly. Not funny-looking. Not monstrous. Her spirit was beautiful. It shone in that photograph, illuminating her face, her being, with a lovely, clear light. You would want to know this person. I could have.

It was terrible to know that I had not been able to see her for all those years, in fact, for most of her life, that my prejudice had obscured my love for her. It was terrible to know that I had lived all those years denying that love, feeling unable to love, as my mother still did. I felt such terrible guilt for all those years of finding her ugly. I felt awful for the way I had carried my mother's guilt and self-hate.

How sad that I hadn't been able to see this until now, so long after Martha's death, but I was so glad to have finally seen it, so grateful. Because the look in her eyes, her strength and her humour, were not just for anyone. They were also for me. When I looked at that photograph, I felt she was speaking directly to me, encouraging me, that she had confidence in me, that she loved me. I needed her strength and her forgiveness. And I knew she would always be there for me. Even if she was dead. Even if she was gone.

I brought the photograph of Martha to show Margot. She looked at it carefully and immediately saw the person Martha was; she saw her strength and spirit and dignity and also her resemblance to me. In an act of exquisite tenderness, she put the photograph on the shelf opposite her bed, and we lay down, and she held me and stroked me. Martha was our witness as we lovingly embraced, as we made love, and that felt completely right.

But still, it was pretty deep and tangled stuff I was sorting out, and I continued to be triggered and confused. What was becoming evident was that after she had disappeared into the institution, Martha and I had become fused somehow. She had become my psychic twin, as close to me, as much a part of me as if we were conjoined – and I was still fused with her, even though she'd been dead for so long. Even now I couldn't tell where I ended and she began. At the same time, rationally, I knew that Martha was dead, and that I had to make peace with a part of myself, the part of me that felt such a loyalty to my sister that I still wore an old pair of her sweatpants when I did yoga – years after her death.

Whatever happened, I could not abandon her. I had to take care of her. That commitment had been a hidden thing all my life, outside even my own consciousness. As a child I had needed that allegiance to make sense of my situation and survive emotionally and ethically, but it had created a psychic structure that was also imprisoning me. Clearly, it was affecting my relationship with Margot and my relationship with myself and probably also my relationship with Mark.

But I couldn't rush where I went with this. I had to go slowly.

At every stage in my developing relationship with Margot, I became upset, sometimes over the most unlikely things, and I started feeling the left-right split in my body again, these two parts of myself that seemed to go off in different directions, that barely held together or communicated with each other. Gradually, I came to understand that the part of me that recognized myself, that spoke as my "I" was only on the right side of my body. Somehow, I had lived with a form of double consciousness, with two different selves on either side of my body, one articulate, one voiceless, which seemed so abnormal, so weird, so wrong, I felt crazy just thinking about it.

How could I bring the two sides of myself – my Martha and Victoria – into an equitable relationship, since one side, the conscious "I," had been so dominant, had refused to even recognize the other? I wanted to be one person, not two. I didn't want to have a left side that felt like it was either not mine but part of somebody else or a corpse or dead thing that "I" (the conscious Victoria on my right side) carried around. Slowly, following the feelings rather than words, holding and caring for that aching left side, I finally came to understand that split.

My left side was not my sister's spirit inhabiting me, as I sometimes feared, it was where I had put my love for her.

I had needed to put it somewhere. It hadn't been safe to let my feelings for Martha flow freely through my being; those feelings could not be allowed to contaminate the rest of me. I had hidden that love from my parents, particularly from my mother, so I would not also be rejected and sent away, and also so I would not hurt my mother and father. That part of me that loved Martha had been reviled and abandoned by me, which was why it felt dead. But it was still alive, no matter how hard I tried to kill it or reject it. It still had consciousness and a will to live. I had identified that will to live with Martha, given it Martha's voice. But it was my own.

Here was the living proof that "the body is the flesh of memory," as somatic psychologist Katharine Young has written. My body continually spoke of my past; it embodied my history.

As I slowly integrated these parts of myself, I could move more and more into a relationship with Margot. But this movement was far too slow for her – she needed and wanted and deserved to have a partner who could be truly present for her and who could fully meet her. I hated how slowly I moved towards her, but I couldn't hurry my own process of healing. In truth, I did not have the emotional or psychic energy for intimacy, given all that being with her brought up. She waited for more than a year and finally came to the decision that she wanted to end our relationship. I could hardly blame her. I understood why she needed to end it, and I knew I had to let her go.

I stumbled home from her house the day that she broke up with me. I felt more physically split than ever, with the left side of my body horribly aching. But somehow, I knew this pain

wasn't about Margot, though the thought of losing her had precipitated it – it was about Martha.

I went to see Athina, a friend who sometimes helped me sort
myself out.

"I need a place for Martha that is outside my body," I said.

Athina gave me an odd look and went upstairs. She returned
with a small ivory box that was plain except for an elaborately
monogrammed *M* on the lid. It was old, probably Victorian, she
said; she had picked it up decades previously at a garage sale in
England.

"I've always felt funny about owning it because of the ban
on ivory."

I took it in my hands and examined it.

"It's odd," she continued. "I was looking at it last night and
thinking that I really don't have a use for it, and I should give it
to someone whose name starts with *M*. I was thinking of various
people I know – Mary ... or Margaret – but neither of them felt
right ... But maybe you should have it for Martha."

It was perfect. Even the ivory. She told me about how ele-
phants gather round to mourn a member of their family, sometimes for days, and she reminded me of that silly saying: "An
elephant never forgets." I knew immediately what I would put
in it. I would retire the sweatpants, cut them up, and save a
small piece to put in the box. I would burn or bury the rest. I
would add strands from the lock of Martha's baby hair that my
mother had saved. These were the very last things I had of my
sister, other than her photographic image.

So I went home with the box and added these relics. I felt
oddly at peace. In fact, I had the strange sensation that a hole
in my heart had been healed. I realized it was my sister's love I
had been seeking first and foremost, although I also cared for
Margot, and she had been very kind to me and had loved me
and cared for me. I will always be grateful to her.

That day, the split in me was healed. I felt the return of the left side, joining the rest of me. Now there was something new in my relationship with myself. In the past, I'd always needed a romantic or sexual relationship to feel whole, but now I sensed that I could be there for myself in an entirely new way. I could feel my own self-love, which I had given away to my sister. There had been a bargain, a trade, just like all those other bargains that my mother and father had made in relation to her.

It was a new experience to be with myself, truly alone with myself, to have no double, no shadow, no second self, to be only me.

Now I have Martha's box, and her spirit or my love for her – or whatever it was that I carried for so long – lives there. It is no longer part of me, no longer something I carry. She's not forgotten, but she's a little further away, more distinct from me. The ivory box is my sister's final resting place, and it feels so good to finally have her with me – not part of me, but with me. I can see the box from my bed, resting on a beautiful Japanese chest that Athina gave me. I will care for it always.

A few months after our breakup, Margot told me she had met someone else. I was happy for her but also sad that things hadn't worked out between us. Would she ever understand how deeply my relationship with Martha had affected my relationship with her? What was hard to accept was that Martha had always been standing in front of her, blocking the light so that it was hard for me to see Margot and who she really was. I could move my sister to the side, inch by inch, but not all at once.

Through all this untangling and confusion in my relationship with Margot, Mark had still been there for me, had loved me with loyalty and patience, had continued to live with me. The love between us was indescribably deep and true, even if it was no longer a physical intimacy. I have come to accept that for me, sister of Martha, some relationships are for life, even if long-term relationships are not necessarily the same as living arrangements or sexual relationships. Even today, Mark and I still uphold the vow we made to each other, to care for each other, for richer, for poorer, in sickness or in health, truly till death parts us. It feels good to uphold that love and compassion for each other, even as we go through all our permutations and changes. And I am grateful that Margot is still part of my life; I love her and appreciate her more and more with every passing year.

Martha. Mark. Margot. Some people will always be with you. All you can do is rewrite the story of your entwinement. This, too, is love.

19

Second Chances

For so many years, my knowledge of my sister had been defined more through her absence than her presence, through the shape of the void she left in my life. I had been able to approach who she was only through echoes and shadows, through my own fear of being carted away or of being seen as crazy or stupid, through my fear of experts, those who had condemned her to exile. I had known her in my own mind as the accusing sister, the crazy sister, or the sister who could not speak. Sadly, through most of her life and my own, I had been so affected by my own trauma in relation to her that I had been largely oblivious to what she may have actually experienced. I was never able to see the real person. I had never asked her what she felt, because I had never considered her capable of answering. Unconsciously, I had understood her abandonment, felt it, and absorbed it, but I had taken it on as my own, an appropriation that was not true empathy. I had not recognized that her pain was distinct from mine. The only way I had been able to deal with it was to make it mine, but that was a disservice to her. Now, finally, as my own pain lessened, I could begin to consider hers.

Boxing Day, 2012. A beautiful, sunny winter day. Mark and I had spent Christmas Day with my parents at their retirement residence near Ottawa and now set out for the two-hour drive to Smiths Falls. The car skimmed along the bare highway on the same route my family had travelled when I was a child, past snowy fields with broken-down fences, the same small gatherings of houses and gas stations at major crossroads, and then the fast food joint that had variously been a hamburger or ice cream stand, where we often stopped on the way in or out. As we moved through the town to its southeastern edge, I recognized the familiar streets – Union, Cornelia, Queen, and then Hershey Drive (which led to the shuttered Hershey chocolate factory of my childhood dreams, now a grow-op for medical marijuana). Then, sooner than I remembered it, the turnoff, where I was startled to see a new sign, which read "Gallipeau Centre."

The Rideau Regional Centre had finally closed in 2009, one of the last three of such Ontario institutions to be decommissioned. I had read on the internet that the site of the former hospital school had been purchased by a local businessman named Joe Gallipeau. He planned to turn part of the facility into a retirement community, while the rest would be available for local businesses. The advertising copy on the Gallipeau Centre website read: "Nestled in the heart of the country-side but walking distance from downtown Smiths Falls, our facility is perfectly located, providing anything you need. With 800,000 square feet of available lease space and over 350 acres of land, the Gallipeau Centre can accommodate almost anything!"

The buildings of the hospital school were now featured in the annual "Doors Open" architectural festival, where the public came to view its "severely handsome" Art Deco architectural style, as well as the gymnasium, eight-hundred-seat auditorium, and indoor swimming pool, for which I had raised $24.35 and which had given my sister so much pleasure. A local community group was now raising funds to restore all three facilities as part of a new multipurpose recreation centre for the town. Their fundraising campaign featured a photograph of dozens of community members standing in the empty pool, holding signs that read "Fill Our Pool!" Martha would definitely have approved.

But these plans had not yet been realized.

The car veered in a smooth arc to the left. As we headed up the long driveway through an arbour of trees, it felt like we were driving back through time. At the top of a gentle rise of land, the sprawling red brick complex suddenly appeared before us in all its splendid isolation, still surrounded by acres and acres of farmland and bush. All had been freshly blanketed in snow. Only the ring road had been plowed, and none of the walkways had been cleared. It was just as I remembered it, except that the swings and teeter-totters had been removed, and there were no cars in any of the parking lots. I had not been there in almost fifty years.

Now I was back at the epicenter of all that family misery. Surprisingly, it felt good to return, to bear witness to all my sister and family had experienced there. Mark took my photograph as I stood solemnly at the front entrance to the main building, under the stone inscription, which still read "Ontario Hospital School." I peered through the glass of the heavy front doors down the endless corridor, narrower and even more forbidding than I remembered. I turned and surveyed the other buildings, trying to remember which one my sister had lived in.

But now the place was deserted. No child cried at night in the dormitories. The sun was shining, and that day there were no ghosts. What struck me most was the silence.

It amazes me now that that day was the first time in my life that I truly asked myself what Martha had experienced at that institution and, in particular, what it had been like to be left there. Staring out at the massive complex of buildings, I began to imagine the enormity of being abandoned there, at the age of twenty months.

You sleep in the car on the way to Smiths Falls, and then you are left here, held here. People push spoonfuls of food into your mouth, change your dirty diaper, wipe your bum and your pudendum, some of the many things that are simply done to you. Those you knew before are like phantoms in a dream. Not

I return to the Rideau Regional Centre, December 2012.

one thing here is real. It is, at first, an utterly meaningless life, shapeless, formless, strange. Not one thing is familiar except your own hand, your foot, your own breath, your fingers. You have lost the one who gave birth to you and everyone and every- thing else you knew. You are a small, helpless child wanting and needing to be lovingly cared for and sheltered and not understanding why your parents are no longer here. You have no language whatsoever for that enormous void, that terrible loneliness, that awful despair that persists day in and day out for a very long time. You are so vulnerable, so dependent, in a strange place with hundreds, no thousands, of others.

The routines become familiar but are completely independ- ent of who you are. People come and go for no apparent reason. You are assailed by strange food, strange smells, strange sounds, strange hands. No one knows who you were before. You lie for long periods in a wet diaper. Cold. Or hot. No one comes. You cry and no one hears. Too many are crying. Shut up, kid! Nothing makes sense. Nothing in your previous life prepared you for this. You must start over or die, become a different you. And yet somehow you do not die. You survive in this new world where no one loves you and where there are so many others all

clamoring for attention. You have no idea of what has happened.
No one has even tried to explain it to you. You become angry, with-
drawn, aggressive, rough. You fight for your space, for yourself.
You fight to survive. Yet somehow you continue to love us in spite
of what we have done to you.

In spite of my distance and neglect, you love me.

In her book *Gender Trouble*, the philosopher Judith Butler says
that some identities cannot exist. They are outside the norm
and are therefore labelled developmental failures or logical
impossibilities, rendering them unintelligible and invisible –
something I have experienced to some degree as a bisexual,
genderqueer person. Yet we come to be only through being
recognized by others.

Through all the years of her life, I never considered Martha's
particular perspective, her identity, her experience, her subjec-
tivity – her "I" – in part because I didn't believe she actually had
one. However, Butler notes that if there is no subject position
from which to speak, then one cannot be recognized as a full
human being with desires, wants, and needs. So it was with my
sister – it was not only her language difficulties that made her
unintelligible to us, to me. We believed that someone else would
always have to speak for her, that she had no legitimate voice.
Her particular perspective did not seem worth attending to. My
family knew her primarily through her difference, yet to us that
difference was a useless rather than a productive difference, a
difference without value, perceived only as a lack. Yet somehow
I unconsciously knew she should have a voice. Perhaps that is
why I internalized her voice for so many years – because in the
world we grew up in, there was no other place for it. I had been
possessed by an injustice.

It was only after her death that she truly existed, that she
truly became human to me. But by then there was no "I" to
listen to.

I had read on the internet that there was a class action lawsuit underway on behalf of those who had lived at the Rideau Regional Centre and their families, and it was partly because of that case that I decided to revisit the site. The suit alleged abuse and neglect and was patterned after a similar lawsuit launched by Marie Slark and Patricia Seth, two former residents of the Huronia Regional Centre at Orillia. My family was not part of the Rideau lawsuit, because Martha had died too long ago to qualify for class membership. In any event, I suspect my parents would not have felt comfortable being part of the lawsuit because they were grateful to the school for taking my sister in the first place and for teaching her how to be independent in her self-care. I think they felt the institution had done a reasonable job of taking care of her, recognizing that no institution is perfect. But I resolved that I would go to hear the testimony and arguments when the case finally came to trial. I hoped to learn something more of what might have been my sister's day-to-day experience and to bear witness to the lives of all those children who had grown up in that institution, so far from their families.

Other than her "Shub up, kib!" I had never had any direct indication that Martha had been ill-treated at Smiths Falls. I'd always had the impression that she'd been a bit of a staff pet – but I knew appearances could be deceiving. How ironic that I had helped organize a major regional gathering for survivors of residential schools, had wept through the anguished testimonies of so many who had been abused and traumatized in such places, but was only now beginning to face the possibility that my own sister might have also been treated callously or abusively in a residential institution. Her "Shub up, kib!" indicated, at minimum, the presence of what researcher Madeline Burghardt, in *Broken: Institutions, Families, and the Construction of Intellectual Disability*, refers to as a culture of roughness. In a world where the residents of the school had no access to the outside world, no recourse, and often little language to even articulate mistreatment or neglect, abuse could easily have been normalized, as it was at so many similar total institutions. Even if she had not been abused herself, Martha might well have been harmed by witnessing the brutalization of others. How lucky she was in leaving the school when she was fifteen, before she became an adult, for all the available evidence indicates that adults were treated the worst. And how lucky that she was a girl, for it seems that things were often far worse for the boys in such institutions, since their caregivers were often former soldiers who had been brutalized by their war service.

I now realized that the ways we had viewed my sister, the ways society had viewed my sister, had been equally violent and were related to the violence perpetrated in the hospital schools. Our psychic violence, our insistence on the normal as the only life worth living, had created an environment that enabled the physical violence and abuse of power that harmed so many. Our prejudice had unnecessarily isolated "the disabled" and erased this violence from our view.

That day, Mark and I drove around the entire complex three times, looking at every building, mesmerized and astounded by the scale of it all. To be there again was to know that I had actually been there as a child, that it was not a figment of my imagination, as it has so often seemed to be. What had tormented me, what had been locked away in a corner of my mind and haunted me for so many years, was still there, swaddled in snow, set off by the dark shapes of the leafless trees, real. I wasn't crazy. It had really happened.

That day I revisited the fairy hill and undid the spell. Martha was no longer there, and I knew I need never go back again. Now she would always rest with me.

After that visit to the institution, something changed in me. For the first time in my life, I wanted to be around people with Down syndrome. I wanted to understand more of who my sister had been. I thought of volunteering with L'Arche, the organization that my cousin Louise has been a member of for almost forty years, even though I was afraid it was too Christian for me. I screwed up my courage and phoned the Toronto office, but was informed that volunteers had to go through a formal interview process and commit to a year of involvement. A year! I didn't know if I could manage more than a day. I wanted to be with people with Down syndrome at least once without having to commit myself, to see how I felt, and if I could even handle being with them at all. Perhaps, like my mother, I still wouldn't be able to see past my old prejudices; perhaps I would never be capable of friendship or acceptance. An alternative first step in joining L'Arche was to attend a worship service. That didn't require a time commitment, but it didn't feel right for me either. So I never followed up with L'Arche.

A few months later, however, I heard about a theatre group named Sol Express. The artist who told me about it spoke admiringly of its creativity and innovation in creating original shows involving people with intellectual disabilities and other artists. I was immediately interested because I was already working with Jumblies Theatre, another innovative company that works with communities in Toronto to create theatre that imaginatively reflects local people's lives. In that work, I sometimes drew upon my ten years of modern dance training while I was a child and teenager.

Working creatively with people with intellectual disabilities was an option I had never before considered – partly, I am ashamed to admit, because I had never believed people like my sister capable of either imagination or creativity. In fact, I would say that ultimately false perception was a crucial marker of the supposed difference between my sister and myself. I believed her to be without the spark of imagination, and for that reason she seemed to me to be truly dull in both senses of the word – not interesting and not truly and fully alive. That seeming lack of creativity was the very mark of the subhuman in her.

But at the Toronto Fringe Festival the previous summer I had seen Judith Thompson's play *Rare,* which featured a cast of people with intellectual disabilities who told their own stories about living with disabilities in a world that regarded them as freaks. Although I had mixed feelings about the play itself, it had been a revelation to see people with Down syndrome on a stage speaking about their lives in their own words. Clearly, people with Down syndrome were capable of far more than I had ever believed possible.

So once again I found my courage, and this time I emailed Cheryl Zinyk, the director and originator of Sol Express, and asked if there was some way I could be involved. I told her about Martha, about my dance and theatre experience, such as it was, and about the book I was writing as part of my own healing process. She immediately responded and kindly invited me to meet and discuss the possibilities. It turned out Sol Express was associated with L'Arche, which bolstered my good impression of both groups and offered me a different way to become involved with L'Arche.

I felt considerable trepidation before that first face-to-face meeting with Cheryl. I had never really talked to anyone who worked with people with Down syndrome before, other than my cousin Louise, and that discussion had been complicated and constrained by broader family dynamics. For someone who had had a sister with Down syndrome, I knew I was remarkably ignorant. What I did know was that there was a whole new field of critical disability studies and disability activism that I was unfamiliar with, and I was worried that my attitudes and language would seem so outdated and offensive that Cheryl would decide I was unfit for involvement in Sol Express. I was also afraid she would judge me harshly because my family had put my sister in an institution and that she would be critical of me for not having been actively involved in my sister's life.

But as soon as I met her, I was put at ease. A warm, open, and generous woman in her fifties, there was nothing intimidating about Cheryl at all, and her years of experience, creativity, and sense of fun were readily apparent. She told me that through

L'Arche she had lived with people who had spent their first twenty years in institutions and had been formed by them. She said she had also known family members who had made the difficult decision to institutionalize. She was a product of the same era as I was and had first-hand knowledge of the attitudes towards disability so prevalent in my youth. I immediately felt her compassionate interest when I spoke of the Rideau Regional Centre and my experience visiting my sister there. Mercifully, she did not judge me or my parents.

As I spoke about Martha's life and the effect that her institutionalization had on me, and why I wanted to become involved in Sol Express, I could feel the pain of those experiences rising to the surface, emanating from every cell of my body. I'm sure she sensed it and felt it, as she immediately acknowledged how difficult the loss of my sister must have been, but mainly she simply listened and helped me through.

"Most of the people in the theatre group have Down syndrome," she told me. "Would you like to come to meet the group and spend a morning with us?"

"Yes," I said.

"We will do our warm-ups and team-building exercises, and you can simply join in. We're starting to work on our new production, so we might be doing things to workshop it. Does that sound okay with you?"

I said that it was, and we arranged the date that I would attend.

My excitement at having made this connection was quickly followed by mild anxiety about meeting the group, which soon deepened into fear and then a state of abject terror. Rationally, I knew such terror was entirely inappropriate but that did not lessen it. What in the world was I so afraid of? It was something about being with a group of people with Down syndrome, though rationally I knew they were probably the least threatening or violent people in the world. Yet the terror was no less real for all that. Ridiculous as it was, I was absolutely paralyzed by it.

I'd known for a long time that I'd been traumatized by Martha being sent away and that I hadn't liked going to the hospital school, but what only became apparent that day was that all my life I had actually been suffering from some form of posttraumatic stress reaction related to the institution itself. The prospect of being with a group of people with Down syndrome reawakened the extreme fright of those early visits, a trauma that was distinct from my parents' pain at Martha's birth or my feelings about her being sent away. There I was again, a young child in a nightmarish through-the-looking-glass kind of world that I might be trapped or abandoned in, a place populated by hundreds of beings who appeared monstrous to me and who swarmed around me and tried to touch me and hug me. Yet what was also confusing was that in some ways it had also seemed to be a normal place, an everyday place – both a hospital and a school, with walls and floors and windows and tables and chairs like any other place, and kindly nurses in uniforms and knowledgeable doctors in white coats – but at its invisible heart were terror and horror and the indescribable pain of abandonment. Williston had talked in his 1971 report about the "profound psychological effect upon both staff and residents when there are hundreds of helpless and hopeless cases in one institution." I must have unconsciously sensed that profound despair, for that was where my terror lived, my terror of others and my terror of myself.

Over all those years of visiting my sister there, it never got any better. My parents tried papering over the abnormal – *I trust there will be no unseemly displays of emotion* – but, really, I had wanted to run away, screaming, as far as I could get. The hospital school became the secret place of insanity in me, papered over, hived off. To me, terror really was a place, insanity was a place, a landscape and a community of people I had actually visited. That was why the terror of insanity came so easily to me.

I had not been with a group of people with Down syndrome since my whitewater rafting experience and, before that, since groups of lonely children and adults had cornered me and overwhelmed me as a child. In fact, I had never ever voluntarily chosen to be with a group of people with Down syndrome in my entire life. I had always avoided them or reacted with dread when I saw them. What if even now I couldn't get past my prejudices? What if they still seemed ugly, deformed, even monstrous to me? And what if I couldn't hide my fear or my disgust? What if they saw that?

I would be so ashamed if that happened. I knew I would have failed as a human being. That was when, shaking and crying, I realized what I feared even more than being trapped with them was that they would judge and reject me, that they would see through me, that they would see that I wasn't "good," that I wasn't a good person at all, that I was the ugly one. Smiths Falls had also been the place where I failed as a human being. I hadn't wanted to see my own sister. I had avoided her, felt superior to her, been repelled by her and all people like her. I had failed to love what seemed, to me, unlovable. I had wanted to leave her there and never see her again. I had felt worthless because I knew I hadn't loved her enough. I had failed to be a good human being and, in a sense, to be a human being at all. In fact, I had proven that I was the one who was subhuman, less than human, that I was the monster. And I knew that this was what my mother also felt deep down, that she was not a good person; she felt guilty whenever she saw someone with Down syndrome, and that was why she reacted so harshly to them. What had it done to us to have carried this trauma, this hatred, for so long?

Once again, I had that strange feeling when you realize something and your whole life begins to make sense. I understood with so much more compassion why it had been difficult for me to feel good about myself, why I had been held back from certain kinds of growth and development, and I wondered who I would have been and what my life would have been like if this had not happened to me. I also understood more of why my mother had become emotionally stunted. Unrecognized, unprocessed pain and self-loathing had twisted and maimed both of us, and as a result it was the two of us who had been "retarded" – held back from full humanity by our own fears.

By the time I actually went to meet the participants in Sol Express, I had let go of my fear. I felt calm and happy as I took the subway and then the bus to the L'Arche building in East York. I knew this was a day that might change my life and I was ready for that possibility. I walked into the brightly lit studio space (the former nave of a large church that had been bought and renovated by L'Arche), was greeted by Cheryl, and felt immediately at home. The day's activities hadn't started yet, and the participants – both men and women, many with Down syndrome – were sitting in chairs on three sides of the room, some talking, one drawing, a couple playing games or texting on their smart phones. Did I say texting? I had not imagined that someone with Down syndrome could ever truly read or write, and here they were sending texts to their friends! This was the first sign to me that I would be continually surprised by the accomplishments and abilities of the people in this group. It was immediately apparent that many of them functioned at a level far higher than my sister had ever been able to attain.

I sat down in a vacant chair and said a shy hello. They had heard I would be coming and greeted me. One of the participants, a very handsome man who appeared to be in his late thirties or early forties, came over and sat beside me and immediately engaged me in conversation. William, as I will call him, asked me if I had ever watched *Mork and Mindy*, a TV show from the 1970s, and launched into a lively discussion of the show, replete with a singing of the theme song and snatches of dialogue. I was drawn immediately to his humour and spirit.

Then Cheryl and Matt, her assistant, gathered us together in a circle, and I was introduced to the nine other participants. We played a name game, where each of us introduced ourselves by saying our name with an accompanying action. Wanda! Keith! Samir! Victoria! I was simply one more participant in the circle. Many of the actions were humorous; some outrageously silly, others wonderfully imaginative, and the group took delight in each person's offering. This was clearly a group that had worked together for some time and had long ago shed its inhibitions.

Next, we passed various movements and sounds around the circle or threw them to someone across from us. It had been a long time since I had had the opportunity to be so playful, and I enjoyed myself immensely. Later, we created a physical tableau that gradually moved across the room as one person at a time left one end of the tableau and through dance moved to the front of the tableau, extending it. Such improvisation was second nature to me after all my years of dance training, and it felt wonderful to go back to it, especially in this context. Soon, Cheryl was using me to illustrate various points, such as incorporating various levels into one's movements. I could immediately see where I could contribute to the development of their show.

At the end of that morning, we played one of their favourite games, which involved recalling and performing the lyrics to popular songs, something I have always been terrible at. One person faced the others, as if on a stage, and began to sing a song. As soon as someone else heard a word or words that they knew were also lyrics in another song, they rushed onto the stage, tapped the singer on the shoulder to displace him or her, and then began to sing the new song. As soon as someone else heard words that formed part of yet another song, that person rushed onto the stage, displaced the second singer with a tap, and began their song. As we played the game, I was quickly left in the dust. They were fiercely competitive and knew Broadway songs, themes to movies and TV shows, pop tunes, nursery rhymes – all of which they sang with gusto and often with hilarious physical gestures. I was completely humbled by their prodigious memories and panache. When it was my turn, all I could remember were songs from *The Sound of Music*, the payoff of all those repeated viewings with Martha, but they cheered me on. Afterwards, I sat with them at lunch hour and struggled to keep up with the conversation as it ricocheted around the room: who had starred in what movie, in what year; what the theme song was to such and such TV show; who had travelled where last summer on their vacations or to attend a conference.

It was an absolutely amazing, life-changing experience to meet the Sol Express performers, to dance and do physical theatre with them. I cried all the way home and then on and off for the next two days. I was so moved, so deeply affected, so grateful. I felt I had been touched at the very point where I had once been split in two, like a tree that had been riven right down the middle by lightning. It felt so special to be able to use dance to connect with them and heal from that painful period in my past, to be able to physically celebrate my love of life with people like my sister, when so much of my relationship with her had been interrupted, deformed, destroyed, to move from so much buried pain to love and joy and laughter. Just having a respected place for all those feelings was a whole new experience. It seemed like working with Sol Express was the most healing thing I could ever possibly do.

For the next several days, there were lots of tears at odd moments and times when the faces of each of the participants would come to me, etched so vividly in my mind. I was so struck by the unique personality of each one after all those years of seeing only the disability they shared. What I wanted most was to go back to Sol Express as soon as possible, to learn more, to be with them, to dance with them.

Cheryl let me know the next day that everyone had felt comfortable with me, and she asked me if I would be interested in continuing to work with them, focusing particularly on dance, as they developed their June performance. Of course, I said, I would be honoured and thrilled to do so.

20

How Far You've Come

On March 21, 2013, less than a week after I'd first visited Sol Express, the first ever World Down Syndrome Day was observed. The United Nations had chosen that particular date because the twenty-first day of the third month corresponds to the third or extra chromosome (trisomy) on the twenty-first gene, the marker of Down syndrome. A new and energetic Toronto-based parent activist group called Circle 21 had organized a huge event in Toronto and connected with other organizations around the world. The mayor of Toronto and the premier of Ontario both announced World Down Syndrome Day that morning, and the Toronto Stock Exchange opened with it. In Hollywood, actor Tom Cruise tweeted his thousands of followers about it.

That evening, Cheryl and I joined 250 to 300 well-heeled Torontonians at the Crescent School's Centre for Creative Learning, in leafy North Toronto, for a celebration of the day. Yes, a celebration! We mingled and mixed while listening to a jazz guitarist and bass player, drank wine from a cash bar, and nibbled on canapés served by enthusiastic young people with Down syndrome. There were T-shirts for sale that proclaimed "A New Kind of Perfect!," scores of colourful balloons, a silent auction of artwork by artists with Down syndrome, and an entire wall hung with huge arty photographs of adorably cute Down syndrome kids. As part of the silent auction, *Down's Upside,* a beautiful and expensive coffee table book with more beautiful photographs of children with Down syndrome was raffled off for more than $125. The people for whose benefit all this had been organized were moving effortlessly through the crowd, excited to see their friends and community, laughing and joking, hugging their friends and family. I recognized a few from Sol Express. I saw a radiant young woman in a gorgeous sparkly dress and stylish haircut. I felt like I had fallen asleep and woken up in Oz.

I picked up a pamphlet from the Down Syndrome Association of Toronto:

> Down syndrome is not a disease, disorder or medical condition. It is wrong to refer to people "afflicted with" or "suffering from" it. Down syndrome is a chromosome variation that has no known cause and occurs once in every 691 live births. Down syndrome is not related to race, nationality, religion, or socioeconomic status ... Early intervention, quality educational programs, a stimulating home environment, good health care, and positive support from family, friends, and the community enable people with DS to develop their full potential and lead fulfilling lives. In adulthood, many people with DS hold jobs, live independently, and enjoy community life, just like everyone else.

Other pamphlets advertised an incredible panoply of services and activities, including alpine skiing, bowling, floor hockey, powerlifting, snowshoeing, bocce, figure skating, golf, soccer, track and field, "business support and coaching to persons with developmental disabilities working in social entrepreneurships throughout Toronto," and "a wholesale bakery and catering company that brings together persons with disabilities and job coaches." A farm vacation program featured an alpaca walk, daily barn chores, egg collection and sorting, performing arts, gardening, baking, woodworking, swimming and water games, canoeing, hiking, dancing and drumming, international theme days, movies, art sessions with guest artists, and a take-home souvenir book. Other organizations offered training in singing, filmmaking, independent living, the visual arts, yoga, dance, digital imaging, resume writing, library fun, and meditation. And then, of course, there was Sol Express, for the lucky ten participants who could be part of it. If only Martha had been alive and living in Toronto, how she would have loved all this.

There was also information on the latest educational research: "Effective methods exist for teaching each individual," one pamphlet said, advocating teaching to the person's strengths and inclusion in regular classes. I wondered what Martha could have achieved if she'd had this kind of education, if she had had more speech therapy to help her speak clearly, if we could have helped her articulate her hopes and dreams. Maybe, like some individuals with Down syndrome today, she could have completed high school, even gone on to postsecondary education as some people with Down syndrome are beginning to do. Maybe she could have had a regular job and even married or had a long-term partner.

My head was reeling as I made my way to my seat in the auditorium for the performances that followed the reception. The talented cast of *Rare* performed a scene from the show, and a group of dancers did a rousing Gangnam Style dance that brought the audience to its feet. Then there were speeches by young adults with Down syndrome, like Angel Blainey. The program notes said: "Angel is a very accomplished happy teenager. She loves sports, arts, and especially creating recipes in the kitchen. She has just come back from Hawaii where she went zip lining and snorkeling in the ocean with sea turtles and dolphins." Another speaker, Emily Boycott, was an "accomplished Special Olympian" who had travelled to Shanghai and Athens for competitions. They were astonishing teenagers – talented, confident, and articulate – who had a stream of accomplishments and read from speeches they'd written themselves. One of them said forcefully, confidently, "I am a human being. I am not a mistake."

The evening was almost relentlessly upbeat, but there were a few presentations that at least alluded to the challenges of raising a child with Down syndrome, even today. A video made by a mother documented her child's first day of school. It was humorous and affectionate, but her child was still in diapers and had trouble with stairs and needed help eating and dressing. I watched the young girl's older sister with attention as she helped her mother with her sister's care and played with her; her younger sister needed help but was obviously loved and appreciated. The film reflected a life of "wonderful perfect ordinariness," as one speaker put it.

There were only a few moments when I felt the ring of the hard truth of my own family's experience; there were clearly things that were still hard to say. In one of the videos, a mother spoke of the huge shock of the diagnosis and admitted that for a while after the first month she had wanted her daughter to die. In another, the father of a young man who worked in a factory and played hockey with a regular men's hockey team recounted how his son now did everything his parents were told he would never do, including being physically coordinated and travelling on his own.

Everyone clapped long and loudly when it was announced that the last institution in Alberta for people with intellectual disabilities would be closing (in the end, it didn't, and there are still institutions similar to the Rideau Regional Centre operating in several provinces). All the people with Down syndrome in attendance appeared to have been raised at home or home-schooled or had lived in small group homes but were still in contact with their families. Yet the parents were mainly white, well-off, and college-educated, and their children were the elite of children with Down syndrome – there were obviously still issues of exclusion, privilege, and opportunity. I couldn't help wondering, where are the others? Where were the people who couldn't afford to home school their kids or pay for expensive lessons or vacations? Where were the kids with Down syndrome whose parents were working at one or more precarious jobs and had little time or leftover energy to support them in their studies or advocate for them at school? There were still many ugly truths, such as that an estimated 40 percent to 70 percent of girls with intellectual disabilities will be sexually victimized by the age of eighteen, that many adults with developmental disabilities live in isolation and poverty or in group homes not much better than the large institutions, that many still suffer from a lack of choice in living arrangements and unwarranted restrictions on their freedom.

Although I was deeply heartened by the achievements of this group of people, ironically, I was still conscious of being an outsider. I talked to one man who was a single father to his only child, who had Down syndrome. When I told him that my sister had been put in an institution, he said, oblivious to the pain of my family's hard choices: "I could never do that. How could anyone do that?"

The next week, I went to a more intimate Sol Express talent night for the L'Arche community. There were perhaps forty or fifty people in our familiar rehearsal space, many from L'Arche homes, some arriving in wheelchairs or walking with canes and some being assisted by others. It was down-to-earth and homey; almost everyone knew each other, and there was conversation all around me. I imagined my sister as she might have been had she been part of this community. It was a delightful evening, full of appreciation, humour, respect, and love. As I watched the performances, I thought to myself that perhaps there had been at least some of this at the hospital school too; I hope so. There must have been love and affection there, too, some of the time, with some of the staff or other residents – oh, I hope so, Martha, I hope so. At least I know my sister had a good life in the end, after she left the school; she was loved and cherished by others, if not by me.

The next ten weeks of rehearsal were among the happiest in my life. I felt like I was in love. I was in love ... not with any one person but with all of the people at Sol Express and the process of making art with them and, especially, dancing with them. I felt a welling up of love, and of my need to love. It was the love I had never been allowed to feel before, a love that had dared not speak its name (which, in my case, was not only homosexuality, as it turned out), a love I had been ashamed of and that had never had a chance to be, a blocked ability to love that had affected all my relationships. The secret me that I had guarded for so long was suddenly larger, encompassed more people, had a life that was more than mourning. It opened out into joy and the end of my psychic captivity; it was my own rebirth. At the same time, I acknowledged a terrible truth: I hadn't even understood Martha as having feelings, as a soul needing to be loved. Forgive me, my sister, my dear sister. L'Arche had saved me; it had given me a place to put that love, a second chance.

Tuesday became my favourite day of the week, because that was the day I was with Sol Express. Every Tuesday I danced for you, Martha, out of joy and love. I explored and created, gave and received, created meaning and new experience with this wonderful group. I came home restored, happy, steadier, and deeply satisfied. I wondered how I could be so fortunate as to be able to do what I absolutely loved, and how surprising it was that I absolutely loved what I had most feared.

There was a wonderful moment when working with Sol Express ceased to be about the past and started to be about the future. Something had changed, and I was no longer hamstrung by some leftover internal psychic structure but living a new narrative. I felt alive to the new forms I (and we) could create, to the openness of possibility.

One of my favourite things was going home on the bus and subway with the others at the end of the day, because we usually had a chance to talk. It was so different from how I had felt in the old days when out in public with Martha. I felt no embarrassment whatsoever; I was proud to know Richard and Sarah and William and the others. It was such a simple yet wonderful thing to be able to just walk and talk with them, and yet it meant so much to me. They were people who were becoming dear to me.

Each of them I found beautiful in a different way, and the remarkable thing was that I couldn't imagine them other than as they were. Each one was a complex individual, shaped by a particular life history, and as multidimensional and contradictory as any other individual. They could be cranky or petty or bored or insensitive, just like the rest of us.

I also became aware of their ongoing struggles for acceptance and respect. One participant told me that people often taunted him on the bus or subway and asked me why people did that. I could only say some people were ignorant or had a need to be cruel or laugh at others so they wouldn't be the ones laughed at, but, really, I had no satisfying answer. And later I was heartbroken when one of the participants had to move to the other side of the city because the group home he had lived in for twenty years was being changed to a temporary residence. I came to see that the systems in place for people with disabilities, though better than in my sister's day, were still far from perfect.

Sometimes, I felt a pain in my chest. Sometimes, I didn't know what I was feeling. Was it grief, sadness, happiness, or just the discomfort of change?

Going to Sol Express freed up something else in me. A week after beginning with them, I got off the train in Kingston for a brief stopover on my way to give a talk in Ottawa. For the first time in many years, I went to see Eva Zaretsky, the woman who had cared for my sister for twenty-nine years, who had been her second mother. She was delighted to see me. And I discovered that my relationship with her had also changed, that I could finally be with her open-heartedly, without shame or pain. I told her that with each passing year I appreciated even more all that she had done for my sister, and all the love she had given her. I presented her with a little gift, a beautiful book of photographs of the Sol Express participants wearing colourful and whimsical masks they had created, and I thanked her from the bottom of my heart for her kindness and generosity to Martha and to my family. She told me I was always welcome in her home and that she hoped I would visit often. She asked me to convey her regards to my parents.

Just as I had finally gotten over my fears of people with Down syndrome, I learned that it may soon become a thing of the past. For one thing, with fetal testing, most women who know they are bearing a child with Down syndrome choose to abort. Down syndrome is now almost completely absent from Iceland and Denmark. The young actors of *Rare* had addressed this head on, calling for mothers not to abort their Down syndrome children, asserting their right to life, and now that I knew them, I had great sympathy for this position. Other medical advances will greatly alter the lives of those who are born with Down syndrome. The *New Scientist* reported in April 2013 that the first drug specifically designed to lessen cognitive impairment in Down syndrome was being tested on humans. Gene editing may also address specific medical issues arising from Down syndrome, or eliminate it altogether, though such research is highly controversial in the disability community.

A few days before our performance, Matt designed a beautiful poster that showed the main characters of the play entering a cavern in a mountain. As I looked at it, I recognized with a start the parallel with the beautiful quest dream I had had as a teenager where I climbed the mountain with the doctor, danced in the sparkling river at the top, and then went down inside the mountain through the museum to meet the old wise woman who sent me on my way. How odd it was that after Martha's ashes were scattered, I had ended up whitewater rafting with people with Down syndrome, and now here I was involved in a play about frustrated love and siblings who looked after each other and accompanied each other on a quest up a mountain, then went inside it and finally re-emerged to meet a wise shaman, who told the lovelorn girl that she was not alone. And on the stage the whole time was an old wise woman who slowly tore up bits of paper upon which the audience had written their hopes and fears.

It was a beautiful and inspiring production, and the audience loved it. *Torn* featured poetry, original music played by live musicians, acting, clowning, and dance. Everyone had a part to play, appropriate to their abilities. It was entirely fitting that I

That's my body forming the entrance to the cave in this poster for *Torn*.

was a clown representing Pride, one of the Seven Deadly Sins encountered by the sibling protagonists, and later a seething, churning red blot of emotion as I and another dancer roiled under a stretchy, red fabric.

So many important people in my life came to see *Torn*, particularly those who had witnessed my pain and helped me in my struggle to heal: Mark; my son, Ariel; Athina, Margot, and even those who didn't really know my story, like my aunt's new partner and some of my students. But by far the most significant thing for me was that my sister Kate drove from Ottawa to see it and afterwards came backstage to meet the cast. Only she truly knew what this meant to me, what an enormous healing this was.

Her own relationship with Martha had been different and far easier than mine because by the time Kate was born, Martha had already been sent to the institution. Kate had never suffered that wrenching separation and confusion that I had, but she had experienced the misery of our trips to Smiths Falls and our tortured family dynamics when it came to Martha. Now, her eyes were shining with tears as she told me how much she loved the performance, how Martha would have loved it, and how much she would have loved to perform in it. We cried together, knowing that Martha had never reached her full potential, had never had that opportunity – and there was also a surge of regret that others weren't able to see it – particularly my mother and father.

But mostly I was ecstatic, filled with a sense of wonder that I had been able to turn such a painful part of my life into something joyous and beautiful, that I was no longer trapped in the pain – and I recognized that Martha had also given me this. Looking back over the path that I had taken – recovering from my breakdown, doing all that therapy, going back to university and graduating, revisiting the hospital school – I realized that it was not simply that I had recovered from Martha's birth and institutionalization, it's that I was eventually able to work her being back into the fabric of my life.

After the performance, I was ready to make my commitment, and I formally become a volunteer at L'Arche. L'Arche provided a home for me, the first place in my life where both my sister and I were welcome and loved for our unique talents and our common humanity.

Around the same time as the Sol Express performances, Margot invited me to go see the documentary *Softening,* by Kelly O'Brien, at Toronto's Hot Docs film festival. She knew the film-maker and thought I would be interested in the film because it was about a young mother's response to giving birth to a severely disabled child.

O'Brien's son Teddy was born with both physical and mental impairments that arose from an infection in her womb. Teddy couldn't speak or hold up his head; he could only move around the house with the help of a rigged-up contraption that helped him keep his head erect. He would always be dependent on others and require specialized care. His mother was devastated at his birth, totally grief-stricken, and barely managed to con-tinue. As she is quoted saying in publicity for the film, "I'm not really one of those parents of a kid with special needs who thinks it's a gift from God or a blessing in disguise." Yet she was some-how persuaded to use her camera to document the first years of his life, although she couldn't bear to look at the footage or at photographs of those early days for many years. Even in the film she eventually made, she is hardly able to speak her feel-ings. For five years she was as frozen in grief as my mother.

It was the first time that I had heard another mother speak of it, the first time I had seen that grief represented in art. This woman's pain was raw and laid bare for all to see. Kelly O'Brien's camera captures so clearly her son's utter vulnerability and helplessness and also his need for love; it is there in the way he looks at his mother, his father, and his older sister. His look is so open, so vulnerable. And in the most beautiful and searing scene in the film, it is there as he reaches out clumsily, with a look of absolute wonder on his face, to lovingly touch his new-born infant sister. I thought of that huge collection of cast-off people, "the friendless" – those abandoned children at the hospital school, so alone and at the mercy of others – and I wept.

Teddy's mother was frozen in grief, but, as was true in my family, his father was more able to form a relationship, to toss Teddy in the air and make him laugh, to take joy in his laughter. And in the film, as you witness Teddy's response to such playfulness, you can see that despite his severe disabilities, he can feel joy and every other human feeling. His is a life still worth living.

In the question-and-answer session after the screening, the filmmaker said it took her five years to want to know her child; it took her five years to love him. That was the arrow that pierced my heart. For the first time I realized that Martha's institutionalization really hadn't been good for my mother either, even though she thought it had saved her. Now, I saw that it had locked her into that pain forever; she had never had those five years to come to love, because Martha had been sent away at twenty months. That's why my mother had remained frozen. That's why she couldn't heal. Her process of adapting to the reality of my sister's condition was arrested before it could be worked through. Because she never had the opportunity to move through her pain, she believed herself incapable of loving her child. I think that's why she hated herself and was so hard on herself. I think that's one of the reasons her heart constricted over time in the way it did.

It was a devastating film. I started crying as I watched it and then continued after, unable to stop, for there were so many resonances for me. I went home and lay on my bed; bubbles of pain rose and broke like blisters. There again was my mother's inexhaustible grief, her ocean of grief, her frozen grief, her grief without end. I cried even harder when Mark reminded me that grief is unrequited love. And I felt my inner child's helplessness because nothing I could ever do would change that grief; my love had no power, all the feelings I had for my mother could change nothing. I hadn't been good enough to make things right. As far as my mother's grief was concerned, there was no closure anywhere.

.The other thing I saw in the film was how the mother leaned on her daughter, who ran around in her princess costume, just as I had. The question of what the mother needed her daughter to be was not asked in the film, though perhaps it was implied. Like me, she was the smart one, the strong one, the dependable one, the repository and symbol of her mother's hope for the future. She carried it all for her mother; she shone, she excelled at all things, especially goodness. I hoped she would not crash and burn as I had.

Through Sol Express, I also met a researcher doing her PhD research on the impact of institutionalization on families of people with developmental disabilities. She was interviewing former residents and their families and interviewed me; later, surprisingly, my parents and Kate also agreed to be interviewed. It was a new feeling that our painful experience was of interest to someone, was deemed worthy of study. Perhaps our experience would even help others in the future.

Kate was at first worried that the researcher would think my mother was a horrible person for some of the things she would likely say about Martha. But the interviewer was wonderfully compassionate. She had encountered such attitudes before and had come to understand them. What she gently suggested to my sister and me was that it had been too dangerous for some mothers to love their own children. And I thought, yes, that is the right way to think of it. And even in spite of that, in some ways, she did.

One day, my mother began spontaneously talking about Martha, something she never used to do. I'd noticed that she had become less reticent and more emotional; something had been freed up in her through the passage of time, or perhaps it was the Alzheimer's that helped her forget her pain. Even dementia has its upside, I realized.

I was startled by her sudden excursions into memory, but grateful, too, because there was still so much about my mother's experience that I didn't know or understand. There was so much that my parents had never talked about or that I had been afraid to ask. My mother was willing to share now, but with both of my parents much of the past had either disappeared or it would reappear in strange new forms, such as when my father asked my sister Kate, "Remember when we used to pick raspberries in the garden in Port Arthur?" He was actually talking about the 1920s, and the girl he used to do that with was his older sister, not his daughter born in 1960. And so I now listened to my mother with both alarm and curiosity. Sometimes the story changed with each telling, though at other times she transformed my understanding.

"When Martha was born, I cried for six weeks," she told me one day, "and then I was ashamed of myself. I had to do something. I had to find a way to keep going."

I thought to myself, *You never stopped crying. You never got over it.* But I listened anyway.

"I started to do research, and I saw that although nothing could have been done in Martha's case, there were a lot of things that could happen during labour that could also result in retardation, like lack of oxygen. And most women had to labour alone, because the men were not even allowed in the labour room. They had to sit in the waiting room or even go home. They couldn't help their wives at all, and they could only visit during visiting hours. So a group of us tried to make some changes, and that's how I ended up president of the Natural Childbirth Association. And we did make some changes, and I'm proud of that: we got fathers into labour rooms, and we promoted pre-natal classes so women and their husbands would know what to expect."

That was the first time I'd heard her make that connection between her activism with the Natural Childbirth Association and Martha's birth. I was so glad to hear it, to know that she did not just suffer and endure and feel horrible about herself. She had also tried to make things better for others; she had tried to make her experience useful, and it was – it did change things. She had made the best of it, on her own terms. I admire her for that, and I am proud to trace my own activism through this lineage.

But she was only warming up. She told me several other stories and clarified some points of chronology that I'd been confused about. Then she told me that after Martha's birth her own father had gone "on a toot." His brother, my great-uncle David, who worked around the corner from my grandfather's hair salon, received a call from a friend, who told him that my grandfather "wasn't doing so well" and had been seen lurching drunkenly across the Laurier Bridge and that someone had better go find him and take him home. And then she told me that the friend told David that my grandfather had said, "What have I done that such a thing was visited on my daughter?"

Wait a minute, I said to myself, *wasn't it my father who got drunk after Martha was born, and wasn't it his friend Victor Stirling who heard my father say, "What have I done that such a thing was visited on my daughter?" and wasn't he speaking about what had been visited upon Martha, not my mother?* Did both my father and my grandfather get drunk? Did all the men get drunk? Was that their way of coping? Did they all say the same thing, in the same words, or had the story become mixed up with other things? Which was the true story, if either? As she spoke, I could feel this narrative I had been trying to reconstruct slipping away from me. I would never know the full truth of what happened, and certainly not my mother's experience. Those days in 1958 and 1960 and 1973 were irretrievably gone.

Another day, my mother handed me a small notebook she had found among the possessions she had brought with her to the retirement residence. Either she had found it accidentally tucked in with other things, or perhaps she had even deliberately held onto it. It was a small yellow spiral-bound notebook with "Martha's notebook" written on the front in my mother's delicate handwriting. I opened it up and saw the familiar letters, the columns of printing, that now seem like poems to me.

[in green marker]
GO
C
victe

[in red marker]
CONTEN
SI
febwar2
1989 VOY1
1008Z
39
...
[in black marker]
GOOD
BYE
BLAHS
COLDT-
[in red] EDITORIA
L4

[in yellow marker]
WE
JACL
OR

[in red marker]
SEE
OOOO
MPM

[in red marker]
snow
white

I smiled as I read my sister's long-ago scribblings, the reference to me (Go see Victoria), the women's magazine table of contents banishing the blahs, and the fairy tale ending.

"I want you to have it," my mother said, and I gratefully accepted her gift.

21

Remember
Every Name

On December 9, 2013, I sat in the visitor's gallery of the provincial legislature to hear an all-party apology by Ontario premier Kathleen Wynne, opposition leader Andrea Horvath, and Conservative leader Tim Hudak for the treatment of residents of the Huronia Regional Centre, the sister institution to the one my sister had attended. The oldest and most notorious of such institutions, Huronia had operated for more than a century, closing only in 2009, the same year that the Rideau Regional Centre shut its doors.

The public apology was one of the conditions of the settlement of the class action lawsuit launched by former Huronia residents and their families. A similar class action for former residents of the Rideau Regional Centre was also winding its way through the court system but had not yet come to trial, though once the Huronia case was settled out of court, there was more hope that the Rideau case would also reach a settlement before the vulnerable and aging former residents were called on to testify.

Three months earlier, in September 2013, I had gone to the court house to hear the first day of the Huronia court case. I had only contacted the law firm and the litigation guardians a few days earlier, although I had known about these court cases for almost a year. It had taken me that long to find my courage. I did not know what to make of the class action because what the litigants were saying about the treatment of residents was so at odds with the mental image I had grown up with about the Rideau Regional Centre, still the "hospital school" to me in now-discredited politically incorrect parlance.

I had learned a lot about myself and about Down syndrome in general and a bit more about my sister's later life with the Zaretskys, but it bothered me that I still knew almost nothing about her time in the institution during the most formative years of her life. Now, I was finally ready to learn what I could about what her life may have been like there, and I also hoped to meet other siblings of people who had been institutionalized. What was their experience? Had anyone else ever felt as I had?

That day in September, about forty people gathered in the waiting room outside the court room, and I met the litigants and the litigation guardians for the class action for the first time. What struck me first was the palpable terror of the two litigants, former Huronia residents Marie Slark and Patricia Seth, at the prospect of having to testify, and then I was struck by their grim determination to do so. They were clearly well supported by their litigation guardians, Marilyn and Jim Dolmage, who were also quietly determined. The assembled crowd was dismayed to discover that the court had been unexpectedly adjourned to the next day, without explanation, and the litigants and their supporters were suddenly deprived of their purpose, unsure of what was happening.

No one wanted to simply turn around and go home, especially since representatives of the media were there, an opportunity not to be wasted. Groups of "survivors," as they were now called, gathered together and talked to the media and one another, and from them I learned for the first time about their experiences in their own words. Various former residents came forward to speak, some of them encountering each other for the first time in decades, yet all telling similar stories. One of the litigants spoke of Huronia as being like a prison, of being forced to clean toilets with toothbrushes, of being given the "water treatment" as punishment, of being forcibly drugged for misbehaviour. Another man wept as he recounted the posttraumatic stress he still suffered from witnessing a deaf and blind resident being hit and killed by a train as the resident tried to run away.

As former residents spoke, others identified themselves and corroborated their stories. They talked of still having nightmares, of being treated like dirt. I had a strange sense of déjà vu because I had been involved for many years with Indigenous peoples' struggles and had heard so many similar stories about residential schools. Then I wrestled with my own initial disbelief, my desire for it not to be true, even my suspicion that the survivors must be exaggerating or that such abuse had been isolated, only to gradually realize that such stories were too prevalent, too detailed, not to be true and systemic. Now that previous experience circumvented easy denial on my part of abuse and neglect in the case of the "hospital schools." Sadly, it seemed that the people who worked in such institutions and who I had imagined as cheerfully professional were not necessarily any more enlightened than the general population when it came to their attitudes towards people with intellectual disabilities, and some were clearly twisted people who horribly abused their power to inflict their anger, disgust, and hatred on extremely vulnerable people. Regardless of whether or not an individual had suffered physical or sexual or emotional abuse, what was becoming clearer to me was that the system of isolation and incarceration was itself damaging to human flourishing.

A number of the people present had come to honour a sister or brother who had been institutionalized. The litigation guardian Marilyn Dolmage had had a brother at Orillia. He died there at the age of eight, and she showed me a photograph of a beautiful little boy that she had met only once – when she saw him dead in his casket. A quiet man who appeared to be in his eighties told me he was there for his sister, who had died at Huronia more than fifty years previously. Here were others who were as haunted as I was by what had happened to their siblings so many years ago. The isolation many of us had lived with for decades was ending.

The next morning, we assembled again, but this time the lawyers announced at the outset that the case had been settled out of court, so there would be no trial and hence no testimony. The settlement offered was $35 million (up to $35,000 for individual claimants, depending on the severity of abuse), a government apology, and a memorial plaque to be raised at the site of the Huronia institution. A confirmation hearing was set up for December.

I was relieved for the witnesses that they would not be subjected to cross-examination but also disappointed that I would not hear their testimony about life at the institution. The litigants also had mixed emotions. They wanted and needed to tell what they had gone through, and it was important that their voices be heard, that this painful history be fully documented and not forgotten. Luckily, in the days before and immediately after the tentative settlement, there was a flurry of media attention, in particular a dogged string of articles in the *Toronto Star* about Huronia and the class action. Clearly, someone at the paper was keeping up the public pressure, refusing to let the story die, putting pressure on the government for a public apology.

One morning, I picked up the newspaper and then couldn't take my eyes away from the shocking photograph on the front page. It showed the Huronia graveyard, the ground completely covered with stone grave markers, all lying flat on the ground and squeezed together so there was no space between them. They were all without names, blank except for four-digit numbers. I couldn't get the image of those nameless grave markers out of my mind. There in front of me was clear and vivid evidence of the cruel attitudes that had so traumatized me as a child, the belief that people like my sister were not worth knowing or remembering, their very existence so shameful that no one would acknowledge their relationship to them, even in death. They were out of sight, out of mind, their very identities obliterated in a final violent erasure, as if they had never been.

Ironically, the institution began to put names on gravestones after 1958, the year of my sister's birth. Previously, only registration numbers were marked, "to protect the privacy of

Nameless, numbered grave markers at Huronia Cemetery.

the resident and their family," I read somewhere. I could imagine some superintendent or bureaucrat saying that, in a tone of unctuous professional compassion, but clearly the numbered markers were really intended to make sure no one found out that you had a person with an intellectual disability in your family. To me, those words were an abomination, exemplifying the appalling secrecy and shame I had grown up with and the trauma I had experienced in witnessing my sister's dehumanization, not to mention the incalculable harm my sister experienced because of such attitudes. In the image of the numbered graves, I finally had something I could show people to express what we had lived through and been harmed by. Such treatment was so painfully disrespectful, and yet that photograph helped me understand why I had been so upset at what had seemed to me to be the cavalier disposal of my own sister's ashes by my parents. I felt terrible pain when I looked at that photograph, but I also felt vindicated. Finally, it was visible. It was recognized. It was known, no longer a shameful secret.

Going to the courthouse and meeting the litigants, the litigation guardians, and other siblings, friends, and family finally gave me the courage to contact the Ministry of Community and Social Services to request access to my sister's institutional file. Maybe I would find letters written by my father to the institution, asking why his daughter should have learned the words "Shut up, kid!" Maybe there would be records of her competitions in the Special Olympics. Maybe I would find out things I wished I'd known earlier or wished I'd never known.

I sent the required documents proving I had a legal right to my sister's records. It took eight months and a second application before I finally gained access to my sister's file. In the meantime, I turned to the people involved with the court cases to learn what I could about daily life in the institutions. I talked with Vici Clarke, the litigation guardian for the Rideau lawsuit. She was also a sibling: her brother had been sent to Rideau briefly, and both were still haunted and traumatized by that experience. I spoke with another sibling who strongly suspected from her brother's behaviour and reactions that he had been sexually abused at another institution, but since he couldn't speak, this was difficult to verify. Vici told me about David McKillop, the litigant for the Rideau class action, who had been sent to Rideau at the age of five because he had autism. He was now in his sixties and married but unable to have children because of a physical assault that had occurred at the school. In the class action, he stated that Rideau was like a prison, with the dorms locked day and night and basic privacy lacking for toilets and showers. He alleged that he was physically and mentally abused by staff members, punished and humiliated for doing nothing wrong. He also said that he witnessed staff members instruct other residents to physically abuse or attack other residents, that there was an environment of fear.

David was associated with People First, the most militant activist group for people with disabilities, and I began to collect some of People First's slogans, such as "Nothing about us without us" or "An institution is not just a place; it is the way people think" or "Is it because I can't learn or you can't teach?" or "Labels are for jars, not people." Later, I watched the powerful film *The Freedom Tour*, in which members of People First toured western Canada in a bus, interviewing institutional survivors in an effort to raise awareness about the need to close institutions in Alberta, Manitoba, and Saskatchewan.

At the Huronia settlement confirmation hearing in December, the litigants, Marie Slark and Patricia Seth, made a formal statement: "Finally, we have a voice," they said, adding that in the institution they were taught "to keep quiet or get hurt ... No amount of money will give us our lives back. This must never happen to people with disabilities again." And the lead lawyer, Kurt Baert, also gave a prepared statement, in which he said that such institutions were unsafe and unhealthy warehouses for some of the province's most vulnerable citizens, places where they were left to fend for themselves, often without their most basic needs being met, and that many residents were worse off when discharged than they had been when they went in. I thought back to how my sister's speech improved so dramatically within months of her release and what her life might have been like if she'd had better education from the start. The lawyer spoke of reports over the years documenting abuse and neglect that had never resulted in adequate reform. It was a bleak picture, and one very much at odds with what we thought about the Rideau Regional Centre at the time my sister lived there, a place we tried to think of as cheerful and well intentioned, even as it horrified us.

After the successful confirmation of the Huronia lawsuit, the premier announced she would make the formal apology the following Monday in the Ontario Legislature. When I arrived at the legislature on that December morning, I awaited the apology with a mixture of curiosity and skepticism. I wanted to witness this historic occasion, and I also hoped to meet more former residents and their families. But I was also going for the apology itself, even if it was directed primarily to former residents of Huronia. I wanted to be apologized to, I realized. I also wanted my dead sister to be apologized to, so I brought her framed photograph along with me, though I wasn't allowed to take it into the visitor's gallery and had to leave it in my backpack in the cloakroom. But I told myself I would listen to the apology for her as well as for me, that she would be with me in spirit.

I was proud to sit in the gallery with the people associated with the Rideau class action: Vici Clark; her mother, Marion; David McKillop, and David's wife, Eileen. I scanned the galleries for faces I knew and saw a few from L'Arche and one person from Sol Express. There were many other people with intellectual disabilities there, many former residents of Huronia, who otherwise would never have seen the inside of a government legislature. For the first time, they were there not as problems, or dependants, but as citizens.

While we waited, Vici's mother told me some of her own memories of Rideau. I was startled when she described being swarmed by crowds of children in the corridor, and how she, like me, had been horrified and then ashamed of her reactions. It was not just me who had felt that! Unlike my parents, she had fought to keep her son at home and in the community, but her son had been forced to go to Rideau for eighteen months to certify him as toilet-trained and thus eligible for other community services. While there, he was assaulted and had his nose broken. She had been fighting for her son from day one, it seemed, always trying to keep her child out of the system.

That people with intellectual disabilities matter as much as anyone else was what Vici's mother had insisted and fought for, what the premier was now saying, what the disability activists were fighting for. I had so needed my own mother and father to say that, to clearly say they loved and valued my sister. I had so needed to hear them say, "Martha matters." It was also what I had so needed to say to them, to insist upon, but never had, not in so many words. Martha had remained part of our family, but most of the time she had only been endured.

Sadly, my mother in particular hadn't known how to love Martha, and nobody had been there to show her how to do that. I hadn't loved Martha either. We had needed role models. As disability scholar Madeline Burghardt wrote me, "Love is a choice, not a feeling, and if we are told (over and over through cultural discourses, etc.) that some people are not worth loving, then we have not been presented with loving someone 'different' as a choice at all."

Some of my parents' calculation in deciding to institutionalize Martha had been to ensure that their other children's lives would not be dominated by Martha's needs – though, as it turned out, my life was still dominated by the pain of her absence and her dehumanization. Still, in talking with other siblings, I saw that I had indeed enjoyed a freedom that some other siblings hadn't. I had always taken my extraordinary freedom and opportunity to do whatever I wanted with my life for granted, yet my burden was that my freedom had come at the price of Martha's unfreedom. I could do anything, it seemed, my sister nothing. In the terrible logic I had grown up with, I could have my freedom, but not my sister, or I could have my sister, but not my freedom. My mother believed she had the same choice, and she chose her freedom. That is how the choice appeared to my parents in 1960, when only London, Toronto, Barrie, and Oshawa had sheltered workshops (then the only available option for community engagement), when keeping a child with Down syndrome at home was a much bigger and lonelier commitment – particularly for mothers – than it is today.

Finally, the premier and opposition leaders arrived, and in due course the apologies were given. They were both satisfying and unsatisfying, for what words could ever make up for what had happened? Were they truly heartfelt? I knew the apology had been crafted in such a way that the government could apologize without incurring legal liability, which irked me. But still it mattered that the words were said. It was healing to hear them, particularly certain phrases, such as "the deeply flawed model of care" and "the pain you still carry today." Yes, it was good to have those things recognized and acknowledged in public. It was good to hear those in power, those representatives of the broader population, say they were sorry.

Afterwards, at the reception at Queen's Park, I told another researcher about my desire to learn about my sister's stay at Rideau. She promised to introduce me to a former resident at Rideau, a male, who she said had been repeatedly raped for the first three weeks of his stay there, the assaults badly tearing his rectum. *OK,* I thought, with a sinking heart, *it's clear that boys were horribly abused there. Is it too much to hope that the girls were not?* I was too depressed to follow up on her offer.

I thought back to my sister and that embarrassing period when, as a teenager and young woman, Martha would sometimes crawl on the laps of boys – even my brother. We always assumed that my sister's inappropriate, overt, and suggestive behaviour with young males was simply because she didn't know any better, that her lack of restraint was naive and innocent behaviour, just one more indication of her low intelligence. But it was possible that her behaviour had been a sign of something else entirely. It had never occurred to me that she might have been sexually abused at Rideau, causing her to lose her sense of appropriate boundaries. I hope that was not the case. I don't know if that possibility ever occurred to my mother or father, given how hushed up institutional sexual abuse was in those days. It was only much later that its prevalence became public knowledge. I have since talked with people who have first-hand knowledge of female residents who were impregnated by staff at Rideau.

Again, I felt the great wall of the unknown, the past a great blank nothingness of what is forever lost. I sent David McKillop Martha's picture, but he told me he was not in touch with any of the women who were at Rideau when Martha lived there (he knew fewer women survivors because of the institution's policy of sexual segregation). Perhaps somewhere, with a lot of effort,

I could find a staff member or former resident still living who remembered her, but what then? Her past was gone; it had disappeared down the sinkhole of time. I googled "Rideau Regional Centre" on the internet and saw the names of several former staff members listed as deceased in the online books of condolences set up by funeral homes: one for a woman who had worked at Rideau for thirty-one years, another a former teacher. At the library at Smiths Falls, the librarian I talked to had also worked at Rideau for a couple of decades ... but long after my sister's stay there. I found some reminiscences by former staff members in the library's holdings: "It was a happy place," one staff member remembered. "I loved my job." I pray that she knew and liked my sister. But I also knew that such statements were also often indicative of the inability of many staff members embedded within the institutions to examine or acknowledge that the system itself was a fundamentally unjust and wrong-headed model of care. I later talked with another sibling whose sister had been horribly drugged at Rideau and who struggled in vain to receive decent compensation for her sister through the class action process.

I reluctantly came to accept that while I might find out a bit more, I would never truly know what it was like for my sister to live in that institution. I might be able to fill in a few more details, but most of my sister's life – and certainly her subjective experience of it – was lost to me. I will never be able to retrieve it.

There was still a lot to learn from the Sol Express performers, however. The dynamics of the group had changed, as everything changes, and for a while things didn't go as smoothly, or perhaps I just wasn't as starry-eyed – it was no longer my moment of discovery. The complications of everyday life reappeared. Some days, I didn't even feel like going. Now, there was the sheer hard work of living together, working together, and finding ways to accommodate our petty differences, even at Sol Express. I knew this was the phase of integration, working all that I had learned into my day-to-day life. I feared that my second production with Sol Express would be a terrible letdown after the first.

But it wasn't. It was different. The new production was inspired by the lawsuits, the premier's apology, and the sorry history of institutionalization, which the Sol Express participants had thankfully never experienced. But they knew about the attitudes that had spawned the institutions, because they are still around. We did not want to further traumatize members of our audience or theatre group who had been institutionalized, so we worked through metaphor, with the theme of birds, inspired in part by Maya Angelou's poem *The Caged Bird Sings:* we were caged birds, birds that became used to our cages and forgot that freedom existed or died without tasting it, or who still sang of freedom, newly freed birds that rejoiced in our liberty, or birds who had never been caged. Miraculously, it all came together in a beautiful and original new production. At the end, I walked in the mournful procession honouring those who had suffered and died in the institutions, and I joined the other Sol Express participants in a joyful dance of freedom for those who had been released. It was so healing to be part of that honouring and remembering, an honouring and remembering that included my sister and included me.

Others were also determined to honour and remember the survivors of the institutions. A group of Huronia survivors, relatives, and concerned citizens formed a committee known as Remember Every Name to restore and protect the neglected graveyard at Orillia and to mark the actual gravesites of the more than 1,400 people buried there. As I had seen in that shocking newspaper photo, many graves were identified merely with case numbers rather than names, but most had no gravestones or markers at all. Now, following a request by survivors, an archaeological company had been hired by the government to locate unmarked graves and search records to match a list of names with their birth and death dates. Remember Every Name was determined that every Huronia resident buried there would be honoured and remembered, their names marked in stone.

Finally, eight months after I applied for it, the photocopy of my sister's institutional file arrived – all 373 pages of it, an intimidating package. I stayed up all night reading the many medical tests that documented my sister's frequent illnesses at Rideau and the notices of when her ward was put in quarantine. I saw that she almost died of pneumonia in 1969, when she went into severe cardiac and respiratory distress. I read the assessments of her intelligence and social development made by various "experts" from the day she had arrived in my father's arms to shortly before she left the institution. I read my parents' letters to the superintendent seeking information or permission to bring her home at various times and learned only then of the birthday parties they had arranged for her but never attended. I saw my parents through the social workers' eyes – a painful, painful transit – and learned how my sister had ended up at the Zaretskys. I was confronted by my parents' adamant refusal to take Martha back and how little involvement they had in her life, though I also saw how little information the institution shared with them and the perfunctory tone of the institution's responses to their letters. I stared endlessly at the two photos, one of a small bewildered toddler and the other a defiant eleven-year-old girl; I stared at the thirteen years of my sister's life reduced to 373 pages, offering me only a limited and distorted view. I was so grateful for that sheaf of papers, but in some ways it made the loss of knowledge about her life so final.

Maybe I will meet someone else who will remember my sister from her days at the institution, but it has been a long time now, over forty years since she was discharged. I might have asked

Mrs. Zaretsky what she remembered from when Martha first arrived from Smiths Falls – but I can't now, because my sister's saviour and protector has died. Maybe I'll locate a staff member who will remember Martha clearly, or more likely only vaguely, since she was one of thousands of children who passed through those crowded wards. Or maybe I'll just let it be.

Still, when I least expect it, there are new discoveries. Out of the blue my mother told me that the round wooden tabletop that we used to lay on our regular dining-room table to enlarge it for family gatherings had been made by boys at the Ottawa sheltered workshop that my parents helped to set up. That was the table at which we celebrated so many birthday celebrations, Thanksgivings, Christmas dinners ... the table where my parents, siblings, aunts, uncles, grandparents, cousins, babies, friends, and Martha, too, had shared so many feasts, so many stories, so much laughter, where we had given thanks at various moments in our lives ... such wonderful memories. Down syndrome had never been far from us, even if we weren't always aware of it at the time.

At Mrs. Zaretsky's memorial service, I met her son for the first time, and he told me he had worked for the Ministry of Community and Social Services in the 1970s to deinstitutionalize as many disabled people as possible. In those days, keeping children at home was not necessarily better, he said – more times than he cared to remember he had found people with intellectual disabilities hidden away, even tied up, in the back-rooms or basements of their parents' houses, hideously neglected and abused. Mistreatment was not the sole province of the institutions; in some cases, they might even have been the lesser evil, though far from an ideal model of care.

Another discovery was even more startling. An old friend wrote me: "I really only saw Martha a few times. And when I did, we [all] danced to Beatles music. My prevailing memory of her is one of her joy in dancing." But how could that be? I have absolutely no memory of us all dancing together. In fact, I had confidently written in an earlier draft of this memoir that I had never danced with Martha, which seemed to epitomize my inability to accept her for who she was, meet her on her own terms, connect with her, love her, and be joyful with her. But here was the evidence that it was not just my parents' memory that was fickle. I am so glad to learn that I did dance joyfully with Martha, even if I can't remember it. I treasure the fact that she loved to dance as much as I do – in that joy we were truly sisters.

In the end, I continue to contemplate the totality of my sister's life and my relationship to her. I think about how there's more than one way to lose someone. There's early death. There's institutionalization. There's Alzheimer's. There's addiction. There's cancer. There's heart disease. There are accidents. Murder. As pop psychologist John Bradshaw once said, life is really a long series of farewells. Nothing lasts. Everything changes. You lose everything in the end, including the world, and in the end the world loses you. Endings and beginnings, destructions and creations, memory and forgetting, closing down and opening up, both loss and new possibility exist in every moment of our lives, and it is perhaps that truth that is the most profound that Martha taught me and continues to teach me. Out of pain can come new beginnings.

Even though I could go on and search for more information about my sister's life, I no longer need to. I've done what I needed to do. I've let go of that old pain. The me that was so traumatized by my loss of Martha, by her dehumanization and my own, has found a kind of peace.

For so many years that hurting child I was could hint only through the mute language of the body, the bewildering ache in my left arm, at my lonely, wordless grief. Now, finally, after all those years, I've explored and understood my private pain. The me who could not speak has spoken.

Now, finally, I know that my pain is not unique, but part of a collective experience, and my telling but one strand of a collective healing.

And Martha?

I wish I could say to her the opposite of "Shut up, kid!"

She should have the last word.

marTha
Daddy
mommy

Postscript

The compensation awarded to survivors of Huronia, Rideau, and other institutions proved to be disappointing and much lower than that awarded to residential school survivors and other survivors of institutional abuse. Many survivors received only $2,000. The funds left over from the settlement were disbursed for the general benefit of survivors through an adjudication process that included some input from the litigants and litigation guardians. In 2017, L'Arche Toronto Sol Express received some of this funding to research and develop a new play, *Birds Make Me Think about Freedom,* which built upon our previous work inspired by the premier's apology and which was guided by and based on the experiences of institutional survivors, their families, and friends. I was the co-lead of this project, with Cheryl Zinyk.

Birds Make Me Think about Freedom won a Patron's Pick Award at the 2018 Toronto Fringe Festival and subsequently received Canada Council funding for further development. It was performed in March 2019 at "Flying to Freedom," an event hosted by Community Living Ontario to mark the tenth anniversary of the closing of the institutions in this province. Further performances are planned in Toronto and elsewhere in Ontario. The Family Alliance of Ontario's Uncovering the People's History project is also gathering stories of survivors and family members to responsibly share them with the broader public. It can be contacted via its website.

Acknowledgments

I offer my deepest thanks to my partner, Mark Fawcett; my children, Claire and Ariel; my brother, Eric; and especially my sister Kate. Thanks also to Graig Moriarty for all his help.

I owe more than I can say to Cheryl Zinyk, Matt Rawlings, and the performers of Sol Express; Marilyn, Jim, and Leah Dolmage; Marie Slark and Pat Seth; and Vici Clarke, David McKillop, Colleen Orrick, and Madeline Burghardt. My profound gratitude to the late Jean Vanier and all the people who make up L'Arche around the world, especially L'Arche Toronto and my cousin Louise Cummings. I cannot thank the woman I have called Eva Zaretsky (now deceased) and her daughter Kathy enough for their twenty-nine years of loving care for my sister; they have shown me the way.

I wish to heartily thank those who read and commented on earlier versions of the manuscript: Madeline Burghardt, Margaret Christakos, Marilyn Dolmage, Mark Fawcett, Margot Francis, Kate Freeman, Claire Freeman-Fawcett, Athina Goldberg, Ruth Howard, Elizabeth Langley, Simon Ortiz, Soraya Peerbaye, Shelagh Rogers, Cheryl Zinyk, and Rachel Zolf. This book was transformed through their comments and suggestions. I also thank Beth Lavender of Smiths Falls Public Library for her research assistance.

I owe my profound gratitude to Darcy Cullen, acquisitions editor at UBC Press, for believing in and advocating for this book, and I also wish to thank my three anonymous external reviewers, substantive editor Diane Young, production editor Holly Keller, my perceptive and very helpful copy editor Lesley Erickson, proofreader Judith Earnshaw, designer Jessica Sullivan for the beautiful cover (with assistance from Mark Fawcett), publicist Kerry Kilmartin, editorial coordinator Nadine Pedersen, publisher's assistant Valerie Nair, marketing manager Laraine Coates, and Melissa Pitts, director of UBC Press. Together, they helped me turn a manuscript with potential into the book I wanted it to be and made its publication a reality.

Sincere thanks to the Canada Council, the Ontario Arts Council, and the Toronto Arts Council for their generous support. And, lastly, I want to acknowledge and thank my late parents for everything they taught me and all the love and encouragement they gave me over sixty-one years.

A Note on Sources

The key sources of information on my sister's life before, during, and after her institutionalization at the Rideau Regional Centre, Smiths Falls, come from a personal file of mementos saved by my mother, June Freeman, now in the possession of Kate Freeman; my own collection of memorabilia; and Martha's resident file from the Rideau Regional Centre. I received Martha's redacted institutional file on May 2, 2014, through a Freedom of Information Request to the Ontario Ministry of Community and Social Services; most names from this file have been changed to protect privacy. All photographs are from Freeman family sources, except for the school photos and two institutional photos from Martha's resident file.

Details on the Rideau Class Action and settlement can be found on Koskie Minsky's website; in "Settlement Reached in Rideau and Southwestern Regional Centres Class Actions," news release, Ministry of the Attorney General, Ontario, February 24, 2014; and in the official notice to Rideau survivors at https://cltoronto.ca/wp-content/uploads/2014/01/LONG-FORM-NOTICE-OF-FAIRNESS-HEARING-Rideau-2.pdf. The texts of the Ontario government apologies to Huronia and Rideau survivors are available on the Ministry of Children, Community and Social Services website and in "Ontario Apologizes to Former Residents of the Rideau and Southwestern Regional Centres," archived statement, Office of the Premier, Ontario, April 17, 2014. Details of the Huronia settlement are outlined in "Settlement Reached in Huronia Class Action Lawsuit," news release, Ministry of the Attorney General, Ontario, December 3, 2013, and on Koskie Minsky's website.

Quotes from the *Rideau Regional Centre Memory Book, 1951–2001, 50th Anniversary* (Smiths Falls: Record News EMC, 2001) are used with permission; comments by former RRC administrators John McHugh and Claude Harpin are from *VOX: Voice of Staff and Friends of the Rideau Regional Centre* 5, 1 (1974) and 17, 1 (1986), respectively. Glenn Lockwood's *Smiths Falls: A Social History of the Men and Women in a Rideau Canal Community, 1794–1994* (Smiths Falls: Town of Smiths Falls, 1994) also provides information on the development and history of the Rideau Regional Centre. Information on the Gallipeau Centre at the former Rideau site was accessed on January 2013 from its website. The late Gordon Ferguson's book, *Never Going Book: The Gordon Ferguson Story – Lessons from a Life of Courage, Strength and Love* (Brockville: Brockville and District Association for Community Involvement, 2016) describes life at Rideau from the perspective of a male survivor. Two sibling accounts were published along with an earlier version of my story, "Martha Matters: Surviving My Sister's Institutionalization," in a joint article: see Madeline Burghardt, Victoria Freeman, Marilyn Dolmage, and Colleen Orrick, "Unheard Voices: Siblings Share about Institutionalization," in "Institutional Survivorship," special issue, *Canadian Journal of Disability Studies* 6, 3 (2017): 92–117.

Quotes from the filmscript of George Gorman, dir., *One on Every Street* (Fletcher Film Productions and Ontario Department of Health, c. 1960), are used with permission from the Ontario Archives and the Harry E. Foster Foundation. Other films referred to are Douglas Jackson, dir., *Danny and Nicky* (Ottawa: National Film Board of Canada, 1969); Brad Rivers, dir., *The Freedom Tour* (People First of Canada, 2008); and Kelly O'Brien, dir., *Softening: Loving a Child with Special Needs* (Kelly O'Brien, 2013). I listened to first-person accounts by Ontario institutional survivors via the CBC Radio documentary, by David Gutnick, *The Gristle and the Stew: Revisiting the Horrors of Huronia* (2011), and on video via the Remember Every Name's YouTube channel. Lyrics from "The Twist" (1959) by Hank Ballard, used with permission of Alfred Music and Hal Leonard Corporation.

Excerpts from letters sent by doctors to the Honourable J.W. Spooner can be found in "Smith's Falls – Ontario Hospital School, 1962–65," Ontario Archives, General Subject Files, "J.W. Spooner, Minister of Municipal Affairs," RG 19-4-1, B269569. All names except the minister's have been changed.

The following newspaper articles are quoted or referred to in the text, listed in chronological order: Victoria Glover, letter to the editor, *Toronto Daily Star,* September 29, 1949, 6; Pierre Berton, "What's Wrong at Orillia? Out of Sight, Out of Mind," *Toronto Daily Star,* January 6, 1960, 31; "Probe of Hospital Precautions Promised," *Ottawa Journal,* September 23, 1964, 3; "Rideau Regional Head Retires: Hundreds Say Thank You," *Ottawa Journal,* May 26, 1969, 4; "Viewpoint: Retarded Resident Writes," *Record News,* February 3, 1972, 6, written by an anonymous resident of Southwestern Regional Centre and previously published as "A Resident's Eye View," in *Grapevine* (OHS Cedar Springs), Winter 1971; "Dr Vanier: Prejudice Is World Sickness," *Record News,* February 10, 1972; "A Record – News Feature Story: School within a School at Rideau Regional Hospital," *Record News,* February 24, 1972; "The Coroner Says There Will Be No Inquest" and "Search Fails – Area Girl Dies," *Ottawa Journal,* January 17, 1975, 1; "Doomed from Birth to Death: Medical Research – The Tragic Link between Down Syndrome and Alzheimer's," *Globe and Mail,* May 5, 2007, A1; Beth Marlin, "The Place Was Run Like a Prison," *Kingston Whig-Standard,* October 9, 2010; Simon Makin, "Memory Drug Trialled with People with Down Syndrome," *New Scientist,* April 11, 2013; Rachel Mendleson, "Huronia Lawsuit: Who Was Child 1751?," *Toronto Star,* September 18, 2013, A1; Tim Alemenciak, "Remembering the Dead at Huronia Regional Centre," *Toronto Star,* December 29, 2014.

I have drawn extensively on the following sources on the development of Ontario's institutions for people with intellectual disabilities: Thelma Wheatley, *"And Neither Have I Wings to Fly": Labelled and Locked Up in Canada's Oldest Institution* (Toronto: Inanna Publications, 2013); Walter Williston, *Present Arrangements for the Care and Supervision of Mentally Retarded Persons in Ontario* (Toronto: Ontario Department of Health, 1971); Harvey G. Simmons, *From Asylum to Welfare: The Evolution of Mental Retardation Policy in Ontario from 1831 to 1980* (Toronto: National Institute on Mental Retardation, 1982); Angus McLaren, *Our Own Master Race: Eugenics in Canada, 1885–1945* (Toronto: Oxford University Press, 1990); and Robert Welch, *Community Living for the Mentally Retarded in Ontario: A New Policy Focus* (Toronto: Ontario Provincial Secretariat for Social Development, 1973). A new book on the violence endemic to such institutional spaces is Kate Rossiter and Jen Rinaldi's *Institutional Violence and Disability: Punishing Conditions* (Abingdon, UK: Routledge, 2019). The concept of total institutions comes from Erving Goffman's *Asylums: Essays on the Social Situation of Mental Patients and Other Inmates* (New York: Anchor Books, 1961).

For the impact of institutionalization and attitudes towards disability on families, I read Madeline Burghardt's 2014 York University PhD dissertation, "Narratives of Separation: Institutions, Families, and the Construction of Difference," which has been published as *Broken: Institutions, Families, and the Construction of Intellectual Disability* (Montreal and Kingston: McGill-Queen's University Press, 2018). Other perspectives on families and disability that I drew on included Jeanne Safer's *The Normal One: Life with a Difficult or Damaged Sibling* (New York: Free Press, 2002); Steve Luxenberg, *Annie's Ghosts: A Journey into a Family Secret* (New York: Hyperion, 2009); and Pearl Buck, *The Child Who Never Grew: A Memoir* (New York: J. Day Co., 1950). For perspectives on mother blame, I consulted Ruth Kolker, "Blaming Mothers: A Disability Perspective," Ohio State Public Law Working Paper No. 295, May 13, 2015; Molly Ladd-Taylor and Lauri Umansky, eds., *Bad Mothers: The Politics of Blame in Twentieth-Century America* (New York: New York University Press, 1998); and Linda M. Blum, "Mother Blame in the Prozac Nation: Raising Kids with Invisible Disabilities," *Gender and Society* 206 (2007): 202–26. Joy Schaverien's *Boarding School Syndrome: The Psychological Trauma of the "Privileged" Child* (London: Routledge, 2015) provides an insightful analysis of another form of traumatizing institutionalization.

Information on the history of attitudes towards Down syndrome and other developmental disabilities is drawn from John Langdon Haydon, "Observations on an Ethnic Classification of Idiots," *London Hospital Reports* 3 (1866): 259–62; Philip Margulies, *Down Syndrome* (New York: Rosen Publishing Group, 2007); David Wright, *Downs: The History of a Disability* (Oxford: Oxford University Press, 2011); "Celebrate Being: About Down Syndrome," Canadian Down Syndrome Society pamphlet, n.d.; Burton Blatt and Fred Kaplan, *Christmas in Purgatory: A Photographic Essay of Mental Retardation* (Boston: Alleyn and Bacon, 1966); David Lawrence Braddock and Susan L. Parish, "An Institutional History of Disability," in *Handbook of Disability Studies*, edited by Gary L. Albrecht, Katherine D. Seelman, and Michael Bury (Thousand Oaks, CA: Sage Publications, 2001), 11–68.

Quotations about changelings are from John Gay, *Fables* (London: Kegan Paul, Trench and Co., 1882) and Fran and Geoff Doel, *Folklore of Northumbria* (Stroud, UK: History Press, 2009). The definition of "changeling" at the end of Chapter 4 is adapted from Dictionary.com. Definitions of "moron," "idiot," and "imbecile" are from the *American Heritage Dictionary*. The historical correlation of these terms with IQ scores is documented in Robert J. Sternberg, *Handbook of Intelligence* (Cambridge: Cambridge University Press, 2000).

The story of the wild boy of Aveyron is found in Jean Marc Gaspard Itard, *An Historical Account of the Discovery and Education of a Savage Man: Or, the First Developments, Physical and Moral, of the Young Savage Caught in the Woods Near Aveyron in the Year 1798*, translated by R. Phillips (London: Richard Phllips, 1802). The Jukes family story was told by R.L Dugdale in *The Jukes: A Study in Crime, Poverty, Disease and Heredity*, 4th ed. (New York: Putnam, 1888).

The work of disability studies scholar Rosemarie Garland-Thomson, especially *Staring: How We Look* (New York: Oxford University Press, 2009) and *Extraordinary Bodies: Figuring Physical Disability in American Culture and Literature* (New York: Columbia University Press, 1997), has deeply informed my understanding of the social construction of disability. Jane Nicholas, *Canadian Carnival Freaks and the Extraordinary Body, 1900–1970s* (Toronto: University of Toronto Press, 2018) confirmed my childhood memories of the Central Canada Exhibition in Ottawa. Other works helped me understand the links between attitudes towards various forms of difference, including Lennard J. Davis, "Constructing Normalcy: The Bell Curve, the Novel and the Construction of the Disabled Body in the Nineteenth Century," in *Enforcing Normalcy: Deafness, Disability and the Body*, ed. Lennard J. Davis (London: Verso, 1995), 3–16; Erving Goffman, *Stigma: Notes on the Management of Spoiled Identity* (New York: Simon and Schuster, 1963); Katie Aubrecht, "Disability Studies and the Language of Mental Illness," *Review of Disability Studies* 8, 2 (2012): n.p.; Richard Sandell, Jocelyn Dodd, and Rosemarie Garland-Thomson, eds., *Re-presenting Disability: Activism and Agency in the Museum* (London: Routledge, 2010); Katie Aubrecht and Janice Keefe, "The Becoming Subject of Dementia," *Review of Disability*

Studies 12, 2–3 (2016): 137–54; Sally Chivers, *From the Silvering Screen: Old Age and Disability in Cinema* (Toronto: University of Toronto Press, 2011); Judith Butler, *Gender Trouble: Feminism and the Subversion of Identity* (New York: Routledge, 1990); Gary William Kinsman and Patrizia Gentile, *The Canadian War on Queers: National Security as Sexual Regulation* (Vancouver: UBC Press, 2010); Robin Morgan, ed., *Sisterhood Is Powerful: An Anthology of Writings from the Women's Liberation Movement* (New York: Random House, 1970); Ian Hacking, *The Social Construction of What?* (Harvard: Boston University Press, 2000); and Aristotle, *Generation of Animals,* translated by Arthur Leslie Peck (London: William Heinemann, 1943), 175.

The following works helped me think about the body and its responses to trauma or shame: Siri Hustvedt, *The Shaking Woman or a History of My Nerves* (New York: Picador, 2009); Elizabeth Probyn, *Blush: Faces of Shame* (Minneapolis: University of Minnesota Press, 2005); and Katharine Young, "The Memory of the Flesh: The Family Body in Somatic Psychology," *Body and Society* 8, 3 (2002): 25–47.

Quotes from Jean Vanier and information about L'Arche came from Vanier's website and the L'Arche Canada website. Other information on current struggles against institutionalization came from the Institutional Survivors website, Remember Every Name's Facebook page, and the People First of Canada website.

VICTORIA FREEMAN is a writer, theatre artist, educator, and public historian. She is the co-creator, with L'Arche Toronto Sol Express, of *Birds Make Me Think about Freedom*, a play about the experiences of peoples institutionalized for intellectual disability, which won a Patron's Pick award at the 2018 Toronto Fringe Festival. She serves on the advisory board of Uncovering the People's History, which documents the stories of institutional survivors and their families for Family Alliance Ontario. She also co-wrote the *Talking Treaties Spectacle* with Ange Loft of Jumblies Theatre, which was performed in 2017 and 2018 at Fort York in Toronto. Her previous book, *Distant Relations: How My Ancestors Colonized North America*, was shortlisted for the 2000 Writers' Trust Shaughnessy Cohen Prize for Political Writing. She teaches in the Canadian Studies Program at Glendon College, and in the History Department at York University, in Toronto.

Author photo: Mark Fawcett